A CHANCE TO FIGHT HITLER

What Hans Ibing tells us of his dramatic and unique experience in Spain is an important addition to the recorded history of the Canadian volunteers who went to fight fascism. Just as compelling are his story of immigration and his personal odyssey in the aftermath of the war – a colourful thread in the fabric of this country's social history over five decades.
    — David Yorke, editor of *Mac-Pap*, Ronald Liversedge's memoir of the Spanish Civil War

David Goutor's biography of Hans Ibing adds to our growing knowledge of the role of Canadians in the important and still very much contested history of the Spanish Civil War. The often altruistic, "premature anti-fascist" volunteers found themselves entrenched in the opening salvos of the fierce battle soon to engulf the world.
    — Gregory S. Kealey, professor emeritus, Department of History, University of New Brunswick

David Goutor is assistant professor in the School of Labour Studies, McMaster University. He researches and teaches about working-class formation, union and leftist movements, immigration, and transnational migratory labour systems.

A CHANCE TO FIGHT HITLER

A CANADIAN VOLUNTEER IN THE SPANISH CIVIL WAR

DAVID GOUTOR

Between the Lines
Toronto

A Chance to Fight Hitler: A Canadian Volunteer in the Spanish Civil War

© 2018

First published in Canada in 2018 by
Between the Lines
401 Richmond St. W., Studio 281
Toronto, Ontario M5V 3A8
1-800-718-7201
www.btlbooks.com

All rights reserved. No part of this publication may be photocopied, reproduced, stored in a retrieval system, or transmitted in any form or by any means, electronic, mechanical, recording, or otherwise, without the written permission of Between the Lines, or (for photocopying in Canada only) Access Copyright, 56 Wellesley Street West, Suite 320, Toronto, Ontario, M5S 2S3.

Every reasonable effort has been made to identify copyright holders. Between the Lines would be pleased to have any errors or omissions brought to its attention.

Library and Archives Canada Cataloguing in Publication

Goutor, David, 1969–
A chance to fight Hitler : a Canadian volunteer in the Spanish Civil War / David Goutor.
Includes bibliographical references and index.
Issued in print and electronic formats.
ISBN 978-1-77113-395-1 (softcover). – ISBN 978-1-77113-396-8 (EPUB). –
ISBN 978-1-77113-397-5 (PDF)

1. Ibing, Hans. 2. German Canadians – Manitoba – Winnipeg – Biography. 3. Spain – History – Civil War, 1936-1939 – Participation, Canadian. 4. Biographies. I. Title.
DP269.47.C2G68 2018   946.081'092   C2018-902802-5
                                                    C2018-902803-3

Cover design, cover illustration by Maggie Earle
Text design and page preparation by Steve Izma
Printed in Canada

We acknowledge for their financial support of our publishing activities: the Government of Canada through the Canada Book Fund; the Canada Council for the Arts, which last year invested $153 million to bring the arts to Canadians throughout this country; and the Government of Ontario through the Ontario Arts Council, the Ontario Book Publishers Tax Credit program, and the Ontario Media Development Corporation.

Contents

	Introduction	1
1	Turbulent Times	7
2	Turning Left	39
3	The International Brigades	65
4	The Long Trek Home	101
5	Settling Down	119
6	Rarely Looking Back	151
	Acknowledgements	161
	Notes	163
	Index	189

Introduction

ON A DOCK IN THE PORT OF LE HAVRE, sometime in early December 1938, a scene was unfolding fit for a spy novel. Two men hid behind a freight shed, watching passengers board a Canadian Pacific Railway (CPR) ship headed to Halifax. They waited as customs agents and the ship's purser checked tickets and passports before allowing passengers up the gangplank. The two had to be patient; they could not move until the purser and the officials left. Hans Ibing, one of the men behind the shed, had a ticket for the voyage – but he had no valid papers for international travel. Two years earlier, Ibing had signed up to join the International Brigades fighting for the Republic in the Spanish Civil War; as an ardent anti-fascist and member of the Communist party, he was an enthusiastic volunteer. He had lived and worked in Winnipeg since migrating in 1930, yet he had not attained Canadian citizenship and the visa he had used to come to Spain had long expired. There was a good chance his life depended on finding a way to get on that ship.[1]

Ibing had snuck into France in September after his service as a truck driver in the Republican Army's Regiment de Tren was over; he spent most of late 1938 in a Paris safe house for veterans of the International Brigades. But the French authorities did not want many veterans of the Brigades on their soil, and they handed Ibing an expulsion order: he was given only forty-eight hours to get out of the country. Ibing was convinced that if he could not get out France, he would be deported to his country of birth, Germany. For a Communist veteran of the Brigades, being handed over to the Nazis would be a death sentence.[2]

The day after getting his expulsion order, Ibing rushed around Paris between police stations, the German embassy, and French government offices looking for help. He received none. The local Communist organizations that were supporting veterans from Spain then took Ibing to the CPR's travel offices. They knew a CPR agent who might offer assistance. The agent (whose name Ibing never learned) took up his cause: he not only provided a ticket, but also said he had a plan to slip Ibing onto the ship without having his documents checked. The CPR agent travelled with Ibing to Le Havre the next morning, and, standing with him behind the shed at the dock, coached him through the key phase.[3]

Timing would be everything. They had to wait out the purser and the customs agents, then wait still longer, right up to the point that the ship was pulling away – only then would the sailors have little choice but to wave Ibing through without worrying about his papers. Ibing recalled holding on as "there were still a few stragglers coming on board."[4] He clutched his suitcases, which were merely props so he would look the part of a typical passenger who just happened to arrive at the last second. In reality Ibing, like most veterans of the International Brigades coming out of Spain, had almost nothing to his name except the clothes on his back.

Finally the purser and the officials left and the last passengers were on board. The coast was almost clear, and the two remaining sailors started to pull up the gangplank. The CPR agent told Ibing, "Now is the time! Run!"[5]

❧

In 2008, as Ibing was reaching the age of a hundred, his experiences in Spain long behind him, he heard that I was thinking about writing his biography. His story fit with my areas of interest as a historian of immigration, labour, and the left in Canada – and, having married his granddaughter in 2000, I was part of the family. Nevertheless, he was surprised. "Why write about me?" he asked. "I'm just an average person." He had a point, at least on one level. Ibing was only a private in the International Brigades in Spain and held nothing more than a couple of low-level positions in local Communist organizations in Winnipeg and Toronto. Even in the small world of

Canadian Communism, Ibing was not an influential political figure, and he never harboured ambitions to become one.

Yet Ibing's life is also a great illustration of a historical truth: many people who see themselves as merely average live extraordinary lives. Indeed, Ibing's story will take us through some key moments in Canadian history and in twentieth-century history in general. Ibing's youth in Germany was shaped by social and political upheaval during the Weimar Republic and the rise of Nazism. At age twenty-one, he joined the last part of a great wave of European migration. In Canada, Ibing experienced the crushing effects of the Great Depression and joined the growing membership of Communist organizations in the 1930s. Then he, along with thousands of volunteers from around the world, joined the International Brigades to defend the Spanish Republic. During World War II, he joined the effort of Canadian Communist organizations to rally support on the home front for the fight against Hitler, particularly, in his case, within the German-Canadian community. Though never doctrinaire, Ibing remained in the Communist party until 1953, when a trip to East Germany left him so appalled that he lost his faith in the cause. Ibing came to enjoy the benefits of the Golden Age of capitalism. He would live his last years enjoying being a grandfather, and rarely looking back, unless prodded to do so, at the struggles of his youth.

❦

Given my close connection to Ibing, one might expect this biography to be derived from lengthy interviews or from hearing him reminisce at the family dinner table. But Ibing was reluctant to talk much about his past. He was especially resistant to conjuring up the most difficult parts of his life – growing up in Germany and, above all, the Spanish Civil War. Indeed, it was only in researching this book that I was able to appreciate how much these experiences must have scarred him. Ibing regularly characterized himself as a profoundly unnostalgic person. Even in his nineties, he preferred to focus on the positive aspects of his life in the present. If he did talk about the difficult times in the past, it was often as a general reference point to help him appreciate how much better things became for him starting in the 1940s.

There were exceptions. At times Ibing would readily recall his life in Winnipeg in the early 1930s, his escape from Paris in late 1938, and his experiences in Toronto in the 1940s and 1950s. Less frequently, he would talk about his conversion to Communism. The sections on these events are therefore spiced with his comments and witticisms. Ibing would occasionally recount small parts of his experiences in Spain, but he was rarely willing to dwell on the subject. When I first raised the possibility of doing detailed interviews about his life (around 2003), he was clearly uncomfortable with the idea.[6] He agreed to an interview with me in 2005, in large part because I assured him that we would focus on "easier" subjects, such as his migration to Canada, his experiences in Winnipeg, and his activism in Toronto during the war.

Thankfully, records remain from three other interviews Ibing participated in. Ibing was one of a number of Canadian volunteers interviewed in the late 1960s by Mac Reynolds for the CBC Radio Archives.[7] In 1980, Arthur Grenke, an archivist for Library and Archives Canada and a scholar of the German-Canadian community, conducted an extensive interview with him.[8] In 2002 Michael Petrou did a shorter interview with Ibing for his study of the Canadian volunteers, *Renegades*.[9] Ibing spoke at length about his political convictions and his activism in these interviews, but he was usually less forthcoming about his experiences in the war. In the interview with Grenke, however, he *did* go into detail about his time in Spain – at times breaking down in tears.

Ibing also left a number of written statements about his experiences, including several detailed notes in his personal papers that he left to the family. He wrote fourteen pages of reminiscences for the official history of the Mackenzie-Papineau Battalion, published by William Beeching in 1989.[10] These moving reminiscences were rich in detail about the war and about his motivations for volunteering. Ibing was disappointed that Beeching's book used very little of his writing; he was pleased that Mark Zuehlke drew a bit more on those reminiscences and told parts of Ibing's story in his 1996 book on the Canadian volunteers, *The Gallant Cause*.

This book relies heavily on secondary literature not only to provide context, but also to help reconstruct many events about which Ibing offered only fragmented accounts. This was a significant yet pleasurable challenge: the historical scholarship on the themes in this book has been a joy to explore.[11] I can make no pretense of being an objective analyst of this subject. Ibing was part of my family, and he had a profound influence on my wife and me. Yet while Ibing often acted heroically, he brushed off any notion that his service in Spain or in the anti-fascist cause in general would merit unconditional praise. Knowing Ibing for many years was invaluable in helping me to understand how he grappled with the issues of his time – how he kept his calm through numerous crises, insisted on asking what was the right thing to do, and developed a great appreciation of the prosperous years he started to enjoy in his forties. As his story will show, few people deserved a piece of this prosperity as much as Hans Ibing.

1 Turbulent Times

Early Years

Hans Ibing's generation of Germans would grow up in an environment of almost constant crisis. Born in December 1908, he had only a few memories from very early childhood that were not marked by war or political upheaval. Although some crises touched him relatively lightly, others would bring hardship to his family and shape his life. The determination and resilience that the Ibing family showed through Hans's early life is remarkable.

Hans Ibing's family roots were in the working class of Germany's heavily industrialized Westphalia region. His grandfather on his father's side was a shoemaker and his father became a printer. As was typical for skilled craftworkers of the time, Hans's father, Gustav, went through a long apprenticeship and a longer stage as a journeyman, which required him to travel widely around Europe. The family kept some of his postcards from this period "from far away – France, Switzerland, Austria and many parts of Germany."[1]

Just after the turn of the century, Gustav Ibing settled in Mainz, a town of 100,000 on the Rhine River, about fifty kilometres east of Frankfurt. Hans was born the youngest child of three and the only son. He has no memory of his mother, who died when Hans was only two. Gustav would remarry not long after and have two more daughters, and Hans was raised by his stepmother, Berta.

By the time Hans was born, Gustav Ibing had become well established as a printer and, like thousands of skilled German craftworkers, found an outlet for his political and social interests in the Social Democratic Party (Sozialdemokratische Partei Deutschlands, or SPD), then a rising force nationally.[2] Indeed, his work in Mainz was printing the local party newspaper, the *Mainzer Volkszeitung*.

However, Hans recalled Mainz as a conservative city which, outside of a base of working-class voters, was quite hostile to the SPD. The family faced further social obstacles as Protestants living in a predominantly Catholic region. Although the Ibings were hardly active in the church, they were regularly reminded of their place in the social order. Hans recalled that the majority Catholics would "let you live among them [and] at the same time let you know that you had to be grateful that they allowed you into their midst."[3] The Ibing family also faced personal struggles – in addition to the death of Hans's mother, his father suffered a severe case of tuberculosis that put him in a sanatorium for several months.[4]

Despite these difficulties, Gustav Ibing earned an increasingly prominent role in the *Mainzer Volkszeitung* and SPD politics. Indeed, Hans describes his father as "a remarkable man in some ways" with a gift for politics and public speaking, and a "social conscience" that was the "motivation in his life." Not long after Hans was born, his father became a regular writer for the paper. By 1914, he was the editor.[5]

The outbreak of the war disrupted Gustav Ibing's career ascension, as he was called into military service. On the whole, however, the impact of World War I on the Ibing family was relatively light. Due to his health problems, Gustav was placed into the army reserves and stationed in a quiet spot along the Danish frontier, well away from combat duty. Hans even remembered taking trips to the north to visit when his father was granted weekend leaves. Berta Ibing worked steadily during the war, mostly in local munitions factories, and the family seemed to avoid suffering too much hardship.[6]

Gustav returned to Mainz just as the German Revolution of 1918–1919 was unfolding. In the fall of 1918, the German war effort was faltering; soldiers were fleeing or surrendering en masse, and after a sailors' mutiny in the port city of Kiel at the end of October, worker and popular revolts were

Turbulent Times | 9

The building where the Ibings lived near Mainz, Germany, 1912.

spreading. Unable to cope with the crisis, the imperial German state system collapsed; the Kaiser abdicated and SPD leader Friedrich Ebert became chancellor. But there was no new governing structure in place and almost anything seemed possible – a radical socialist revolution, a civil war between the far left and the reactionary right, or a descent into anarchy. The SPD took the lead in establishing a parliamentary democracy. Revolutionary activity was suppressed and Ebert led a provisional government until elections for a new assembly were held in January 1919. The SPD easily took the largest share of the vote and headed a coalition of democratic parties that had a working majority. The coalition established the constitution of the new Weimar Republic.[7] As all of this unfolded, Gustav resumed his position as editor of the SPD newspaper in Mainz and also won a seat on the city council. He was thus becoming a prominent figure in the area. Like all of the major parties, the SPD counted heavily on the daily press. Local papers like his *Mainzer Volkszeitung* were part of extensive propaganda machines that included weekly magazines, periodicals, and flagship national dailies such as the SPD's *Vorwärts* (*Forward*).[8]

But getting involved in politics was also a dangerous and difficult proposition, given the widespread turmoil and the shakiness of the new Weimar Republic. "Fear and hatred ruled the day in Germany," writes noted historian Richard Evans. "Gun battles, assassinations, riots, massacres and civil unrest denied Germans the stability in which a new democratic order could flourish."[9] Anger and political division seeped into every aspect of daily life – and no member of a politician's family, not even a child, was spared. "I received a lot of unjust treatment while I was going to school there because of my father's politics," Hans recalled.[10]

Hans Ibing did not provide much detail of the abuse he suffered in these years, but understanding the depth of the bitterness and divisions of the time helps one appreciate how difficult it must have been for the son of a prominent SPD figure. The most fraught issue was the fall-out of defeat in World War I. No one in Germany accepted defeat and the sense of national humiliation that came with it. In early 1918, Germans had been convinced that victory was near, as a favourable peace agreement (the Brest-Litovsk treaty) was finalized with Lenin's new Soviet Russian government, and the German army was able to redeploy entire divisions from the east to prepare for a spring offensive on the Western Front. When that offensive failed in the summer, media reports and state propaganda gave little sense of how depleted and demoralized the German army had become, and how much the Allies had been bolstered by the arrival of the American forces. Defeat came as a complete shock to the public – a shock that in turn contributed to the political chaos that followed.[11]

While SPD leaders headed the transition to the Weimar Republic in the midst of this upheaval in Germany and a continuing economic crisis, they also had the terms of the peace handed to them by the victorious Allies. The public held out hope that since Allied forces had not breached German borders, the terms of the armistice and the final treaty would not be too punishing. There was widespread shock when the armistice required the Germans to hand over their military equipment and their fleet; meanwhile, the Allies would continue their naval blockade, which was causing serious hunger around Germany. Under the Treaty of Versailles of 1919, Germany signed a "war guilt clause" taking sole responsibility for starting the conflict. Germany was made to pay heavy reparations to the Allies, not only in hard currency, but also in the form of material output, including coal for French industrial centres. In addition, the Allies were to occupy a large swath of western Germany until the late 1920s; France held a particularly large area near its border.[12]

In Germany, Versailles was met with almost universal dismay and outrage. Across the political spectrum, there was what has been called an "inner rejection of the peace." Germans felt a deep sense of national humiliation, and were angry that the terms of the treaty seemed to violate their "democratic right of self-determination," which U.S. President Woodrow Wilson had vowed to make a universal principle in the postwar international order.[13] Germans on the political right especially found defeat to be unbearable, and when the reparations and the occupation were added on top, ultra-nationalist extremism and a lust for revenge flourished. These passions were aimed internationally against the Allies, but even more against perceived internal enemies of the Fatherland.

The myth of the "stab in the back" became a central part of the worldview of embittered right-leaning Germans. According to the myth, the heroic soldiers had been betrayed by the sailors' and workers' uprisings of 1918, and then leftist politicians completed the sell-out in signing the Versailles treaty.[14] The dire situation on the front for the German army and the broad impact of the United States joining the war were ignored or simply denied, as were the political manipulations of German military leaders at the end of the war. Once top commanders Field Marshal Hindenburg and Major General Ludendorff recognized that defeat was imminent, they fled their positions of power and left the SPD leaders of the new government to deal with the fallout. Many military leaders were determined that "the parties of the Left have to take on the odium of this peace. The storm of anger will then turn against them."[15]

Given the extent of bitterness and recrimination after the war, it is difficult to imagine the scale of the "unjust treatment" that the son of a prominent SPD figure such as Hans Ibing had to endure. Indeed, in Mainz, there was no escaping these political issues: the town was in the zone occupied by the French after the war. The sense of outrage was further deepened by the fact that part of the occupying force was made up of black troops from French colonies in Africa. Hans, who was ten years old when the occupation began, recalled the presence of French colonial troops mostly as a source of curiosity; it was the first time he had seen black people. But for many Germans, having black Africans (who were widely seen in these years as "subhuman" throughout Europe) play the role of occupiers came to symbolize Germany's humiliation. There was a deluge of racist propaganda, and the myth of widespread rape of German women by French colonial troops took hold in the minds of nationalist Germans.[16]

For SPD leaders, it was essential to find their own ways to fight back against the occupation. Mobilizing resistance in the occupied zones was important to strengthening the Weimar government's hand in ongoing diplomacy with the Allies; it would show the Allies that they could not continue to dictate terms to Germany and count on the economy running smoothly and generating a reliable flow of reparations. SPD leaders also hoped to unify the country in opposition to the occupation, which in turn might hasten Germany's recovery from defeat. Above all, leading the resistance would help defend the SPD and its supporters against charges that they had "sold out" the Fatherland and would continue to allow it to be subjugated in foreign affairs. The SPD focused its resistance on the reparation payments, because as historian Ian Kershaw puts it, the issue "was like oxygen to the nationalist right."[17] Thus the social democrats mobilized popular protest and organized worker slowdowns in the occupied zone. Not surprisingly, Gustav Ibing spoke out loudly against the occupation – and this made him a target for the French authorities.[18]

A crisis point came in 1923, when the Allies, led by France, expanded their occupation into the Saar and Ruhr valleys primarily in response to the Germans falling behind on their reparations, including their coal shipments; an additional 100,000 French and Belgian troops were dispatched into the enlarged occupied zones. Part of France's new effort was a suppression of resisters, including the arrest of prominent opponents of the occupation – such as Gustav Ibing. The Allied forces were vigorous in executing the crackdown, expelling almost 150,000 Germans from the occupied areas.[19] But when the French arrived at the Ibing family house, Hans remembers them being polite and relatively gentle for armed police, especially considering they had missed their target: Gustav was gone when they arrived. Nevertheless, the French searched the house thoroughly and evicted the family from their home.[20]

Hans suspected that his father got wind of his looming arrest, as Gustav was out of sight until he was reunited with Hans, his stepmother, and his sisters at a small town near Frankfurt. But they were now refugees as the crises gripping Germany were becoming increasingly severe. In 1923 there were aborted attempts at revolution by the Communists on the far left and the Nazis (in the Beer Hall Putsch) on the far right.[21] And the economy, which remained generally depressed in the early 1920s, could not withstand the new troubles that year brought. The passive resistance campaign, whereby workers and officials refused to produce for the French occupiers, had a particularly damaging effect. Much of the economy ground to a halt, and Germany launched into a catastrophic period of hyper-inflation. Through the early 1920s, Germany's currency had slipped to the point that one American dollar was worth seventeen thousand German marks in January 1923. By September 1923 one dollar was worth 98.9 million marks and by December, 4.2 trillion marks.[22]

The chaos generated by the financial crisis made this a horrible moment for the Ibing family to lose all their possessions aside from a few suitcases thrown together in the panic of forced expulsion. Goods and property were the only things that kept their value while the currency inflated out of control. Being left homeless made the family even more vulnerable, as a massive crime wave broke out and the most basic sense of civil order started to crack. Desperation grew to the point where people stole whatever they could from wherever they could. There were cases in which packs of armed young people – some as large as two hundred – raided local farms in the hope of grabbing food to bring home.[23]

But if Gustav Ibing's political engagement got the family into this crisis, it also gave them a way out. The German government adopted a policy of compensating resisters of the occupation.[24] The SPD was keen to protect its leading opponents of the Allies, and Hans recalled that it moved quickly to look after his father. The structure of Weimar governance created ample opportunities for leading parties to find a political seat for prominent members. For instance, the highest municipal political positions were often appointed by the major parties in city councils or regional governments. The SPD found Gustav Ibing such a spot in Bad Frankenhausen, a small town in a rural area of Thuringia (in what would later become East Germany). A power struggle between the town's SPD council and the conservative provincial governor had left the post of Zweite Bürgermeister (roughly the equivalent of deputy mayor) sitting vacant.[25]

Hans Ibing in 1926, age 17, when he was living in Bad Frankenhausen.

    Hans Ibing did not recall the expulsion from Mainz and the relocation to Bad Frankenhausen as a uniquely traumatic moment in his life; he usually described it as a hastily arranged, career-related family relocation rather than a brush with catastrophe. Indeed, in interviews and in conversations with his family in Canada, he readily noted the widespread economic hardships and social upheaval surrounding his youth in Germany, but never made particular mention of the scale of the crisis looming over the family's move. This is a tribute to the effectiveness of the SPD's political machine, his stepmother's

16 | A Chance to Fight Hitler

Gustav Ibing speaking at an SPD event in Germany in the 1920s. Specific date and location not known.

wherewithal in smoothing out the transition for the family, and his father's political acumen.

Hans remembers his father's greatest asset as a politician being that "he was a great orator. He could speak without preparation . . . never using notes, on subjects of politics [and] religion."[26] Bad Frankenhausen was also a more favourable political setting for Gustav than Mainz, as the SPD remained strong in the town council.[27] Gustav Ibing held the position of deputy mayor through the 1920s, and eventually became mayor in 1930.

The late 1920s were the period of his early life in Germany that Hans recalled most fondly. The German financial system had stabilized somewhat, and the economy made a noticeable – if creaky and shallow – recovery. The political waters calmed as well, and the Weimar Republic enjoyed a brief window when its survival was not in immediate danger. Local politics in Bad Frankenhausen also became steadier, and Hans found there were benefits to being the son of a prominent local official. He retained fond memories of the family living in the Bürgermeister's house, which was large

A brief happy moment in Germany: a costume ball in Bad Frankenhausen in 1929. Ibing, 20, is in a sailor's costume, front and second from the right. His sister Else is front and fourth from the right.

and beautifully appointed. He also had a strong circle of friends and a busy social life during his gymnasium (high school) years.[28]

Nevertheless, Hans also remembered that the effects of the era's political rancour were everywhere. The teachers at his gymnasium were mostly conservative and often frosty, although they were never so bold as to discriminate overtly against the son of a prominent local official.[29] He also witnessed the spread of Nazi extremism. Myths such as the "stab in the back" continued to circulate, and many young men Hans's age were becoming radicalized. Indeed, he remembered the young as the most aggressive among the ranks of the extreme right, even more than embittered veterans.[30]

Hans Ibing's recollections are in keeping with historians' accounts: a powerful gender identity developed among young men that centred on proving their masculinity through combat in the streets. According to Evans,

The Bürgermeister's home in Bad Frankenhausen.

these were "men in their late teens and twenties who had been too young to fight in the war themselves and for whom civil violence became a way of legitimizing themselves in the face of the powerful myth of the older generation of front-soldiers."[31] Right after the war, the Freikorps (Free Corps) emerged and drew in between 200,000 and 400,000 men. In the early 1920s, a dizzying array of armed right-wing groups of street fighters emerged, including the "combat leagues" associated with a veterans' group called the Steel Helmets, nationalist "fighting leagues," and the Nazis' Sturmabteilung (SA, or Storm Division). Paramilitaries also developed on the left, the largest being the Communists' Red Front Fighting League. The SPD did not have strong traditions of taking up arms in the streets, yet it also started a paramilitary, the Reich Banner Black-Red-Gold. Violence in the streets remained a fact of life even in the relatively stable period from 1924 to 1929, with thousands reported injured in clashes between rival paramilitaries.[32]

Hans consistently rejected the organized thuggery that consumed many of his peers. But it became more difficult to stay out of the turmoil after the international financial crisis of 1929, which brought a new economic crisis

Ibing in 1928, age 19

and a major surge in political violence. Throughout his life Hans never forgot the "misery and desperation of the German people in the 20s and 30s and the ensuing degradation that spawned degenerates like Hitler and his movement. It was much worse than the Great Depression in Canada."[33]

Hans was able to avoid the severe unemployment of the time, finding a spot, thanks to his father's connections, as a clerk in the municipal administration. But in his mind, it was a dead-end job; he wanted to learn an industrial trade as his father and grandfather had. He appreciated how fortunate he was to have any income, but the job "was too much paperwork and it just wasn't [his] line."[34] The job was not engaging enough to keep him from seeking to get out of Germany before Hitler and his "degenerate" followers gained greater influence. The Hitler Youth stood out in his memories as "bullies, and loudmouths, and they'd try to intimidate other people." Hans reflected, "That was not in my nature. So in 1930 I left. I didn't want to stay there anymore."[35]

Canada – through a Narrow Window

Hans Ibing's political motivations for leaving were unusual among German migrants in this period; many Germans with left-leaning backgrounds did not have such foresight. Once the Nazis took power in 1933, their first targets were their political opponents. The Nazis' first concentration camps, including Dachau, were primarily built for members of leftist parties and other socialist organizations.[36] Millions tried to flee – most without success. Throughout his life, Ibing would express his conviction that it was vital that he got out when he did, as he would have died had he stayed in Germany either as a political prisoner or later in the army on the Eastern Front.[37]

But there was also a much brighter aspect to Ibing's interest in emigration. Like many people who migrate in their early twenties, Ibing left with a sense of both escape and adventure, and without much advance planning. He recalled that the idea to emigrate came not from him, but from a friend from his gymnasium years. This friend had already started the process, making contact with groups organizing migration to Canada, and Ibing decided to join him. "We didn't know what we were getting into," Ibing said, "except we thought there couldn't be much wrong with going to Canada." When one interviewer pressed him about what he brought to prepare for life in Canada, Ibing quipped, "Just one suitcase with my belongings, and . . . no furs or anything like that."[38]

Hence a combination of politics, happenstance, and youthful free-spiritedness shaped Ibing's decision to migrate, but broader trends in German emigration and Canadian immigration policy also played crucial roles. German emigration to the New World had been well established since the early nineteenth century, when economic changes and shortages of land started pushing people to seek new opportunities overseas. Up until World War I, the majority of German migrants came not from Germany itself, but from rural German-speaking enclaves around Eastern Europe. Most were drawn by the large amounts of available land in western Canada, where they aimed to start homesteads. Emigration was shut off during the war years, but after 1918, as the hard realities of the defeat, occupation, and economic depression set in, a wave of "emigration fever" spread among the German public. Emigration societies and agencies that were dormant during the war were again up and running strong by the early 1920s.[39] And a number of new trends in emigration after the war made it likely that someone like Ibing would consider crossing the Atlantic. Although most migrants continued to be German-speaking farmers from around Eastern Europe, a growing proportion came directly from Germany itself and did not have extensive agricultural experience.[40] Ibing fit the demographic profile of a typical German emigrant during this period: he was a working-age male and unmarried. His destination was also reflective of another trend: Canada became an increasingly popular choice among German migrants as the 1920s went on.[41]

Canada's rise up the list of destinations was in part the product of the basic impression that most Germans had of Canada as a "wide open" place that needed more people to "fill it up."[42] This image had particular appeal in Germany, which faced a severe housing shortage in the early 1920s.[43] Agencies that recruited immigrants to Canada eagerly played to the German public's impressions, producing no end of flashy promotional literature promising a fresh start in the New World. Ibing recalled reading "information folders" that "emphasized the vastness of the country," and "the wonderful conditions in Canada." He added with a chuckle in one interview, "They were embellished quite a bit."[44]

The German government took a similar view. Through the late 1920s the Weimar government criticized "misleading" promotional material, and the authorities made efforts to stop immigration agents from distributing it. In addition, the Weimar government's Reichsstelle für das Auswanderungswesen (RA, or Reich Office for Emigration Affairs) produced its own literature insisting that Canada was actually "an unsuitable land for German emigration." The RA's *Nachrichtenblatt* (*News Sheet*) contended that new settlers would struggle to prosper given the cold winter in the Prairie West, "which more or less turns the land into a frozen desert." Yet the government's counterpropaganda campaign did little to dispel the idea that, as one commentator put it, if Germans were "a people without space, then Canada could be called a land without people."[45] Comments like these also show that both Canadian recruiters and German emigration promoters paid no heed to the presence of Indigenous peoples, who had been brutally forced off the land to make way for white settlement.[46]

On the Canadian side, the increase in German immigration in the late 1920s was the result of a push by Ottawa to attract large numbers of immigrants from Europe. The particular program under which Ibing came to Canada was the Railway Agreement, by far the largest of its kind in the 1920s. Under its terms, the government supported the massive immigration recruitment of the Canadian Pacific Railway and the Canadian National Railway (CNR). For the railways, immigration was a lucrative business: they owned much of the land in the west; they would carry the produce and supplies generated by new growth in settlement and agriculture, they owned many of the mines and other resource extraction operations, and they ran the shipping lines that carried immigrants.

These efforts to promote immigration were, in turn, the result a series of shifts in policy through the late nineteenth and early twentieth centuries. Just a few years before the 1927–1930 high tide of German migration to Canada, any significant influx of Germans would have been inconceivable. During World War I, hostility toward "enemy aliens" and "foreigners" in general ran extremely high. This hostility in turn drew on a deep vein of xenophobia and racism toward "unassimilative" immigrants that had been manifest since the late nineteenth century.[47]

Before the war, however, this hostility was mostly outweighed by the strong consensus – especially among policy makers and business leaders – that large-scale immigration from Europe was essential in order to spur economic development and to help settle the Prairie West. Indeed, the period before 1914 saw the largest waves of immigration in Canada's history.[48] The Anglo-Canadian majority's views of German immigrants were ambiguous – but Germans were generally seen then as coming from a more "civilized" and "assimilative" culture, and they were not one of the main groups that anti-immigrant agitators targeted when they protested against "foreigners" coming from Europe. Germans were one of the main targets of Canada's recruitment efforts in Europe, and by 1911 they constituted the third-largest ethnic group in Canada after French and British.[49]

But attitudes changed during World War I. As xenophobia and racism spiked, there was no doubt that Germans were "enemy aliens." When the War Measures Act was invoked in 1914, the government used its new powers to force about 80,000 "enemy aliens" to register with authorities and put 8,500 into internment camps.[50] There was also a major effort to expunge evidence of German culture; the most famous example was the renaming of the Ontario city of Berlin, which had a large German population. The city was thereafter called Kitchener, after the British general who became a hero during the Boer War.[51]

The revolution in Russia and the Bolsheviks' seizure of power in 1917 and the postwar labour revolt in Canada (especially the Winnipeg General Strike of 1919) created new fears about "foreign subversives."[52] As this xenophobia ran high throughout the Western world, many governments enacted new policies to exclude "foreigners." Ottawa was no exception, amending the Immigration Act of 1919 to grant itself "sweeping powers" to exclude "immigrants belonging to any nationality or race deemed undesirable."[53] It used these powers to impose a policy of "Anglo-preference" in immigration. Immigration from Europe dropped well below prewar levels, and the influx of Germans, specifically, was minimal.

As the 1920s went on, a surprising shift in policy was brewing, one that would create a new opening for German migrants such as Ibing. The long-time proponents of large-scale immigration – including political and business leaders – regained their voice. Again, they argued that immigration was needed to revive the economy.[54] Media commentators and business leaders contended that new waves of immigrants were needed to boost western settlement and provide labour for resource industries. The CNR and the CPR were particularly vocal. In the mid-1920s the government began to loosen its restrictive policies regarding immigration from Central and Eastern Europe, and then struck the Railway Agreement in 1925.[55]

The support for large-scale immigration as a part of nation-building proved remarkably persistent, and the view that Germans were suitable immigrants proved even more so. Germans remained classified as non-preferred immigrants when the Railway Agreement started, but in 1927, as recruitment under the agreement expanded, Germans were moved into the preferred category. The number of immigration agents working for the CPR in Germany went from two in 1925 to fifty-one at the end of the decade. And the CPR's agents were extremely active in the regions where Ibing lived.[56]

Indeed, memories of wartime antagonisms seem to have faded by the late 1920s, at least when it came to immigration. Canadian recruiters even worked hand in hand with conservative and nationalistic German emigration associations, which were well known for their efforts to sustain migrants' loyalty to the Fatherland after they moved elsewhere. Ibing, of course, with his socialist roots and his desire to get away from the fractious climate in Germany, had no interest in these associations or in staying connected to German political interests once he left, but the fact that Canadian immigration promoters would work with such groups shows just how much Ottawa's policy had shifted. Immigration agents also promoted Canada – especially the Prairie West – as a place where German migrants would not be forced to assimilate, where they could keep their German culture in the New World.[57]

The organization that recruited Ibing was the Canadian Lutheran Immigration Society, which was relatively moderate on religious and political questions. German religious societies – and the Lutheran one in particular – were effective at recruiting migrants under the Railway Agreement. Crucially for Ibing, they also remained quite active through most of 1930, even as the

Canadian government wound down its immigration recruitment in response to the onset of the Great Depression.[58]

The process of Ibing's migration to Canada was typical for someone brought over under the Railway Agreement. Since Germans were now preferred migrants, the administrative and security procedures were light, and requirements on the books that may have caused problems were hardly enforced. The Railway Agreement was presented to the Canadian public as aimed primarily at recruiting agricultural workers and settlers for the Canadian west. Accordingly, migrants who did not settle immediately on a homestead had to work as hired hands on a Canadian farm. In addition, all immigrants were required to produce witness statements or certificates from local officials that they had experience in agriculture.[59]

The first requirement was not a problem for Ibing, who agreed in advance to do agricultural labour; in fact, one of the only things he knew about Canada was that "they had a ruling that people who came from Europe had to go to the farms first."[60] But like many of the German migrants in this period – and many immigrants coming under the Railway Agreement – he did not have experience in farming. It did not seem to matter; the requirement was simply ignored or evaded so easily that Ibing did not know about it. He made no mention of having to engineer documents showing that he had a track record in farm work. He never recalled his lack of such experience causing him any trouble or making him find a way to circumvent the rules. According to Canada's immigration records, when Ibing arrived in Halifax and gave his information to the immigration officers, he did not bother pretending to be a farmer and named his previous occupation as "clerk."[61]

Ibing's voyage across the Atlantic to Canada was also typical of those of hundreds of thousands of immigrants in this period. The ship carrying him, the *Crefeld*, was a "packet boat" – part freighter and part passenger ship – run by the Norddeutscher Lloyd company. In his thorough study of German immigration to Canada, Jonathan Wagner chose the *Crefeld* as a good example of a ship commissioned under the Railway Agreement to carry immigrants to Canada; the CNR and CPR did not have enough ships to carry all of the new immigrants and thus had to hire other carriers. The *Crefeld* spent the late 1920s and 1930 making constant runs between Canada and Germany.[62] All of the passengers on Ibing's trip were immigrants; according to the Immigration Office's list of arrivals in Halifax, about three-quarters were German, the majority of them from Germany itself, and the rest were Finns, Swedes, and a number of Swiss.[63]

On the way to Canada: Ibing, 21, on the *Crefeld* from Bremen to Halifax in 1930. Ibing is sixth from the right, smiling but with his eyes shut.

Conditions on the passage were generally tolerable; as historians have noted, by the 1920s ships carrying migrants were much better equipped to cross the ocean than had been the case for migrants in earlier periods.[64] Still, the boat was overcrowded and not well suited to carrying so many people on the North Atlantic. Ibing remembered that at one point the seas became so rough that the crew had to shut down the ship's motors and ride out the waves; they told him that the waves were lifting the rear propeller right out of the water.[65]

The timing of Ibing's trip, however, was quite notable. As he would frequently say in conversation with his family, he "just squeaked in" before the gates to Canada were closed. The margin could not have been slimmer, as Prime Minister R.B. Bennett's cabinet imposed restrictions on immigration days after Ibing's ship had left Germany. In other words, immigration was effectively banned while Ibing was crossing the Atlantic. When the ship arrived in Halifax on August 21, 1930, the passengers were not initially allowed into Canada. It was only when officials determined that the boat had in fact set sail before the new policies were announced that Ibing and the other passengers were issued landing permits.[66]

The Depression

Ibing's biggest initial impression of Canada was that it was incredibly vast – he recalled that the train ride to Winnipeg seemed to go on forever. "It was kind of awesome" he commented in one interview, "the size of the country, coming from Germany, where you can travel from one end of the country to the other in no time at all."[67] But he also quickly registered that times were tough in his new homeland. Indeed, if Ibing's luck was good in helping him gain entry into Canada, it was terrible in terms of providing new opportunities upon his arrival.

Since he was not part of any kind of chain migration (that is to say, he did not follow other family or community members who had arrived earlier) Ibing had almost no connections in his new homeland. Thus initially he relied upon the agents and organizations involved in the business of facilitating the settlement of immigrants, and got immediate exposure to how players in this business could blur the lines between public and private interests or take a flexible approach to many of the rules. Upon arriving in Winnipeg, Ibing and his friend from Bad Frankenhausen were picked up by a local immigration official, who took them directly to a rooming house he operated as his own private business in Winnipeg's North End. Ibing stayed there for a few days and made his first awkward attempts to adapt to the new country. He walked into one local restaurant, and when a young woman greeted him from behind the counter, he gave his warmest smile and said "Goodbye!" It would take time to learn even the basics of the language – but this awkward initial greeting did not ruin his hope of getting to know the young waitress.

Ibing waited about a week before getting picked up by representatives of the Lutheran Immigration Board, which would ship the migrants out to serve as farm hands around the Prairies.[68] Ibing was sent to work for a German farmer near Stornaway, Saskatchewan. This move severed his only personal connection in Canada; his friend from his hometown was sent to a different farm and Ibing never saw him again.[69]

The Lutheran Immigration Board had promised all immigrants one year's work in Canada, but Ibing worked on the farm near Stornaway for little more than a month.[70] He generally kept fond memories of being a farm hand; it was "a brand-new experience." He enjoyed working outdoors, even if he had to start at five in the morning, six days a week. Still, the main result of his time working as harvest help was to confirm that his future ambitions did not involve farming. His primary tasks were to shovel grain into the granary and to pile and bale massive amounts of hay for the livestock to consume over the winter. The intense agricultural work took a toll on Ibing, who had spent the previous months working at a desk. "I ached," he recalled; "my muscles were not used to that kind of thing." The constant work with shovels and pitchforks was particularly hard on Ibing's hands, which became "swollen with blisters and the blisters broke" and yet he "had to go out every day and keep on working."[71] He also felt isolated on the Prairies and grew bored with the lack of social events or recreation in the area. He recalled the people in Stornaway as very religious and mostly straight-laced. On Sunday "the only place you could go was church." Even on Saturday nights, there was little more amusement to be found other than young people getting a little moonshine from the local bootlegger, or someone playing "an old piano in a church hall."[72]

Ibing did not seem aware that the Lutheran Immigration Board was sup-

Ibing (with child on shoulders) on a day off from farm work in Saskatchewan in 1930, not long after he arrived in Canada.

posed to supply a year's work on the farm; if he had found out, he likely would have been relieved that the promise was broken. He returned to Winnipeg with enough savings to get another spot back at the immigration official's rooming house and to get out and enjoy a bit of Winnipeg's social life. He visited local German clubs and made a few friends with other German migrants in his neighbourhood.[73]

But finding and holding work would be an enormous challenge. Indeed, his experiences in the job market in late 1930 serve as a telling illustration of the desperation of the times. The economic crisis that had begun the previous fall continued to deepen, with unemployment already hitting new heights. The Prairie West, whose economy (including in its cities) depended to a great extent on agriculture, was devastated by a collapse in grain prices, especially for wheat. Winnipeg's budget for relief of the poor exploded; by 1931 it was more than fifty times greater than in 1928.[74]

Recently arrived immigrants such as Ibing were among the most vulnerable. They were least established in the labour market and many had not yet settled into a local community or support network in Canada. Ibing recognized those challenges at the time, but fortunately he did not seem aware that the onset of the Depression led to another wave of xenophobia. As he looked for work in Winnipeg, Ibing would have been chilled if he had heard about the resolution the Manitoba legislature passed unanimously in 1930 that took aim at immigrants just like him. According to the resolution, Canada's unemployment crisis was a result of "the flow of immigrants into Western Canada, many of whom had been admitted as agricultural labourers, and who have undertaken farm work for a short time only."[75] The increasingly common way for the government to deal with unemployed recent immigrants around the country, and in Winnipeg particularly, was to deport them to their country of origin.[76]

Many recent immigrants received help finding work from the CPR, the CNR, and other agencies working under the Railway Agreement. The railways were not acting out of benevolence: they also had an interest in avoiding transportation costs when the government ordered unemployed immigrants to be deported back to Europe. The railways' efforts could take place on a large scale; CNR officials in North Bay and Winnipeg, for example, placed recent immigrants in northern Ontario lumber camps.[77] But they also happened on a smaller scale, such as when the immigration official who ran the boarding house placed Ibing in a job in a creamery of a grocery store.

The store was run by an American chain named Piggly Wiggly (Ibing would always giggle when recalling the name to his family). It was tedious, menial work, the main task being to wash out returned milk bottles. He once recalled that "for weeks and weeks" all he saw was an endless stream of stinking used milk bottles. At times, he was also charged with refilling the bottles, loading them on a wheeled cart, and placing the cart in the cooler. One day, while Ibing pushed the cart through a "dark corridor" in the store, one of the wheels got caught in a hole in the cement floor, and at least a couple dozen bottles "just slid off" the cart and crashed spectacularly in the hall. In the 1930s, one such mishap was disastrous for a worker. The managers insisted that Ibing pay for the damage. When Ibing objected, as he did not have any extra money and felt he was not at fault, he was promptly fired.[78]

To get established in any kind of job would require a combination of luck, ingenuity, and help though a few fledgling ties Ibing developed in the immigrant German community. He found temporary work as a helper in a large butcher shop. Run by an Eastern European Jewish family, the shop's main business was as a wholesale supplier to restaurants in Winnipeg's immigrant communities. One day late in the work week, Ibing heard that the shop's delivery driver was quitting and a replacement was needed to start Monday. Ibing always enjoyed recalling what happened next, as he did in detail in his interview with archivist Arthur Grenke. His boss asked him if he could drive a truck, he recounted. "So I said 'Sure, I can . . . I can drive.' I lied to him . . . I had no idea. I couldn't drive a car or a truck or anything."[79] Now stuck with little more than a weekend to learn how to drive, Ibing turned to a local connection he had made, a fellow German immigrant who worked as a salesman and had a car to travel around the region as part of his job. After Ibing came to him and explained his predicament, the salesman took him to "one of the big parks in the city" and for two hours he showed him "how to shift gears and how to drive." Ibing said, "That was all my preparation for the job. Of course, I still didn't have a licence."

In addition to being a remarkably quick study behind the wheel, Ibing needed plenty of good fortune on his first day. He had to show his boss that he could get the truck out of the garage and through the narrow alleyway behind the shop. He started the motor, tried to chart his path, and told himself, "Well anyway, here goes." He then jerked the truck into gear so quickly it "just shot out of the garage," had to swing the steering wheel "like wild" to avoid a fence, but somehow "got it in front of the store" – and by passing that test, Ibing become one of the fortunate people, especially among recent immigrants, to land steady work in the early 1930s in Canada.[80]

Ibing would hold the job for the butchers, apart from one brief period, for the next six years. His pay started at five dollars a week, but it was enough to get by, as prices for goods and services remained depressed along with the rest of the economy. Always careful with his money, Ibing recalled the fine details of how he spent on his meagre wages. He moved into a better rooming house (on Euclid Avenue, also in the North End), which still cost only about a dollar a week. For that price, he recalled, "you even got your laundry done," usually through a local Chinese laundromat. A good meal was usually a quarter, but he spent a lot of his time finding places "where you could eat all you wanted for fifteen cents or ten cents sometimes."[81]

The work itself also had its upsides; he was outdoors and on the move for large parts of the day. Ibing recalls that traffic was generally light at the time and driving was fairly easy, once he got a little experience. But he did rack up a fair number of speeding tickets when he had to rush. Ibing also got to know the city, especially the Eastern European immigrant neighbourhoods where he made most of his deliveries. Mostly he supplied Ukrainian restaurants, although he also delivered to Russian and Slavic places, and a few Chinese-owned restaurants that served "Canadian-style food."[82]

Ibing was constantly aware of how he could have had it worse, and how "you had to stick to the job if you were lucky enough to have one."[83] The

Ibing (right) with a friend at a park in Winnipeg, 1933.

economy continued to tumble downward until 1933, by which time per capita income in Manitoba was one-half of what it had been in 1929. The recovery that followed was remarkably shaky and uneven.[84] The railway companies gave up finding work for immigrants, due not only to the difficulty in finding jobs but also to the backlash from the media and the public who believed that any available work should go to Anglo Canadians.[85]

Despite the scale of the crisis, suspicion and resentment of those who needed relief ran remarkably deep. Prime Minister Bennett readily stoked the bitterness. "The people are not bearing their share of the load," he declared in 1931. "Half a century ago people would work their way out of their difficulties rather than look to government to take care of them. The fibre of some of our people has grown softer and they are not willing to turn in and save themselves."[86] Relief for the unemployed remained in the hands of municipal governments that had scant resources and generally clung to suspicions that generous welfare programs would erode the work ethic and create a "dependency problem." City officials in Winnipeg worried that providing relief would lead to a "blunting of personal initiative and to the mental attitude [among recipients] that they do not need to worry since they are bound to be cared for."[87]

Recent immigrants were among the last in line when relief was made available; mistrust of outsiders went so far that most municipalities, drawing on precedent going back to Elizabethan-era Poor Laws, refused relief to people who could not prove they were established residents of that municipality.[88] Many of the German migrants Ibing got to know were among the unemployed and desperate. Some came to the retail section of the butcher shop to redeem grocery vouchers, as the shop "was in a poor area and things weren't too expensive there." He recalled that no one ever received money, and only married people could even get relief vouchers to bring to the store.[89] Unemployed single men were viewed not only as shiftless but also as a potential source of unrest in the cities; they were regularly denied assistance unless they were willing to go to remote labour camps set up by the government.[90] Ibing recalled seeing hundreds of single men sleeping in shelters or in shanties clustered near the railway yards, lucky if they would get served meals from the local soup kitchens – and the kitchens usually served only one meal per day.[91]

What Ibing did not seem to know was that there was more at stake in sticking to the job than surviving the Depression. Staying employed also ensured he was safe from being deported back to Germany, where the Nazis were growing in strength and would eventually seize power in 1933. Ibing never mentioned the matter of deportations of immigrants needing relief, but the practice continued apace.[92] In Winnipeg the scale of deportations reached the point that in 1932 it attracted local media scrutiny and political controversy. Consular officials in Winnipeg from a number of countries, including Germany (then still under the Weimar government, although it was teetering) started to question why so many of their migrants were being sent home. Investigations by local newspapers and city councillors found that immigrants were routinely asked to sign requests to be deported voluntarily as a condition for receiving relief. But the public was especially scandalized by cases of "respectable" British immigrants getting shipped back to the mother country. In early 1934, Winnipeg ended its policy of automatically reporting immigrants needing relief to the immigration offices that would then deport them.[93] But overall the approach to welfare hardly softened, and many immigrants were cut off from relief programs.[94]

Ibing saw much of the misery of the Depression first-hand at the store and while on the job driving around Winnipeg. He routinely drove through back lanes of the city to deliver to the rear doors of restaurants. There he would see more unemployed and homeless people huddled in the alleys. He rarely felt threatened – although he often had to co-ordinate delivery times with the staff of the restaurants to make sure someone kept an eye on the truck. Otherwise, some desperate person might steal some of the meat.[95]

But for all of the obvious advantages of sticking to the job, the work routine was arduous. Ibing usually started at six in the morning and worked twelve hours a day, six days a week; indeed, Saturday was the busiest day, often keeping Ibing out on deliveries until eight at night. He began each day by processing the orders, which involved cutting some of the meat himself. Then he would load the truck and head out on delivery for the day. Not surprisingly, the frigid winter mornings in Winnipeg were the hardest. The truck did not have heating (let alone windshield defrosting), so Ibing scraped layers of ice off the windows in the mornings; he would have to constantly scrape again through the day as the Winnipeg's notoriously cold winds kept freezing the windows up.[96]

The weekly grind of the job left little time for socializing or pastimes. A number of the German customers at his store belonged to a local social club and encouraged him to get involved. Ibing came to their dances and socials when he could, but it was difficult to attend regularly as most events were on Saturday evenings, after his toughest workday. The club was part of the socialist German Workers and Farmers Association (GWFA); Ibing had no interest in joining the right-leaning nationalist German clubs as he thought they were sympathetic to Hitler. But he could not spare the time to get more active and was still not interested in the political aspects of the association's work.[97]

After about four years, the demands of the job were starting to wear on him. In early fall of 1934, he decided to try his luck further west by riding the rails – hopping onto an open car on a freight train and getting a free ride down the rail line. He first went to Saskatchewan (he did not recall precisely where) to work on the harvest again, and then started to drift toward Alberta and British Columbia. As was typical of young men riding the rails at the time, Ibing had no clear plan. Instead he was mostly driven by boredom, frustration, and a sense that prospects had to be better somewhere down the rail line. And like thousands of others, he drifted all the way to the coast without finding any work.[98]

Ibing experienced plenty of the dangers of riding the rails. One time while riding on top of a train, he heard urgent shouts coming from the men closer to the engine at the front. He was not able to make out what they were saying but did notice that others were getting their heads down. He decided to duck as well – right before the train sped into a tunnel. "If I hadn't caught on," he once recounted to his family, "I would have lost my head."[99] Each time Ibing came to a city and could not find work, jumping onto another train to get to the next town could be a struggle. Ibing recalled plenty of CPR police officers watching spots where the train was moving away slowly. Most were sympathetic and did not make much trouble for people riding the rails, but once in a while, there would be a bad one who would chase them off the train. Ibing would thus be forced to lie low and hope for better luck getting on the next train, or sometimes he would find the highway and hitchhike westward.

Ibing hitchhiked through most of the Rockies.[100] One day in the mountains, he strayed from the main road looking for a shortcut – and soon regretted it. He came face to face with a massive grizzly bear. Ibing did not try to run; he and the bear just stood there for a moment watching each other. But then the bear decided simply to move on, perhaps thanks to some remarkably good luck, or perhaps, as he once joked at the family dinner table, because the bear's stomach "was still full from the last guy who had come by." Once the bear was out of sight, Ibing scrambled back to the road heading toward the coast.

By the time he reached Vancouver, Ibing had used up the last of his meagre savings and had to rely on the soup kitchens. But he recalled that the kitchens would not help for long; "they would not feed you once they knew you," he once told me. In another interview, he recounted that "after three days . . . you got a ticket – a railway ticket or a bus ticket – to a labour camp and that's where you [were to] stay."[101] But Ibing was determined to stay out of the camps, so he got back on the rails and headed back to Winnipeg. His return trip was much more direct; he had little reason to make stops, as he knew work would be even scarcer with the harvest season coming to an end. He was often cold on the lonely ride, especially at night, and likely fighting hunger. Once back in Winnipeg, Ibing made a new search around the city, and then decided to return to his old employer, who was happy to take him back. His boss "sort of liked" him, as Ibing was a reliable employee. "I didn't want to go back to him," Ibing confessed, "but that was the last resort."[102]

In the fall of 1934, Ibing was a few months away from his twenty-sixth birthday, but he had already survived more than a lifetime's worth of tribulations. It was remarkable that he kept body and mind together through his early years, but by this point in his life, he was eager to get out of the dismal conditions he was facing. So Ibing started to seek broad-ranging change through politics, looking for a movement that offered hope for a better world.

2 Turning Left

The Best Hope for Change

Not long after he settled back in Winnipeg, Ibing turned in a new direction. It was a gradual change over about a year and a half, beginning in the fall of 1934 when he joined the German Workers and Farmers Association. At first Ibing, who had been resolutely apolitical, was involved mostly in the association's social events. But then his politics started "drifting further left."[1] Later that year he became a member of the Canadian Labour Defence League, which defended Communists and their supporters from government prosecution. Sometime in 1935 he would go on to join the Communist Party of Canada (CPC) itself.

Ibing was acutely aware of the singular circumstances of the era. In interviews and in conversation with his family, he highlighted how hard it is for people in our time to appreciate the severity of the suffering in the Depression era and the deep despair that set in. He also understood that politics took on a particular shape when capitalist democratic systems seemed to be faltering, the Soviet Union was a force to be reckoned with, and the fascist threat was growing.

As with many immigrants who joined Communist organizations in this period, Ibing was drawn to the left partially by his political roots in his homeland. "I had that kind of background," he observed, citing his father's career and being raised in a socialist family.[2] In Germany, he had also borne witness to the "violent striving for power of the Nazi party."[3] In discussions about his politicization, Ibing also emphasized the "depression times" he lived through in Winnipeg, the "rottenness" of the conditions, and the widespread misery. The word he used most frequently to capture the general sense of the time was "hopeless," especially as the 1930s ground on with few signs of recovery. People like Ibing were pushed to seek alternatives, and "the only hope they could see was socialism because . . . [the existing capitalist] system then was so bad you couldn't supply the necessities of life. It couldn't supply work for the people."[4]

As with most people who join a cause and decide to risk their life fighting for it, his motivations were intensely personal – they stemmed from his family, his early experiences, and his own sense of right and wrong. But Ibing's personal story does not quite explain all of his decisions; how his life fit into the broader context of this unique period also shaped his politicization. For instance, Ibing's upbringing in an SPD household in Germany may explain his attraction to leftism in general, but it hardly explains his embrace of Communism in particular. Quite the contrary: when Ibing was growing up, his father's social democrats and the Communists were engaged in a fierce and often violent rivalry. Their enmity is one of the most famous, and tragic, stories in the history of the left. A key source of the animosity was the upheaval that followed World War I, when those on the far left saw an opportunity to create revolution in Germany, just as the Bolsheviks had in Russia in 1917. Far from satisfied with the abdication of the Kaiser and the creation of the Weimar Republic, they wanted to seize this moment of upheaval and turn it toward much more sweeping social and economic transformations. Since Gustav Ibing's SPD played a key role in the founding of Weimar, radical socialists tended to see them as part of the system that needed to be overthrown. SPD leaders, on the other hand, came to fear that in the event of a revolution, they would fall victim to the same kind of Red Terror that was occurring in Soviet Russia; starting in the fall of 1918 the Bolsheviks had thousands of their "class enemies" or "counter-revolutionaries" arrested, many of whom were shot. The SPD thus encouraged remnants of the German army and the Freikorps, the largest right-wing paramilitary group, to brutally suppress the far left's postwar insurgencies. In the first uprising in early 1919, revolutionary leaders Karl Liebknecht and Rosa Luxemburg were murdered; in a second wave of unrest in the Ruhr Valley in 1920, more than a thousand Communist militants were killed, the majority of them prisoners that were executed. Thereafter, any sense of common cause was outweighed by bitterness and mistrust.[5]

In the late 1920s and into the 1930s, the SPD and the Communists continued to struggle against the Nazis and other far-right groups – and with each other. Under the Third Period initiated by the Communist International (Comintern) in Moscow in 1928, Communist parties labelled all capitalist states and parliamentary parties as fascist. Parties such as the SPD were deemed "social fascists," and Moscow ordered German Communists to work ceaselessly to bring down the "fascist" Weimar Republic and its social democratic backers. More generally, Communist parties in the Third Period were directed to create as much instability in Western democracies as possible in the hope of spreading revolution.[6] These divisions on the left, and the Communists' intense focus on destabilization and revolution, further reduced the Weimar Republic's chances of surviving the mounting crises it faced in the early 1930s. Basic societal trust disintegrated under the crushing weight of economic depression, paramilitary street violence grew, and centre- and right-leaning voters abandoned parliamentary parties in droves and gave their support to the Nazis.[7]

Ibing's main response to the political unrest during his youth had been to leave for Canada. He was aware of these internal conflicts on the left, but he was not politically engaged in Germany and did not witness the final stages of Weimar's collapse. He became politicized in a different context, and choosing Communism in the mid-1930s in Canada had drastically different implications than it would have had in Germany a few years earlier. In the broadest terms, he did not see a looming threat of a fascist takeover in Canada, or the need to worry that backing one leftist political party over another might create serious openings for the Canadian extreme right. As Ibing became politically active in this period, he saw anti-fascism as an international issue rather than a domestic one. Canadian social democrats and

Communists also developed a fierce rivalry, though it did not become as violent or as relentlessly destructive as it had been in Germany.[8] Indeed, during roughly the same time period as Ibing was becoming politicized, Communist parties everywhere were ordered to abandon their Third Period approach and adopt Popular Front policies focused on fighting fascism.

Canada had its own notable history of labour and left activism. Although Ibing rarely mentioned Winnipeg's thriving leftist political culture in interviews, there is no doubt that, as a member of the working class in Winnipeg, he was surrounded by it. Class conflict had simmered in the city through the early twentieth century and the war years, and then exploded on May 15, 1919, when workers responded to a call for a general strike to support local building and metal trade unions by shutting down the entire city. Roughly 35,000 workers eventually joined the Winnipeg General Strike; it was the largest disruption in a massive wave of postwar labour unrest, and it would spawn a series of sympathy strikes in western towns in the following weeks.[9] A major counteroffensive by employers and all three levels of government defeated the strike after six weeks, yet support for leftist politics was hardly driven out of the city. Indeed, through most of the interwar period, leftist politicians continued to count successes in local elections and steadily held over one-third of the seats in city council.[10]

The strongest left-leaning electoral forces in the city were social democrats who strove to create a structure rather like the SPD's in Germany: an independent socialist party tied to the labour movement.[11] Their Independent Labour Party (ILP) held a lock on most aldermanic seats in the working-class North End, and regularly elected J.S. Woodsworth (starting in 1921) and A.A. Heaps (starting in 1925) to federal Parliament. After the ILP joined with other groups to form the Co-operative Commonwealth Federation (CCF), Woodsworth became the first leader in 1933.[12] On the municipal front, in 1934 the left scored a major victory, as the ILP (still running under that name) delivered its candidate John Queen to victory in the mayor's race and leftist parties had a working majority in the city council. Hence by the end of 1934, the city's mayor and two of its members of Parliament were socialists who had been arrested at different points in 1919 for their efforts in support of the Winnipeg General Strike.[13]

These breakthroughs for labour-left political parties in Winnipeg undoubtedly encouraged Ibing to become active himself. But as with his background in Germany, they made his choice of the Communists over other brands of socialists particularly interesting. Indeed, the Communists took a back seat to social democrats in Winnipeg. They were junior partners in the left's working majority after the 1934 municipal election.[14] In the 1935 federal election, Heaps scored an impressive victory in Winnipeg North in his first campaign as a CCFer, soundly defeating a challenge from no less than the Communist Party of Canada's general secretary, Tim Buck.[15] But beyond its success in Winnipeg, labour socialists and the CCF struggled to get established, and it remained a distant goal to become the political force that the German SPD had been. On the national level, the Communists were actually better organized and more established than the CCF.[16]

For Ibing, the basic consideration was which party could deliver rapid change and sweep away the wretched social and economic conditions people were facing. "People thought in terms of revolution in those days," he explained, with some humour. "The CCF wasn't that kind of a party. It was a party for gradual change. . . . But it didn't have too much teeth, and young people, they are looking for something that brings quicker results." While he did not adopt the contemptuous attitude toward the CCF that other Communists did, Ibing "never gave them much thought" in the 1930s.[17]

It was the Communist Party of Canada that was showing plenty of teeth. Although Ibing was never asked about which particular CPC initiatives impressed him, a number of historians have noted that the party earned credibility for its remarkably vigorous mobilizing efforts among workers in the early 1930s. The party's work was in keeping with another part of Moscow's Third Period strategy: agitating among non-unionized industrial labourers and the unemployed. Communists in Canada spent less time attacking "social fascists" than did Communist parties elsewhere, especially after their "confrontational posturing" precipitated a drop in CPC membership and the arrest of key party figures, including Buck. Instead, through the Workers' Unity League (WUL), Communist activists led organizing drives in many sectors of the economy, including in the leading mass-production industries of auto, steel, and rubber. WUL organizations were involved in by far the majority of strikes in the early 1930s, many of which led to violent confrontations with police.[18]

In the eyes of someone looking for results, as Ibing was, the Communists' credentials were bolstered even more by their agitation among the unemployed. The WUL created unemployed associations, which organized protests and processions such as the Manitoba Hunger March in 1932.[19] The Communists gained still more traction in the relief camps among increasingly frustrated young men who remained stuck in miserable conditions as the Depression ground on. By 1933, there was unrest in camps around the country, culminating in the most spectacular Communist-led protest of the era, the 1935 On-to-Ottawa Trek. The trek started when a group of about 1,500 relief camp strikers came to Vancouver and after a two-month protest produced little response from any level of government, about a thousand of them headed east on empty freight cars to demand "work and wages." The trek drew strong support – and more trekkers – as it headed through the Prairies until the Royal Canadian Mounted Police (RCMP), under orders from Prime Minister Bennett, stopped it by force in the Regina Riot on July 1, 1935. The authorities instigated the riot in large part out of fear of what would happen when the trek reached Winnipeg, with its well-earned reputation as a hub of radical activity.[20] In the face of such repression, another Communist-allied organization, the Canadian Labour Defence League, gained popularity by defending party activists and other labour militants against prosecution by the authorities.[21]

The impact of the Soviet Union drew Ibing even more toward Communism – and away from social democracy – than the CPC's activities within Canada. The response of social democratic governments in Europe to the Depression hardly inspired confidence. Historian Tony Judt (himself a noted social democrat) goes so far as to claim that through the 1920s and 1930s, the moderate or "democratic" left in Europe had no meaningful economic policy at all. Social democrats failed to offer a clear program to get the collapsed global economy back on its feet.[22] When people such as Ibing were looking for new hope and quick results, the real beacon seemed to be the Soviet Union. As capitalist economies were unable even "to supply the necessities of life," as Ibing put it, the Soviet Union appeared at the time to be developing its economy, building a new society, and showing what was possible under socialism. When asked in one interview about his model of socialism in the 1930s, Ibing responded, "Everybody thought in terms of the Soviet Union in those days. And there was no other way to look at it. There was no other example."[23]

At the time, a crucial part of placing hope in the Soviet model was that Stalin's atrocities, such as the starvation of millions due to the collectivization of agriculture in the Ukraine, remained out of sight. In addition, most of Stalin's murderous purges within his party had not yet taken place. "The example of the Soviet Union was only in our minds because none of us had ever seen . . . what was really going on in the Soviet Union. We didn't realize [what] was being . . . covered up," Ibing explained in one interview. Ibing did acknowledge that he heard a few rumblings about Stalin's repressive tactics in the 1930s, but these were easily cast aside: "As far as we were concerned everything was . . . in a blissful state."[24]

Ibing was correct that the Soviet Union was widely viewed as a beacon of hope at that time. As renowned historian Eric Hobsbawm puts it, there was a sense even among mainstream political leaders throughout the Western world that capitalism was facing a "crisis of progress" and major structural reforms, at a minimum, were going to be needed if it was to survive.[25] Elected leaders and influential thinkers looked for ways to increase the role of governments in alleviating suffering and planning the economy. Prominent commentators saw particular promise in the Soviet model and its economic advances. Influential Canadians who visited the USSR in the 1930s, including Sir Frederick Banting, came back to praise the work of Soviet planners. Leading social democrat and future CCF leader J.S. Woodsworth did raise concerns about protections of individual rights in the Soviet Union after his visit in 1932 – but overall, he claimed "to have witnessed a successful socialist system at work."[26] As the Depression ground on and suffering and instability deepened, the sense grew that the 1930s were bringing "the twilight of liberalism in the west," while the USSR became "the exemplification of social engineering for human purposes – of the force of human hope for a better society."[27]

Ibing's politicization was also influenced by the relationship between leftist parties and European immigrant communities in Canada. The CCF had a deeply Anglo-Canadian character and drew on many British labour and left traditions. CCF publications were full of content about new ideas and debates in Britain, which "most CCFers still considered 'the old country.'"[28] Perhaps unsurprisingly, the CCF counted very little support among European "ethnic groups" in Canada. The Communists, in contrast, had deep roots in many immigrant communities, including the Ukrainian and the Eastern European Jewish communities.[29] In the early 1930s, Communism also started to attract a smaller yet significant number of new members from the German community. As recent German immigrants became politically active, they would in turn help to draw Ibing toward Communism.

Most German migrants who had come to Canada before World War I showed little interest in unions or leftist politics, since they were from rural backgrounds and saw their futures in independent farming. The largest Marxist party in the early twentieth century, the Socialist Party of Canada, did have a German-speaking section, but it was small and short-lived.[30] But the 1925–1930 wave of migrants changed the politics within at least parts of the German community in Canada, especially in the cities. A larger proportion of these new immigrants had experience with industrial labour; by the early 1930s, the contingent of immigrants with industrial working-class backgrounds were still not a majority, even among recent arrivals, but they had gained enough strength to sustain labour and left-leaning political organizations. When the Depression hit recent migrants hard, they had a further incentive to get active – and many of these migrants saw greater hope in Communism.[31]

The most influential of the new organizations was the German Workers and Farmers Association, and its most influential local was probably Winnipeg's. Many of Ibing's friends were members, and he spent much of his free social time at the local's events. Indeed, Ibing's experience was a good example of someone becoming politically active through social and cultural events organized by an immigrant leftist group. What historians call "hall socialism" could be applied literally to Ibing's case, as his first active participation in the GWFA was volunteering for events to help pay for the "the little hall" they had. He joined the association in 1934 and then become more involved in explicitly political activities.[32]

As Arthur Grenke – one of Ibing's interviewers – has shown in detail, the GWFA was closely tied to the Communist Party of Canada and the Canadian Labour Defence League. The bond with the CLDL was particularly strong because the defence league defended foreign workers threatened with deportation for being unemployed or for alleged subversive activity.[33] Ibing claimed that over half of the members of Winnipeg's GWFA local were active Communists. Not long after joining the GWFA, Ibing joined the CLDL, and in 1935, he joined the Communist party itself.[34]

Hence a combination of broad trends in economic, immigration, and left history helped draw Ibing toward Communism – but one factor was notable for its relative absence: ideology and party doctrine. Like many converts, Ibing did go through a period when he was "holier than the pope, as they say" in his faith in Communism. But this religious-type devotion was to the model of the Soviet Union and to Communism as a way of making a better world.[35] Ideology and partisan agendas meant much less to him than the basic cause of social justice. When one interviewer asked about how he defined socialism or understood particular points of Marxist ideology when he was a Communist, Ibing displayed little interest in the subject. When pressed, he wanted to focus on broad humanitarian principles: he insisted that the most important thing about any social system was that it have a "human aspect . . . it has to do something for humanity."[36] For him, this was the key characteristic of socialism, that it have "a strong [focus on] a humanitarian goal." He added that there is no point to any "ism" unless it "can improve things." In the 1930s, the draw of socialism was that it seemed to have "some more human[ity] to it. An atmosphere where people could be a lot happier than they were in the capitalistic system."[37]

This trait was shared by a significant proportion of those who joined the CPC in these years; they had little time for Communist theory, and mostly saw the party as the best hope for change and the best outlet for their activism. Even as prominent a WUL organizer as Jack Scott remembered that although he read party literature and some Marxist texts, after several years of activism in the early 1930s, he still "didn't have a well-developed sense of Marxist theory or even what communism was."[38] Ibing seems to have been consistently well informed about the party's position on most issues, but official policy statements did not inspire his politicization. An idealized vision of the Soviet Union and of Communism as a means to create a new society meant much more to him.[39] Yet there was one part of the Communists' platform that *did* play a vital role in Ibing's conversion to the movement, because it mattered more to him than almost any other cause: fighting fascism.

There Was No One Else Against Hitler

It is no coincidence that Ibing became politicized around the same time as the Communists were undergoing a major change in their broad approach. Starting in May 1934 the Communist International in Moscow signalled a shift in policy away from the heavy focus on an imminent revolution that characterized the Third Period; the shift was formally announced at the Comintern's Congress the following July.[40] In this new Popular Front period, fascists were seen as threats not only to the Soviet Union, but also to the entire world; it thus became the duty of Communists to unite with progressives in their countries in a broad-based struggle against fascism. Social democrats and other non-Communist leftist organizations were no longer "social fascists" – they were now potential allies in an all-consuming struggle against the radical right. Grassroots labour protests did continue in 1934 and 1935, especially among the unemployed (including the On-to-Ottawa Trek), but the Communist Party of Canada devoted a vast amount of effort to creating alliances with any party, organization, or public figure that was ready to join the anti-fascist cause.[41]

It is hard to overstate the importance of the CPC's anti-fascism in Ibing's politicization. He, too, was convinced that the biggest threat to any hope for a more humanitarian world was the rise of Hitler and Mussolini. Ibing's experience with the Nazis in Germany gave him more than a "real dislike, a real hatred for those people"; it also gave him a deep sense of urgency about this struggle. He understood that fascists had to be confronted; otherwise, they would continue to seek power and, once in control of a state, expand their aggression internationally.[42] In other words, Ibing recognized that, as Hobsbawm puts it, "the policy objectives of [Germany's] National Socialism were irrational and unlimited. Expansion and aggression were built into the system and, short of accepting German domination in advance, i.e. choosing not to resist the Nazi advance, war was unavoidable, sooner rather than later."[43]

Even before the start of the Popular Front era, Communists made strident anti-fascism a pillar of their identity. During their feuds with other leftists during the Third Period era, the Communists' hostility toward fascism was ever-present.[44] Their track record in fighting fascism was hardly perfect, as the Communists' inability to stop Hitler's rise in Germany showed. However, the Nazis themselves identified Communists as one of their biggest ideological enemies. Indeed, Hitler both vilified Communists continually and played to fears of Communist revolution to build his political base. The SPD's defeat at the hands of the Nazis deepened the sense that other leftist parties were ineffective at holding back the rising tide of fascism, and that social democrats could not cope with the crises of the era.[45]

The mainstream parties in the West were even less credible as guardians against the rise of fascism. Indeed, the response to the rise of fascism by the political establishments in Western democracies ranged from feebleness and passivity to acceptance and sometimes sympathy. Many Western political leaders were more concerned with stamping out threats from the far left than from the far right. The Conservative prime minister of Canada, R.B. Bennett, was obsessed with the threat of Communism; he directed the authorities to suppress it by force and called on Canadians to "put the iron heel of ruthlessness" down on "organizations from foreign lands that seek to destroy our institutions."[46] Such fears of radical leftist insurgencies in Western democracies stemmed not only from the creation of the Soviet Union and the emergence of Communist parties, but also from a series of other upheavals, including the workers' uprisings in Germany, the short-lived revolutions in Hungary and Slovakia after World War I, and the Great Strike in Britain in 1926.[47] Although North American societies were generally more stable, their leaders were shaken by general strikes in Seattle and Winnipeg, and the broader workers' revolt in Canada after World War I. And the collapse of capitalist economies in the Great Depression and the crisis of progress added greatly to the sense of vulnerability.

Western leaders were therefore impressed with fascist governments if they could stabilize the economies of their countries and suppress threats from the far left. Indeed, the ruthless destruction of the Italian and German left by Mussolini and Hitler, respectively, rarely elicited complaints – and sometimes earned praise – from Western powers.[48] Even moderate social democratic parties were seen as dire threats to the establishment in many Western democracies. For instance, a popular slogan on the French right was "better Hitler than Léon Blum," in reference to the leader of the French Socialist Party and prime minister in 1936–1937.[49]

Western leaders' dismal response to fascism made an impression on Ibing that lasted through the rest of his life. Several times in general discussions about politics at the turn of the twenty-first century, he cited what happened in the 1930s as clear proof that mainstream politicians in Canada, the United

States, and elsewhere could tolerate any murderous regime if they believed its actions would suit their interests. He also did not forget how, even after fascist powers became increasingly aggressive militarily through the mid-1930s, Western leaders remained tolerant of them, hoping that eventually they would turn their aggression toward the Communists. Ibing recalled that elites in Canada, France, and Britain "weren't friends with Hitler," but they were dedicated to appeasing him because eventually he "would have to fight Russia."[50]

Even compared to Communist parties in other countries, the Canadian party was notably effective early on in making itself the obvious home for anti-fascists and in mobilizing widespread opposition to the far right. The Canadian Labour Defence League, which Ibing joined before joining the CPC, played an important role in this regard: it cited excessive uses of state authority against Communists as a sign that fascist tendencies were seeping from outside into the Canadian elites. It used such arguments to mobilize popular support for its campaigns to free Communist activists from prison.[51] The CLDL was especially effective in getting the public behind the effort to secure the release of Communist party leader Tim Buck in 1934. When Buck was paroled in November 1934, the rally to celebrate exceeded the capacity of Maple Leaf Gardens in Toronto.[52] That fall, the party took other steps to forge alliances against the extreme right, such as creating the Canadian League Against War and Fascism.[53]

A second aspect of the Popular Front strategy was crucial in attracting Ibing to the Communists: changing the internal culture of the party. A hallmark of Communist parties throughout the world was strict discipline and a willingness to use ruthless means to achieve objectives handed down from the Comintern. Although there is much debate (in Canada as elsewhere) regarding just how rigidly the national party adhered to the line announced in Moscow, Communist parties were certainly not models of internal democracy and openness. This kind of ethos did not suit Ibing's character and worldview. He stated repeatedly in interviews (and more often in casual conversation) that he was never a follower by nature; rather, he was "a questioning sort of a person" who "never was one to accept the gospel" handed down from higher authorities.[54] This may have been a reason Ibing did not join the CPC earlier. The Communists' militancy in the early 1930s showed Ibing that they had teeth and promised quick results, and the Canadian party was generally less sectarian than most Communist parties at the time. Still, the tendencies that would have repelled Ibing – such as rigid internal discipline and the use of secrecy and underground activities – were pronounced during the party's Third Period phase, which lasted through the early 1930s.

But in the shift to the Popular Front phase, the hardest of the party's edges were softened. The Canadian League Against War and Fascism, for instance, was more open to non-Communist members – and even non-working-class members – than previous front groups.[55] Starting in late 1935, the party was remodelled to a great extent in the effort to build an alliance against fascism and grow the party base. According to John Manley, a historian of Canadian Communism, "CPC leaders launched an all-out assault on the party's conspiratorial and 'sectarian' culture"; meetings were to have open-ended discussions of politics, and party stalwarts were forbidden from imposing the official line on new members.[56]

These changes undoubtedly helped Ibing to feel that he had a place in the party and allowed him to develop that papal level of faith in the cause. In certain interviews, however, he recalled having difficulty from the outset in toeing the line. He held only one official role in the party at this time, in the executive of the Winnipeg unit of the GWFA. He described the position as giving almost no power, as little more than taking notes and maintaining records – and he stayed in the post only briefly in 1935.[57] "I never was in full agreement with the party," Ibing said in one interview. "I didn't like its leadership. I never got inside with Tim Buck and those men."[58] Manley contends that much of the Stalinist character of the CPC persisted through the Popular Front period; Ibing recalled being uneasy in the 1930s with the party's willingness to say or do almost anything to advance the cause, its view that the ends justified the means. He told another interviewer that "people wanted to bring about socialism by hook or by crook."[59] Even more of a problem was the authoritarianism that continued to be central to the CPC's structure and ideology. Ibing "didn't like dictatorships," and that created doubts for him about both the culture of the party and core parts of the party's agenda, such as forming a dictatorship of the proletariat after a revolution.[60]

It is difficult to determine how serious Ibing's apprehensions became at this time, or how much his recollections of his doubts were a case of projecting backward his later disillusionment with Communism. Like doubts about the Soviet Union, questions about Communist party practices were easy to discount at this moment in history: as the Popular Front strategy was implemented, the overall stock of the Communists around the world was rising still further. The Popular Front inspired what Judt calls a "rebirth of popular left-wing politics," including new waves of worker militancy in parts of Europe and electoral successes in Spain and France.[61] What is certain is that Ibing's reservations were easily outweighed in the mid-1930s by the faith he placed in the Soviet Union and by the imperative to find an organization that would fight fascism. For Ibing, that meant the Communists, because he felt "there wasn't anyone else that was against Hitler then."[62] He may have had early reservations about what the party stood for, but he was convinced about what joining the CPC allowed him to stand against: "It was not that I was such a great ardent communist, you know, I wasn't. I was basically an anti-fascist, and socialist-minded."[63]

The Call to Spain

Through 1935 and early 1936, the aggression of Germany and Italy in international affairs increasingly consumed the attention of anti-fascists such as Ibing. He was never asked by interviewers about which specific crises alarmed him most in these months, but for anti-fascists, the news from Europe was almost entirely bad. Just as anti-fascists expected, Hitler wasted little time in rebuilding the German armed forces. In early 1935, he announced that Germany would no longer respect the disarmament clauses of the Treaty of Versailles. Hitler then prepared to send his army back into the Rhineland, the area – including Ibing's early-childhood hometown of Mainz – that had been occupied by the French after World War I; the remilitarization happened in March 1936. Mussolini started a brutal invasion of Abyssinia (called Ethiopia today) in October 1935, taking control of its territory in about nine months, and killing about 275,000 enemy soldiers and civilians in the process.[64]

Then, in July 1936, Hitler and Mussolini threw their support behind the *pronunciamiento*, or military uprising against the democratically elected government of the Spanish Republic. The immediate impact in Spain of the Italian and German intervention was massive: without their assistance, the rebel generals could not have moved many of their troops from North Africa to the Spanish mainland, and the rebellion likely would have failed. In the ensuing early weeks of the war, German and Italian air support would give the rebels (or the Nationalists, among whom Generalissimo Franco was slowly emerging as the leader) a major advantage against the Loyalists defending the Spanish Republic.[65]

Anti-fascists such as Ibing recognized right away the importance of the Spanish Civil War. The key was the involvement of the fascist powers; Ibing often put it simply: "This was a chance to fight Hitler."[66] As Ibing understood, Franco and the rebels were not fascist in the strictest sense – they had their own right-wing ideology that was distinct to Spain. Still, the Nationalists were brutal, reactionary, and authoritarian, and some militias allied with them, such as the Falange, were avowedly fascist. But what mattered far more was that Hitler had cast his lot with the Nationalists in the hope of installing another Nazi-allied dictatorship in Europe. Mussolini even went so far as to boast that the "Fascist sword had been unsheathed" in Spain.[67] Anti-fascists thus saw a chance to deal the fascist regimes a major setback by defeating Franco. Western governments also understood that the German and Italian leaders could be vulnerable, since, as one senior American diplomat observed, "Having recognized Franco as conqueror when this has yet to be proved, Mussolini and Hitler must see to it that he is successful or be associated with a failure."[68] Altogether, defending the Republic became, as historian Paul Preston puts it, "widely seen as the beginning of a world-wide counter-offensive against fascism."[69]

It also rapidly became evident that Western democracies were not up to leading this counteroffensive. The political dynamics around anti-fascism that drew Ibing to the Communists in 1934–1935 played out even more clearly in the response to the Spanish Civil War. The Spanish Republic appealed for outside help as soon as the war began – but the appeal went unheeded. The British were most adamant in opposing any involvement; British elites were more dedicated than ever to appeasement and the class and ideological outlook that lay beneath it. They were particularly hostile to the idea of fighting Franco and Hitler in order to defend the Republic's government, which was a Popular Front coalition of leftist parties. The British elite's class-based hostility to the Republic was bolstered by the social revolution that broke out in Spain after the election and continued after the outbreak of the civil war, with peasants seizing land and workers taking control of plants. In France, socialist Léon Blum led a Popular Front coalition to power in May 1936, and at first was ready to support the Spanish Republic. But Blum quickly backed down in the face of resistance from Britain and from centrist parties within his coalition, in addition to the furious opposition of the French right. In the United States, the deeply isolationist mindset of political leaders of the period, and strong support for Franco among many on the American right, precluded any serious support for the Spanish Republic.[70] In all of these countries, the attitudes of policy makers stood in sharp contrast to those of the majority of the people – even in the United States, where a poll showed public support of the Republic over the Nationalists at an overwhelming 87 per cent to 13 per cent.[71]

As for Canada, there was not even a pretense that it would get involved. This was in part because, as a Dominion, Canada took foreign policy signals from Great Britain. Canadians were also too preoccupied with the economic crisis, and carried too many bad memories of suffering and social divisions during World War I to consider making commitments overseas. Among the political leadership, as one historian observes, "there were no more enthusiastic appeasers than Canadians."[72] When W.L. Mackenzie King returned to power in 1935, his government may have been less obsessed with the threat of Communism than Bennett's was, but King was convinced that the Nazis were preferable to their radical leftist rivals. In June 1937, King visited Germany; he came away deeply impressed by how revitalized the country seemed and declared himself "tremendously relieved" that perceptions of the Nazis as dangerous seemed overblown to him. "I can honestly say," Canada's prime minister wrote in his diary, "that it was as enjoyable, informative and inspiring as any visit I have had anywhere."[73] King also wrote that Hitler "will rank some day with Joan of Arc among the deliverers of his people."[74]

In Europe, the meekness of the Western powers was clearly expressed in the Non-intervention Agreement. In August 1936, all of the major European powers made broad commitments to keep out of the Spanish conflict and provide no assistance, in terms of equipment or supplies, to either side. In effect, non-intervention violated international law and discriminated against the Republic, because it was still the government and therefore had the legal right to buy weapons and protect itself against an armed revolt. Instead, non-intervention deemed both sides equally abhorrent and barred both from receiving assistance.[75] Further, the agreement turned into a farce almost as soon as it was struck; while France and Britain refused to allow the Spanish Republic to import supplies, Germany and Italy not only continued but greatly expanded their support for the Nationalists, with Mussolini in particular pouring thousands of troops into Spain in late 1936 and early 1937. Yet France and Britain generally refused to even acknowledge how brazenly Hitler and Mussolini were violating the agreement, let alone to take action. As long as France and Britain continued to abide strictly by non-interventionist policies, the Spanish Republic's material disadvantage in the war grew ever greater.[76]

The patent unfairness of the situation seemed to stir something in Ibing that went beyond politics. It was something more personal, at once straightforward and broad-reaching in its importance. "I have always had, from my early youth," Ibing once explained, "the strongest sympathy for the underdog."[77] And this was the role that the Spanish Republic was unmistakably playing by the fall of 1936: left alone to take on a rightist military insurrection backed by fascist nations, while Western democracies looked away. Something resonated with him as he watched the Republicans be "boycotted by France and Britain. They weren't supplied with arms. They couldn't even buy them."[78]

When discussing his views on the Spanish Civil War, Ibing regularly emphasized this sympathy for the underdog. In reminiscences he wrote for William Beeching's history of Canadian volunteers, he went so far as to call it the only answer he had to the question of why he volunteered. Indeed, Ibing believed "there was a natural basis" for these impulses, starting in his upbringing; the "general direction at home" was always "towards the underdog."[79] Ibing's experiences in Germany – as part of a Protestant minority in a Catholic part of the Rhineland, as a child who was singled out for abuse because of his family's socialism, and as a youth who could not bear to witness the bullying and worship of violence around him – reinforced his basic identification with the disadvantaged (even if he had not yet become political).[80] "And of course," Ibing noted in one interview, "I wound up being an underdog myself . . . when I came to Canada" and had to struggle to survive the Depression.[81]

These sympathies would have been aroused further by the brutality of Franco's armies. From an early point, Franco and the Spanish generals showed a commitment to the use of violence that was even more brutal and on a much larger scale than what Ibing had witnessed among the Nazis in 1920s Germany. The Nationalists' leaders were determined not only to seize power, but also to destroy any attachment to the idea and culture of the Republic. This meant creating what Preston describes as "an ocean of political slaughter," including the systematic executions of prisoners (who were often first tortured), and terrorizing and degrading civilian population in areas retaken from the Republican side. While there were also acts of violence by pro-Republican forces, these were mostly smaller outbursts by particular groups and usually discouraged by Republican leaders. In sharp contrast, the Nationalist generals broadcast their commitment to the methodical use of violence for all to hear. Franco famously told American reporter Jay Allen in July 1936 that he would "save Spain from Marxism" even if it meant shooting half the population.[82]

Crucially, the first Western reporters who came to Spain witnessed the horrors and brought them home to their readers. The report that first put the war in the headlines in North America was Allen's in the *Chicago Tribune*; it detailed the mass killings of prisoners in the bullring of the western Spanish town of Badajoz. In twelve hours after taking control of the town in mid-August 1936, the army rounded up and killed 1,800 people, and then killed as many as 2,000 more in the following days. Allen wrote that the "blood was supposed to be palm-deep on the far side of the lane [that enters the ring]."[83] While some Franco sympathizers tried to discredit the reports, the colonel who led the capture of the town was quite frank with a reporter for the *New York Herald Tribune*: "Of course we shot them. What do you expect? Was I supposed to take 4,000 Reds with me as my column advanced, racing against time?"[84]

Ibing's support for the Republic was also strengthened by the political and social changes occurring within Spain. Between the election victory of the Popular Front coalition and the continuing social revolution in many parts of the country, Spain became another place that offered badly needed hope. Ibing was inspired by the initiative of "the Spanish people . . . to build [their country] on a Republican basis . . . they wanted to build up their lives . . . that was the thing."[85] This was another concern that went beyond a narrow sense of loyalty to Communism. Ibing was aware that a mixture of leftist groups was supporting the Republic and gaining strength within it, including the anarchists and what he called "a strong socialist party." He was not preoccupied with how small and weak Spain's Communist party was early in the war; what mattered most was that the "the Republic had features that were socialistic."[86]

In the earliest stages of the Spanish Civil War, support for the Republic was driven at the grassroots level, as a broad range of progressives and leftists in many countries – something vaguely resembling a popular front – quickly identified with the Spanish Republic. Many were not Communists, and many had allegiances to different parties within the Republican side. But as Hobsbawm contends, anti-fascists "from the liberals to the outer reaches of the Left immediately recognized the Spanish struggle as their own."[87]

Stalin, however, initially hesitated to come to the defence of the Spanish Republic. He was gripped by diplomatic and strategic worries: intervening in Spain would require violating the policy of non-intervention and thereby alienating Britain and France. Stalin knew he would need British and French help in the event of a war with Germany.[88] Ibing gave little weight to such geopolitical calculations; for him, Moscow's delays in these weeks were another source of frustration about Communist leadership. Ibing's recollections about the first months of the war conveyed a sense of the urgency of the situation and an impatience to see decisive action to save the Republic.

In late September 1936, Stalin altered course. As Franco's armies stormed toward Madrid, Stalin was alarmed that another victory for the fascists and their allies seemed likely, and perhaps also that he might lose credibility among anti-fascists on the left if he did nothing while the Republic fell. Stalin famously termed the defence of Spain "the common cause of all advanced and progressive mankind" and began – still somewhat slowly – to commit resources to the fight.[89] Moscow formed the International Brigades on September 18, and the first large shipments of military supplies and equipment were sent to the Republic on September 29. The Spanish Communist party's influence in the Republic grew dramatically, and Communist parties all over the Western world began to raise funds and recruit volunteers for the war effort. In the fall of 1936, the CPC's main support organization, the Committee to Aid Spanish Democracy, was up and running and Ibing noticed their calls for donations for the Republican cause or volunteers to join the fight.[90] Ibing did not receive – or need – much recruiting; "nobody told me to go," he stated flatly in one interview.[91] He had no doubt that the situation amounted to a call to duty for people like him. He told his friends in the GWFA that the Spanish Republic "must be supported by every honest anti-fascist," adding "that meant me, too."[92]

Indeed, to a great extent Ibing was ahead of his party in his commitment to Spain. He made his decision to volunteer in early November, just a few weeks after the first units of the International Brigades arrived in Spain. His decision came so soon that the Communists had not yet established any means of getting him to Spain, and Ibing was told he was going to have to go home and wait.[93] A few weeks later, he was informed that tickets had been secured for volunteers on a boat leaving soon from New York City and that there were accommodations where he could stay in the city before the ship sailed. The international support infrastructure was still barely in place and the plans were a bit vague; Ibing did not even know which organization it was that would help him in New York or cover his costs while he was there (he assumed it was an American Communist group to aid Spain). The larger problem was that the Canadian organizations had barely begun to raise funds, and they still did not have enough to cover his trip to New York. But Ibing's mind was made up to go, and he did not want to wait any longer; he paid for the ticket to New York City himself. He quickly said his goodbyes to those he knew in Winnipeg and got on the train heading to the U.S. East Coast.[94]

Volunteers

With the International Brigades newly formed, and regiments from different countries still taking shape, Ibing had no idea when he left where he would be deployed. It was unlikely that he would serve in a Canadian unit: most Canadian volunteers would only start arriving in Spain in the spring of 1937. Ibing had not taken Canadian citizenship – a fact that would affect his options later on. There was a good chance that he would join the Thaelmann Battalion, made up of German volunteers. The Thaelmann was the first unit of international volunteers to fight in Spain, and it served as the foundation of the larger International Brigades.[95] Ibing had much in common with other German volunteers, including his history with the German left and an anti-fascism that was reinforced by direct exposure to the Nazis in Germany. He would frequently emphasize that he understood the threat posed by the Nazis in a way that most people in Canada could not.[96]

But in many respects, Ibing's background and experiences were quite different from those of other German members of the International Brigades. Most German volunteers had been politically active in the losing struggle against the Nazi seizure of power in the early 1930s. They were thus forced into exile and marked by the Nazis as enemies of the Reich. Through 1934 and 1935, they were on the run from either immigration authorities in European countries or the Nazi secret police, whose pursuit was relentless. Ibing's decision to leave Winnipeg for Spain was therefore taken much more freely than that of German volunteers who went to Spain with "nothing to lose but their exile."[97] Indeed, most German volunteers saw the civil war as a new chance to win their desperate and ongoing struggle against Hitler, and therefore a chance to go home again or at least create a safe haven in Spain.

Ibing had considerably more in common with the other 1,700 Canadian volunteers, many of whom would form the Mackenzie-Papineau Battalion in May 1937.[98] In many ways, he did not fit into this group either, and he never ended up fighting alongside other Canadians. Ibing was different not only because he had direct exposure to Nazi aggression in Germany and went to Spain at such an early point, but also because his economic situation was better than that of most volunteers. Ibing had a steady job that provided security to get by month to month. His ability to pay his own way to New York on his way to Spain was quite unusual.[99] He also brought work skills and experience that would be crucial in shaping his role in Spain. In contrast, many Canadian volunteers were unemployed and struggling to survive; a considerable number had been homeless or living in relief camps. Some of these volunteers were involved in the unrest organized by the Communists and became even more politicized after facing violent police repression at events such as the Regina Riot. For instance, Ron Liversedge, an organizer of the

On-to-Ottawa Trek and a volunteer in Spain, claimed that five hundred of the trekkers caught in the Regina Riot went on to join the International Brigades.[100] Ibing had not been involved in militant protests or confrontations with Canadian authorities.

On the other hand, what was quite typical for a Canadian volunteer was Ibing's experience as a recent immigrant to Canada who had felt the brunt of the Depression. The volunteers were usually immigrants from continental Europe or the British Isles, most of whom had arrived during the recent wave of immigration between the end of World War I and the onset of the Depression. The conditions they endured in the 1930s not only politicized them, but also made them likely to head overseas in support of a worthy cause. Most found it almost impossible to get settled and lay down roots in Canada during the Depression, and they longed to escape a deep sense of aimlessness. Ibing's experience riding the rails in desperate hope of finding something better was also common among volunteers. They did not have much – spouses, children, or economic prospects – that would keep them in Canada.[101] Indeed, the future in Canada promised little except more hardship and emptiness. "I was not married, I didn't have relatives in Canada," Ibing recalled, "and I thought, well, [going to Spain] was my opportunity to do something. I was fed up working 12 hours a day, and Saturdays, too."[102]

This mixture of motivations was common among Canadian volunteers. As Jules Paivio, another volunteer, put it, his motivation was "partly a dissatisfaction with a lack of real purpose and this being an opportunity [to have] a real purpose in life."[103] Ibing even held out hope that if Franco and the generals could be beaten back, the new society being started in Spain offered brighter prospects than seemed available in Canada. He expressed hope that he would stay in Spain after the war was won for the Republic, so that he and other volunteer fighters could "have some kind of a future there."[104] This did not mean (as has been charged by right-wing commentators) that members of the International Brigades such as Ibing were opportunists or soldiers of fortune. As Michael Petrou states in his study of Canadian volunteers, "it is unlikely that many . . . volunteered primarily for money,"[105] and few other volunteers mentioned aspirations to settle in Spain after the war. But like Ibing, many did see the Republic and the revolution in Spain as a source of hope for the future – one they wanted to help defend. As William Beeching (himself a volunteer) put it in his history, many saw a chance to "directly participate in a struggle for a new social order in which unemployment and all of the other scourges from which they suffered would be forever eliminated."[106]

But Ibing was not naive about the fact that volunteering meant going to war against a brutal enemy. He was also hardly the only volunteer who was far more dedicated to anti-fascism than to the Communist party.[107] According to Petrou, the majority of volunteers were not long-time party members; most, including Ibing, had joined less than three years before going to Spain. A chunk of the Canadian volunteers were Communist die-hards, but the party itself was often concerned that so many volunteers would not follow official directives. CPC officials complained to Moscow about volunteers who were independent-minded, politically "disinterested," or worst of all, unwilling "to accept permanent authority."[108]

Communism and anti-fascism were part of the internationalization of politics in these years. Millions of people such as Ibing joined Communist organizations that took their direction from outside their countries in order to resist the threat of fascism to civilized society everywhere. It did not matter that they lived in a separate country, or indeed a separate continent, from where fascist parties had taken power: the causes crossed borders and indeed oceans. This stands in marked contrast to the early twenty-first century, when the economy and much of the culture is globalized and yet much of the political discourse is remarkably insular. Although Ibing became politicized in Canada in the 1930s, he drew his inspiration from the Soviet Union, his primary focus became stopping fascism in Europe, and by the end of 1936 he was on his way to Spain to be a soldier in its civil war.

Over the span of just over two years, Ibing's worldview had gone through a dramatic transformation. It was clearly a change driven by both careful reflection about how to bring society out of the misery of the Great Depression and a complex interaction between his life experiences and the particular social and political context of the 1930s. The end point of this transformation was a conviction that if he believed in his political principles, he had to take action – he would have to fight for them. As Ibing put it in one interview: "It wasn't good enough to just talk about Hitler or against Hitler. There was an opportunity to do something. Hitler wanted to take over Spain. And I thought that was my opportunity to do something."[109]

3 The International Brigades

A Perilous Journey

IBING SET OFF TO NEW YORK EN ROUTE TO SPAIN with a sense of optimism and adventure, and an even greater sense of looming danger. He always insisted that volunteers heading off to war against Franco and his fascist allies "went with [their] eyes open" to the perils.[1] But even the most vivid imagination could not have conceived of the extent – and the variety – of difficulties he would soon face. He arrived without knowing much about the groups involved in supporting volunteers, other than their connections to the Communist party. But they looked after him quite well. A strong network of organizations was undoubtedly needed; getting to Spain was a complicated challenge involving several stages: first to France, then to the south and the frontier with Spain, then over a sealed border, and then within Spain to the International Brigades' military headquarters in Albacete.

Ibing stayed in New York for almost two weeks in a "sort of a single men's hotel" with "little cubby holes for rooms with nothing but a little bed and a chair." He took the chance to walk around the city and met other volunteers who were starting "the same adventure," before the ship was ready to take him to Cherbourg, probably right around the turn of the New Year of 1937.[2] For many volunteers, the trip across the Atlantic was supposed to have an air of grave secrecy; they were usually encouraged to conceal their intention to go to fight in Spain.[3] But Ibing never mentioned receiving such instructions, let alone following them. He recalled being part of a large group of volunteers on the ship, and their handlers did not try to stop them from fraternizing.[4]

Volunteers may often have dropped their attempts at secrecy early during their voyages, or perhaps it was because Ibing was in one of the first groups of volunteers to leave the U.S., and official restrictions against travel to Spain were still a few months away.[5]

Ibing recalled the voyage across the Atlantic as one of the only pleasant surprises of his experiences as a volunteer. It is worth noting an irony here that would have delighted him had he learned of it: the ship carrying Ibing and other volunteers from working-class, Communist backgrounds – the *Ile-de-France* – was well known not only as one of the largest ocean liners in operation at the time, but also for its luxury facilities and services. In the mid-1930s, no transatlantic liner carried more first-class passengers. The ship was also the first to be equipped with refrigerators, which made it the first to carry an eminently upper-class item, Brie cheese, from France to the United States.[6] Although the volunteers travelled in the cheapest class and would not enjoy such luxury fare, the food and accommodations were better on the ship than the conditions most of them had experienced during the 1930s. Those who had been unemployed and relying on soup kitchens and charity were especially pleased. "We lived very well on the boat," Ibing recalled. "Of course, morale was great." The ship's service staff were apparently less happy, however, as the volunteers had no money to spare for tips.[7]

The main transit hub for volunteers for the International Brigades was Paris, where the French and Italian Communist parties organized volunteers coming from far and wide. Although Ibing was among the first North Americans to arrive, thousands of volunteers from around Europe had been passing through on their way to Spain for a few months.[8] After a few days in Paris, he headed south on a train known as the "Red Express" that transported hundreds of members of the International Brigades to Spain.[9] His trip was apparently relatively quiet compared with other accounts of the war, in which volunteers shared wine and food and continuously belted out The Internationale.[10] Then Ibing was taken with a small group of volunteers to a town at the edge of the Pyrenees Mountains. It was February 1937 when he crossed into Spain.

Getting over the Pyrenees was a rite of passage of sorts for members of the International Brigades. In the early months of the war, the border was lightly guarded and volunteers could get into Spain without much effort, just a quick hike through the region's orchards. But through early 1937, France faced growing international pressure (especially from Britain) to stop allowing supplies and volunteers to pass easily into Spain. Around the time Ibing made the crossing, the French government closed the border and beefed up patrols in the area. As France and its allies became ever more committed to appeasing Hitler, the French authorities applied the policy of non-intervention more strictly – and more unmistakably against those supporting the Republic.[11] A minority of volunteers were able to avoid the mountains and arrive by sea, but that option closed a few months later after a Republican ship, the *Ciudad de Barcelona*, was torpedoed by an Italian submarine in Nationalist hands; the freighter was carrying about 250 volunteers from Marseille to Barcelona and more than 50 died when it went down in May 1937. Hence the vast majority of volunteers, wherever they came from and whatever their role in Spain, would have to journey through these mountains. The hard trek just to get into the country often served to build up solidarity among the volunteers.[12] As Edward Cecil-Smith, who would become a political commissar of the Mackenzie-Papineau Battalion, put it: "Before they could fight Franco they had to fight the Pyrenees."[13]

When recounting his experiences in Spain long after the war, Ibing tended to vastly understate the perils of the hike over the mountains. His first recollection in one interview was that he "had no trouble climbing the mountains and getting over the top."[14] Ibing was indeed in good shape and better prepared for the challenge than volunteers who had been less physically active. He may have also benefited from wandering through the Canadian Rockies a few years earlier. Given his years of experience making deliveries in Winnipeg's bone-chilling winters, the conditions marching through the mountains from southern France into Spain may not have seemed too severe to him. Still, the hazards were serious, especially for volunteers who crossed during the winter. The easier passes – which were well marked and stayed below two thousand metres – were all guarded by French authorities, so volunteers had to follow tiny paths through the snow and ice at high altitude.[15] In addition, the organizations involved in getting the volunteers to Spain relied on guides who were well versed in the rough business of getting past a sealed and patrolled border. Ibing recalled his guide as "impatient" and constantly pushing the group onward; he "also carried a gun." To Ibing, "he looked like a tough experienced smuggler who knew where the border guards would be and at what time."[16]

Another tactic to avoid French patrols was to make the trips through the mountains at night. Ibing recalled that on the night of the trek, his group of about thirty had to wait until "after the town had gone to sleep." Then they "convened on a dark tree-lined boulevard." They "stood singly or in twos behind these trees so that [they] would not be visible to anybody passing by." A "rattling old bus" arrived and took them up toward the mountains until the road ended, and from there they started their hike.[17] There was at least one advantage of the darkness, noted by Bill Brennan, a Canadian volunteer who made the passage later that winter. "We trudged on over a mountain goat path," he explained. "If it had been daylight and we could have seen the precarious path, many of us would never have made it."[18]

After the war, many members of the International Brigades would tell of comrades collapsing physically or falling down the mountainside or into one of the gorges along the route.[19] Sometimes the groups would stop to aid stricken or injured volunteers; sometimes guides would assure the volunteers that they would organize a rescue later. Sometimes there was little doubt about the fate of the victim and the group would have to simply press forward. Brennan recounted that on his group's trek, some "were left behind to make their own way over alone, later when they regained their strength. Others slipped and fell. Far below – a yell, then the soft echo of a thud, or of splashing water. We stopped and listened. No sound. We went on."[20] After the war, officials of the Non-intervention Committee (an international body struck to monitor compliance with the policy) claimed to have found the remains of two hundred people scattered at different points around the mountain paths.[21]

Ibing's group showed remarkable determination to support one of their comrades who faltered. As the climb wore on and they reached higher altitudes, an American member of the group, whom Ibing described as "over six feet tall" and "very large and overfed" with a "bad heart," began struggling to breathe.[22] Ibing usually just chuckled when recalling these problems and did not bother to offer many details, but another Canadian volunteer who was part of that group, Jules Paivio, was more forthcoming. The American, named Steve, began to stagger, and the layer of ice at the surface of the snow was not thick enough to support him. He continually fell through the crust into snow up to his waist and had to be dragged out. The further they climbed, the more Steve weakened, and the banks of snow he kept falling into became deeper and deeper. The guide took a rope, wrapped it around Steve's waist, and placed men on opposing sides of him. They had to hold the rope but keep far enough away that they would not get pulled down into the snowbank when Steve crashed through the ice – hardly an easy task as they moved along the narrow path. Then they would pull him clear each time he fell.[23] Paivio and another American volunteer stayed with Steve throughout the trek, while others in the group, including Ibing, took shifts providing further help. "Nobody complained or bitched at Steve," writes Mark Zuehlke in *The Gallant Cause*. "They all knew there was nothing the man could do and they were all in this ordeal together."[24]

As they marched on, Steve began slipping in and out of consciousness. His comrades tried a mixture of improvised remedies to keep him going, slapping his cheeks, rubbing snow on his face, and forcing him onto his feet. Other members of the group started to weaken too. Fortunately, the guide proved up to the challenge; Zuehlke describes how he "tirelessly . . . ran back and forth along the column, alternately helping a man at the back of the column who was lagging and then returning to the front to show the way."[25]

It grew still colder as they continued to climb. Then a snowsquall hit. The group had to keep pushing on, as they still had a long section of the climb to go. They could hardly keep their bearings through the snow and the darkness and their growing fatigue. Paivio was getting seriously frostbitten when they reached the summit.[26] Ibing recalled that it was daylight by this point, and once the guide's job was done he did not stand on ceremony – he simply "pointed out a hut . . . and was gone."[27]

The hut was in the distance, far down the mountain. The descent was easier, as one would expect, but it was still on a "mountain goat path." To help negotiate the terrain, the leading hikers would make tracks in the snow for the others to follow. Steve still needed to be propped up as they went so that he did not tumble downward.[28] When they reached the hut, they were greeted by what Ibing called a "family of Spanish shepherds." Their hike was over but they would be kept on the move; they were transported by truck to the nearby town of Figueres and, still on the same day, loaded onto a train to Barcelona.[29]

Republican Barcelona

While most of the group quickly moved on from Barcelona to the International Brigades' main base further south in Albacete, Ibing and a volunteer from Denmark took some time to walk around the city. They got a glimpse into the growing tensions within the left in Spain, especially in the northeastern region of Catalonia. It was at once a brief and complex episode, which few volunteers would have had the background to fully understand. Ibing himself was aware that a wide array of leftist organizations supported the Republic, but his confused reaction shows how little he and many volunteers were aware of the morass of sectarian strife between Spain's different leftist groups.

At that time the war was being fought far from Barcelona, and aside from shortages of food and supplies, much of the city had settled into a steady, almost dull, routine.[30] For many leftists, this was a dispiriting development. A few months before, in mid and late 1936, the wave of popular revolutionary fervour that swept through Spain was especially strong in Catalonia. Structures of the old state were swept aside, industry and agriculture were collectivized, businesses confiscated, churches destroyed, and any vestige of religious authority wiped away.[31] Even Barcelona's legendary football club engineered a "confiscation and collectivization" under the banner of a socialist trade union in order to meet, as the club put it, "the imperatives of the time, which [were] profoundly revolutionary."[32] In one of the most famous passages written about the war, George Orwell described what it was like to visit Barcelona in the fall of 1936, a town "where the working class is in the saddle. Practically every building of every size had been seized by the workers and was draped with red flags or with the red and black flag of the Anarchists. . . . Every shop and café had an inscription saying it had been collectivized . . . servile and even ceremonial forms of speech had temporarily disappeared."[33]

Around Catalonia, a wide array of leftist working-class organizations flourished, most prominently the POUM (Partido Obrero de Unificación Marxista, or Workers' Party of Marxist Reunification), a political party made up of anti-Stalinist far-left socialists; and the CNT (Confederación Nacional del Trabajo, or National Confederation of Labour), the anarchists' massive trade union. The military defence of the area was put in the hands of POUM and CNT militias, which tended to have much less structure and hierarchy, and much greater internal democracy, than a typical army.[34]

By early 1937, however, the revolutionary spirit was dissipating. Many who visited Barcelona at that time were dismayed by the sense of political disengagement, and even apathy about the war, that had settled into the city.[35] But observers also saw serious tensions simmering beneath the surface. As Franco's armies continued to advance, much of the Republican side – including liberals, moderate Republicans, and a number of other socialist and labour organizations – increasingly sought to re-establish a conventional governing structure and a regular army. The Communist party's influence was now massive, thanks to the Republic's continuing dependence on Soviet aid (although the Communists had only a slight base of Spanish supporters), and throughout the war it held firm to its mantra of "Discipline, Hierarchy, and Organization."[36] At the time Ibing strolled around Barcelona, the CNT and the POUM were increasingly losing control to these proponents of a more ordered Republican war effort.

A few blocks from the station, Ibing and his companion came across "a building bedecked with red and black banners and an armed guard on watch."[37] Ibing's accounts are unclear about whether it was the offices of the POUM or the CNT. It was likely the CNT's, since the flags and uniforms were in red and black, the usual colours of the anarchists. And Ibing described the officer who approached the two when they peered into the building's courtyard as the first anarchist he had ever met.[38] Since the officer spoke "perfect" English – Ibing thought he was an American – the guests expected to have a friendly chat. Ibing recalled that he was "under the impression" that there was a level of unity among the leftist groups in Spain, and that anarchists would have shared similar views with a Communist like himself. The impression did not last long: "It soon became evident that [the recruiting officer] not only ridiculed, but actually hated the Communists." The officer then launched into a lengthy sales pitch on behalf of his army. Ibing recalled, "He tried to scare us with tales of the great dangers that awaited us and drew an almost romantic picture of activities at their front. It sounded like an ordinary eight hour day, shift work unfortunately, but with a liberal amount of time off. He did not tell us at that time that the northern front was very quiet."[39]

Volunteers who were worried about the dangers involved in the war or who harboured doubts about their allegiances in Spain might have been tempted by the offer. Ibing was not. He was appalled by the officer's attitudes, and the episode left a couple of enduring impressions. The first was a deep disappointment that the left was so divided. The second was frustration that the anarchists, the POUM, and their allies were only interested in protecting their areas, and "would not fight for the rest of the Republic. . . . They had front line positions where there was no front. They didn't do any fighting until the war came to them."[40] Ibing's impressions may have been strengthened later on by Communist propaganda spread among the International

Brigades that demonized "splinter" groups such as the CNT and the POUM. However, the impact of this propaganda should not be overestimated, as members of the Brigades became famously cynical about the Communist dogma that was forced upon them.[41] In any case, Ibing and his comrade abruptly cut off their visit to the CNT offices and their stopover in Barcelona altogether. They told the recruiting officer that they "were going on to Albacete, and then . . . went back to the station."[42]

Taking Orders

When he reached Albacete, Ibing was no more certain about where he would be assigned within the International Brigades than he had been when he left Canada. Conditions on the Albacete base were chaotic. Military commanders had to share authority with political commissars – Communist officials who would run indoctrination sessions, maintain discipline, try to boost morale, and keep watch for spies and subversives.[43] Moreover, the hallmarks of a hastily assembled, desperately undersupplied army were hard to miss. Many of the buildings were filthy, there was little sanitation, and some volunteers were already getting sick from the poor food. A hodgepodge of weapons were given to the volunteers, many of whom received only a few days of training. They were lucky if they got a uniform that fit; most had to piece something together from collections of boots, hats, and army surplus clothing from World War I.[44]

Similarly, the process of organizing the volunteers was far from systematic. Most were sent to the city's bullring and divided into regiments, usually according to nationality. Since the launch of the Mackenzie-Papineau Battalion was still several months away, many volunteers from Canada who arrived with Ibing in February were put into the American Abraham Lincoln Battalion.[45] If volunteers were recent immigrants to Canada, however, they often found themselves drawn toward regiments from their countries of origin. Many of these regiments were short of volunteers, and their leaders would actively recruit Canadians who were originally from Europe.[46] The precise number of volunteers from Canada who served in European battalions is unknown – but it was large. According to one Canadian commissar in Albacete, there were immigrant Canadians in sufficient numbers to form their own companies within both the Dimitrov Battalion (made up of exiles from the Balkans), and the Dombrowski Battalion (made up primarily of Polish volunteers, as well as Hungarians and Yugoslavs).[47] Ibing was initially placed with the German Thaelmann Battalion and began infantry training with them.[48]

But after a few days, his officers announced that they needed people with experience driving trucks. The Brigades were setting up their First Transport Regiment (or Regimiento de Tren, usually referred to as the Regiment de Tren); they had procured trucks but still had to find drivers. Ibing stepped forward and was quickly reassigned. He thus became one of the large group of volunteers to be deployed based not on nationality but on skills and experience – or as he put it, "according to our usefulness."[49] Had he arrived in Spain a few weeks earlier, Ibing doubtless would have seen combat duty in the Thaelmann Battalion.

The Regiment de Tren was a remarkably diverse group, even by the standards of the International Brigades. It took a couple of weeks to form three companies: the first was made up mostly of Americans; the second spoke mostly French and was made up of volunteers from Belgium, Switzerland, Italy, and France; the third company, where Ibing was placed, was mostly German and Austrian, with some Scandinavians as well.[50] Much of the support staff, or *intendencia*, was Spanish, but the Regiment itself was made up of internationals. This was another reflection of Spain's severe underdevelopment: almost no Spaniards had training as mechanics or experience with larger trucks. The Regiment would begin teaching these skills, and Ibing noticed that as the war progressed, Spaniards would replace internationals "who went sick, missing, or wounded."[51] Ibing would also notice the contingent of Spanish replacements in the Regiment continuously growing – a telling indicator of the casualty rates for the international volunteers.[52]

Ibing spent the next year and a half on the move in Spain. As Ibing put it, his role was simple: he was "considered part of the truck" – and the truck was constantly in demand.[53] Ibing was thus almost always driving, or under orders to stay nearby with the truck and wait to be dispatched again. "Wherever [the army] went, we served them," he recalled.[54] It should be noted that while most of Ibing's driving was for the International Brigades, many of his assignments involved the Republic's Spanish forces. The internationals were only one part of the Republic's larger army, and Spanish and international units often fought together in different battles. A considerable contingent of Spanish forces were mixed into the internationals; reinforcements were increasingly needed as the war ground on.[55] Altogether, it is striking how often Ibing referred to carrying Spanish troops or officers during his work with the Regiment de Tren.

It is difficult to track Ibing's movements and his location in the war's battles with much precision. This is in part because of the usual chaos and confusion that occurs in a war, especially for a transport driver. But in addition to being generally reluctant to recount his experiences in Spain, Ibing was deeply uninterested in the strategic aspects of the war; he had no desire to piece together his particular role in the continual offensives and retreats. During one interview, a CBC producer pulled out a map of Spain and asked Ibing to discuss which battles he joined; Ibing was politely but firmly resistant to even look at the map, let alone retrace his truck's and his army's movements.[56] In another interview, when pressed to recall parts of the war, Ibing tried but would easily lose track of places and strategic positions. Here is Ibing trying to recount the aftermath of one battle in 1938, struggling even to establish what direction he was heading: "The fascists were able to go further, towards the Mediterranean. But then we couldn't get out of the front, the further . . . I don't know the way Spain is situated . . . north, south, east, west, I don't know exactly. . . . We went further out of the Aragón towards the Pyrenees."[57] Still, between the scholarly literature on the war and the recollections Ibing did offer, it is possible to draw out his movements around the Spanish theatre and the role he played.

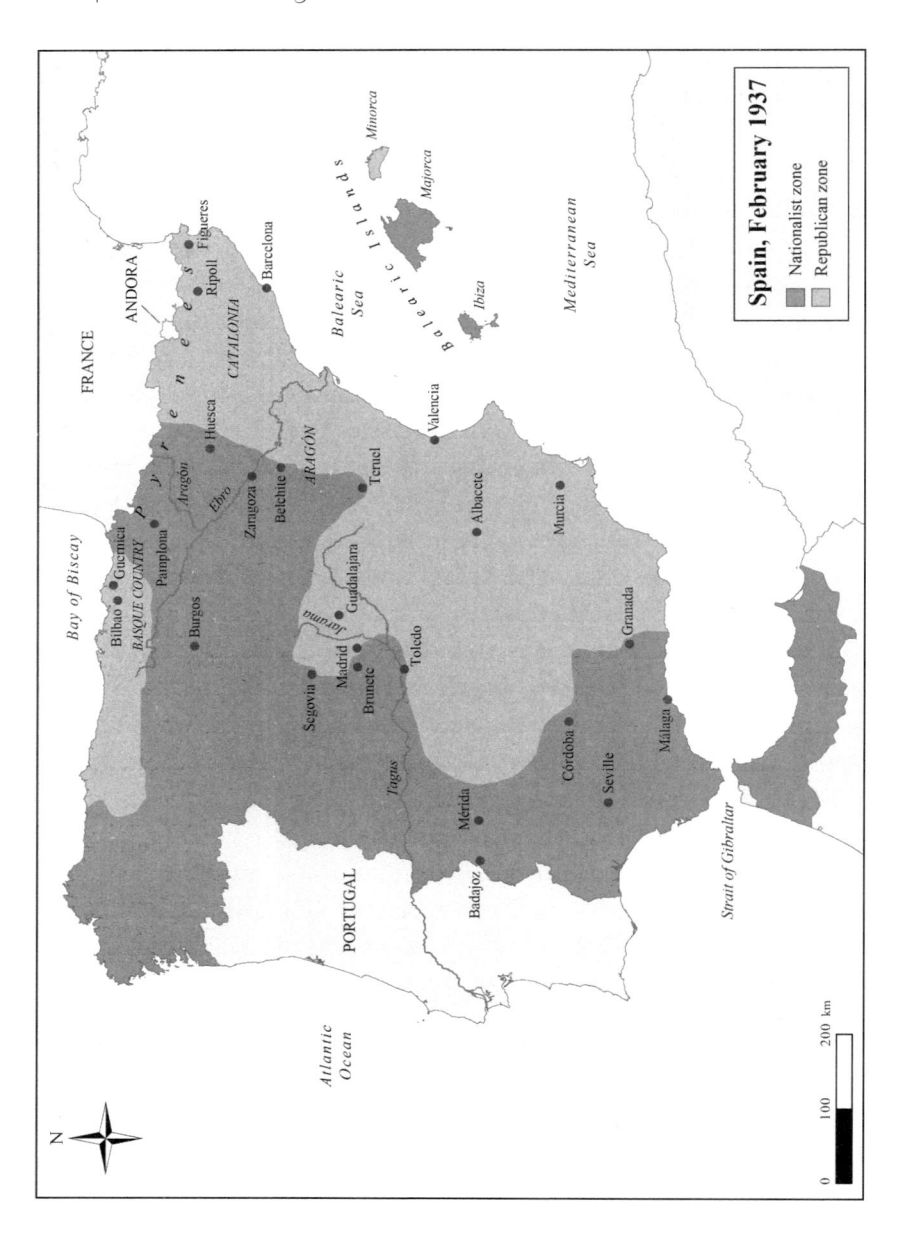

Spain, February 1937
Nationalist zone
Republican zone

Ibing's recollections of his first few weeks of service were the clearest, likely because the Republican armies were enjoying some successes at this time and the demands on the Regiment were still comparatively light. He was first dispatched to the defence of Madrid, which was the "heart of the war" at that point. The International Brigades were heavily engaged in repelling a new Nationalist offensive on the capital, which started in February 1937. The Regiment de Tren's role was moving soldiers and materiel in a convoy into the capital region. The heaviest fighting was just to the east, in the Jarama Valley, where Republican forces were able to fight Franco's army to a stalemate and inflict heavy casualties. The cost to the Republican army, though, was 25,000 troops, a large chunk of them British and American members of the International Brigades.[58] Ibing recalls that after the Regiment de Tren completed its initial mission to bring troops into the sector, it was rarely called upon, mostly because distances within the sector were small and "there was not overmuch use" for the heavy trucks.[59]

Ibing was even granted a day's leave – one of very few he would get during the war – to spend in Madrid. Ironically, it was while on leave that Ibing first came under attack, as Franco's German- and Italian-made planes bombed the capital that day. In his reminiscences for the history of the Mackenzie-Papineau Battalion, Ibing wrote an eloquent description of how he saw "residential buildings split from the top down as if cut with a knife and the furniture still visible in the rooms. . . . Houses were one pile of rubble with death underneath."[60] Ibing was hardly alone in being moved by his exposure to this hideous aspect of the war. The Spanish Civil War was the first instance of mass bombings of civilian targets in a European country. The brutality of the assaults is a prominent theme in literature about the war and in art, most famously in Picasso's masterpiece capturing the destruction of the Basque town of Guernica.[61]

In early March 1937, the Regiment de Tren was sent to Guadalajara, about sixty kilometres northeast of the capital, where Mussolini's Italian army had launched a new offensive. The Republican side mounted a spirited defence, assisted by some strategic errors by the Nationalist command

and by severe winter weather that bogged down the Italian forces. The Republicans scored a decisive victory. Although Guadalajara was not a major battle in strategic terms, it was the first time that a fascist army had suffered a defeat and it heartened the Republican side enormously. It was a humiliating loss for Mussolini, who saw thirty thousand of his troops taken prisoner.[62] Ibing was in the town right after the Italians were defeated. "There were Italians all over the place . . . running around there trying to surrender," he recalled. "Once they were behind the lines they weren't in Franco territory anymore . . . they wanted to be out of it. . . . So they were begging us to tell them where to go, to surrender."[63] He also remembered that most captured Italians were "not hostile"; some were talkative and even "wanted to get on our empty trucks, but we were there to transport our own units."[64]

After these initial weeks, the conditions of Ibing's work began to deteriorate. Franco's armies launched new offensives, turning most of their attack against the large swath of Republican territory in northern and northeastern Spain, and dispelling any doubt that they had the initiative in the war overall. Not surprisingly, Ibing's recollections of his location and cargo during these months were much less clear; he was often unsure of where he was going and almost always surrounded by unbearable misery. The days and nights at the wheel grew longer, and the range of assignments also widened.

One of Ibing's missions that spring was to carry troops or supplies to Barcelona. In May 1937, the tensions between leftist groups had erupted into violence in the city's streets – what historians call the "small-scale civil war within the Civil War."[65] During what came to be known as the May Days, the forces of the Republican government defeated the armed resistance of the POUM, the CNT, and other far-left and anarchist groupings in Catalonia. Since the Communists saw far-left dissenters (whom they called Trotskyites) as especially dangerous enemies, they targeted the leadership of the POUM in the repression that followed. Ibing offered few details about the mission in his written reminiscences, noting only that the transport unit was sent there because "there had been an anarchist uprising in the making."[66]

For Ibing, the May Days did nothing to stir greater sympathy for the anarchists and the POUM. In fact, he would always remain contemptuous of the many commentators, including Orwell (who served in the POUM militias and famously sided with them in the May Days) that blamed the Communists and other Republicans for repressing dissent and the revolutionary spirit in general, and in turn fatally weakening the war effort. Ibing held firm to his initial impressions that the problems lay with the anarchists and the POUM: "They would fight for Catalonia but not for the Republic.... If they had been fighting [with the rest of the Republic's forces] at the beginning, it would have been different."[67] Nevertheless, the Communists' ruthlessness in crushing the resistance made him harbour doubts about their intentions. In his written reminiscences for the history of the Mackenzie-Papineau Battalion, he recalled that a "feeling first occurred" to him in Barcelona that spring that if the Republican side won the war, the Communists may have continued to fight to their "political victory over all of the elements in the Spanish spectrum."[68]

These flickers of doubt did not seriously diminish Ibing's political convictions or his commitment to the defence of the Republic. And there was little time to ponder his reservations, as the war against Franco was about to become yet more desperate. The summer of 1937, Ibing saw a new wave of Republican offensives. These attacks were part of an effort to force Franco to divert some of his armies from their relentless drive in the north. The first was at Brunete in July, to the west of Madrid, and then others followed in the Aragón region, in the northeast. Then in late 1937 and into early 1938, the Republicans launched further diversionary offensives in the Aragón, this time hoping to pull Franco away from his new advance toward Madrid.[69] Ibing recalled being at all of the main battles in these campaigns; he was at Brunete, Belchite (August to September 1937), and the largest, Teruel (December 1937 to February 1938).

Most of these battles followed a similar pattern. They would start promisingly, as the Republican forces were able to break through Nationalist defences and capture key targets. At these moments, morale was high. Ibing's recollections about Teruel were the clearest, including how "at the beginning it was alright, you know, when we conquered Teruel it was quite a thing."[70] But as the battles wore on, confusion and disunity within the Republican command, and above all the Nationalists' enormous advantage in arms and equipment, would keep the Republicans from maintaining their forward progress. Franco would usually make the battle one of attrition, and the Republicans suffered major losses and began to wear down.

Accounts of these battles are littered with details that highlight how difficult the work of Ibing's Regiment de Tren would have been. In his chapter on the Battle of Brunete, for instance, military historian Antony Beevor notes that communication between Republican commanding officers was often poor, particularly regarding their locations; that the "supply services" had no experience supporting an offensive of that scale; and that the general staff had "woefully underestimated the resupply needs of such a battle."[71] Edward Barsky, an American doctor volunteering with the International Brigades, recalled that his medical convoy's trip toward the action during the Battle of Teruel "was colder, rougher and steeper than anyone had imagined. We were menaced by lorries [one of which was likely Ibing's] rushing down the mountains to get fresh troops back to the front."[72]

These key battles ended in demoralizing – and dangerous – retreats. In one interview, Ibing described the retreats as "mostly orderly . . . except in places." But later in that interview, and elsewhere, he made it clear there were many such disorderly places. Even as most of the army was moving back, transport units like Ibing's would often have to stay forward, waiting for groups to leave. They could also be ordered to return to the front to collect more troops. He recalled that his unit was "actually in Teruel with our trucks and everything" when the Republican armies started retreating. They had to "stay in there" in order to "pick up whoever wanted to get out" and then they went back again to get more "of them out and . . . were bombed." He told Grenke, "We lost quite a few trucks there and, of course, the men with it."[73]

Transport units were also ordered, in the midst of retreat, to bring more munitions to the front. These were needed to replenish supplies for artillery and infantry units that stayed forward to provide cover as their comrades fell back. Through it all, drivers like Ibing would fight through masses of troops and civilians fleeing the battle and Franco's advancing army. Barsky, the American doctor, recalled that during the retreat from Teruel "the artillery of the enemy was din in our ears," as his medical convoy pushed its way through the narrowest of roads that were made "practically impassable, choked with tanks, troops, artillery, refugees, goats and donkeys."[74]

After the catastrophic loss at Teruel, cracks in Republican unity and discipline added to the danger. Ibing had a direct and terrifying experience with these problems: he was carrying artillery shells back to the front at Teruel when he was hijacked by a retreating unit. He was stopped by a lieutenant with about twenty-five Spanish soldiers who were "blocking the road."[75] They demanded that Ibing clear out his truck and transport them clear of the battle. Ibing recalled that the lieutenant seemed barely in control of himself: "He wanted to shoot me." The soldiers cleared out the back of Ibing's truck "at gunpoint," and the shells were thrown away.[76] The group was not even clear where they wanted to go: "They just ordered me to drive down the road and after about 50 km they got off, nowhere near the front."[77] Ibing chuckled when recounting parts of this story, adding, "I don't know whether they were deserters or whether they had orders. Of course I didn't speak Spanish so well . . . and in a situation like that you don't ask. You just go."[78]

Through early 1938, conditions got still worse – as did morale for the Republican forces. "We had to give up on Teruel, and from then on it was retreat, retreat, retreat," Ibing recalled, in an observation shared by military historians. Indeed, this phase of the war, from the Republican perspective, is often called the Great Retreats.[79] Franco's Nationalist forces launched a new offensive eastward, continuing through mid-April 1938. This was the first time fascist armies employed the strategy of blitzkrieg, or lighting war, attacking with aircraft, artillery, tanks, and infantry together in a rapid movement. The Republican armies, already exhausted and low on supplies, were in little position to resist; the Regiment de Tren was under particular strain at this point, and the army scrambled backward, trying – often unsuccessfully – to stay ahead of the Nationalists' advances. The literature on this phase of the war abounds in descriptions of how order, communication, and supply lines were impossible to maintain within the Republic's army, and divisions retreated without any cover while "circuses of fighters," as Beevor puts it, dove down to attack them.[80]

By mid-April 1938, Franco's offensive brought him to the Mediterranean coast. The Republic was split in two, with a pocket remaining in the northeast, and another in the central east and southeast. The Republicans still held the main cities, Barcelona and Madrid, as well as Valencia, where the government was stationed. But the Spanish Republic was almost bled dry; an increasing number of its leaders felt resigned to defeat unless Western democracies came to their aid. France opened its borders for a few months starting in March – but hope for further assistance from Western democracies was in vain. In contrast, German forces remained in Spain and the contingent of Italian troops fighting on Franco's side stood at forty thousand.[81]

What Ibing recalled much more vividly than particular battles and strategic twists was the everyday grind of driving his truck during a brutal war of attrition. Indeed, in most of his accounts, the war seems less a series of dramatic confrontations and turning points than one day after another of hard work, physical suffering, and trying to fight off fear and despair.

The Misery of War

Paradoxically, while Ibing usually described the war as involving constant, unrelenting misery, his work was hardly regular and predictable; in fact, the lack of any routine made the experience even more difficult. Only in the first few months did he have a regular schedule to follow, mostly involving going back and forth from the front lines to a regional army base. Thereafter, direct return trips from any single base became increasingly rare. He explained in one interview that as the war went on, he and other drivers would take combat regiments to the front and then be ordered to "stay with them . . . and if

The International Brigades | 83

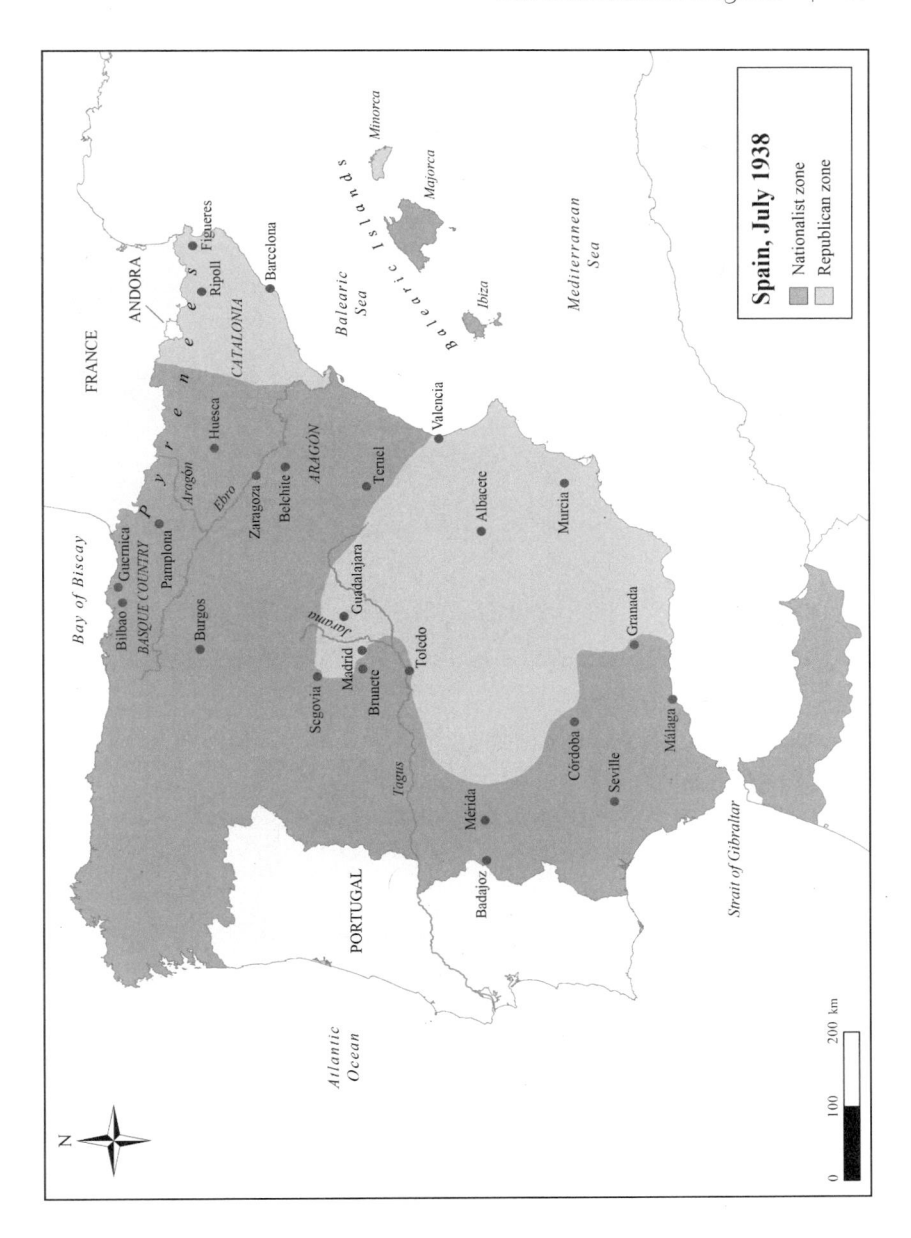

they needed something or they had to take something back . . . we were there."[82] He was also dispatched on a few long-haul missions – he recalled being sent to Barcelona a few times "to pick up a load of something or other."[83] Toward the latter stages of his time in Spain, Ibing rarely saw the Regiment's central base. Indeed, he mostly remembered his time in Spain as a continuous drive from one spot to another, often uncertain about where he would be sent next.

Perhaps the most persistent challenge each day was simply keeping the truck on the road. To maximize carrying capacity, the army had inordinately long beds built for the trucks; they extended a long way back from the driver's cab, hanging far past the rear wheels. When the truck was full with forty or fifty soldiers and their gear, it would sway dangerously along the steep and twisting roads.[84] To make matters worse, the wooden bodies that were installed on the truck beds were poorly built; many of them had only a

A Regiment de Tren truck full of soldiers on the road in Spain in winter. Date unknown.

chain to hold the sides together. The Spanish troops would often disconnect the chain (for reasons Ibing could never discern and dared not ask about), and so on bends in the road, the body would be loose and lean even further, out past the side edges of the truck. Ibing recalled that "the Spanish soldiers seemed oblivious to this kind of danger, or maybe they liked to live dangerously."[85]

In general, the trucks were civilian vehicles that were ill suited to the demands of a war. Working the clutch on the winding roads was a constant challenge, and the strength of the brakes was limited; Ibing recalled that on the steep downhill sections of road, "you quickly had to learn how to shift into second or even first gear to hold down the speed."[86] As with most motor vehicles in those times, Ibing's trucks had no heaters for the driver's cab at the front of the truck and no defrosters for the windshields. His trucks also lacked effective headlights for nighttime driving, which was frequent, since the army regularly needed to move quickly or avoid detection. Ibing recalled often feeling like he was driving in a dark mist when it was cold, which "was enough to give any driver a nervous stomach."[87] The driver's cabs were small and desperately cramped when Ibing transported troops, as two of the commanding officers would insist on sitting up front with the driver. On cold days, these extra passengers would steam up the windshields even more. He recalled many rides when "one side of the driver was pressed against the icy unlined frame of the cab almost numb from the cold while the right arm had to fumble for the gearshift pushing somebody's legs out of the way."[88]

Ibing recalled that, despite all of these problems, the trucks endured "pretty well" in a mechanical sense, breaking down rarely (unless damaged by enemy fire). The trucks' durability was in large part a reflection of the skill of the Regiment de Tren's mechanics in finding and adapting parts from abandoned vehicles or simply improvising with whatever could be found. As the war went on, however, more trucks were captured and supplies of any kind grew scarcer, and the fleet was down to, as one American official in the Regiment put it, "old rattletraps held together with safety pins and string."[89] Ibing's recollections were not quite as bleak (he said little about the mechanics in the Regiment), but he did recall the large number of the Regiment's trucks lost in battle.

Ibing also recalled that riding in the back of a Republican truck was a nightmare for the troops. Indeed, historians' accounts of the war are full of references to troops getting packed into "canvas covered trucks," sitting "under a single swinging light-bulb" as they endured many "freezing, bumpy hours on the road to the front."[90] One of the best accounts of the experience comes from George Orwell. While Ibing did not care for Orwell's political perspective, he would likely have related to his description of a truck journey in *Homage to Catalonia*: "The bumping over the vile roads walloped you to a pulp. No horse has ever thrown me so high as those lorries used to throw me. The only way of travelling was to crowd all together and cling to one another."[91]

The ride was punishing for healthy passengers, but for the wounded it was an unimaginable horror. For Ibing, carrying wounded fighters stood out as one of the toughest parts of his job. Although Canadian doctor (and Communist legend) Norman Bethune developed his famous mobile blood transfusion units during the Spanish Civil War, few of the wounded in Spain were served by specialized vehicles of any kind.[92] A few times Ibing drove trucks converted into ambulances, and at other times he simply had to carry the wounded on the misshapen roads on his regular truck. If that was not bad enough, often Ibing would have to take the trip at the highest possible speed in the midst of a panicked retreat: "It was miserable to have to listen to the wounded back on the truck being shaken up on the rough road and the officer urging you on to hurry."[93]

Ibing offered few other details; accounts from other veterans show why it was one of the experiences he was most eager to forget. Orwell, who was shot in the throat in late May 1937, wrote about the ordeal of his ambulance ride: "What a journey! It used to be said that in this war you got well if you were wounded in the extremities, but always died of a wound in the abdomen. I now realized why. No one who was liable to bleed internally could have survived those miles of jolting over metal roads that had been smashed to pieces by lorries and never repaired since the war began."[94] Harry Wilkes, an American pharmacist working at a medical unit with the International Brigades, gave a clear description of the conditions of one ambulance and its passengers when they arrived: "Inside the truck on the floor were mattresses upon which about 25 wounded lay. Two were already dead. Several others were very low. The rest suffered excruciating pain due to fractures and the ride over the torturing road."[95]

The horrors would not end when Ibing reached his destination at the medical bases. Conditions at the hospitals was another subject about which Ibing said little in interviews, except to note that he worked at them often and that he ended up digging many graves and burying many dead. Indeed, despite the sizable contingent of doctors and nurses who volunteered to serve for the Republic, hospitals were often overwhelmed by seriously wounded soldiers and civilians, many of whom could not be saved. Barsky recalled that during the Battle of Guadalajara in March 1937, two hundred wounded arrived at his hospital in three hours, and four hundred more arrived in the next six days – and Guadalajara was a rare Republican victory.[96]

Ibing found that transporting supplies and materiel was less taxing in many ways, but dangers remained. He noted, for example, that he often carried heavy artillery shells.[97] As he drove along, he must have wondered countless times when he hit a bump if it would be the one to set off an explosion. Perhaps the most physically challenging task was transporting the heavy guns, most of which the Soviet Union had collected from different armies around Europe; it was outdated materiel that the Soviet defence minister plainly told Stalin he was dumping on the Republican army.[98]

Machine guns could weigh over 120 pounds, while the cannon were massive and did not come mounted on wheels. Hence getting them into position was an entirely "primitive" operation: "Everything was manhandled, by . . . sheer manpower. . . . It was murder."[99] At times it also verged on dark comedy. Groups of soldiers and staff would have to heave the cannon up onto the truck beds. Sometimes the immense weight of the cannon would make it crash through the floorboards, so the men would have to pull it back

The Regiment de Tren at work: a truck about to be unloaded in Spain, 1937. Ibing, with his back to the camera, is leaning over the truck's gate at the rear.

off to rebuild and reinforce the boards. Once the cannon was on the truck bed, Ibing would drive it up to the front, usually beyond the end of the roads to reach the best strategic location. The truck would sway more than ever as he tried to reach the spot. Then the cannon was hauled off the back; Ibing recalled that when the weight came off the truck, it would spring upward in a big jump, even though moving cannon required using the heaviest trucks available. The artillery was too immobile to be removed quickly from the front during a retreat; Ibing recalled that most of the cannon he transported would end up in the hands of Franco's armies when the Republicans lost a battle.[100]

As Ibing and his comrades in the Regiment de Tren weaved along the roads, "bouncing through every pothole in Spain," their trucks were visible targets for the enemy, especially from the air. Ibing recalled getting strafed "very often" by enemy airplanes. Being in an ambulance did not bring any greater safety from enemy fire. Both sides in the war regularly used the ambulances to carry officers, soldiers, or munitions, which made them targets like any other vehicle.[101] But some volunteers described bombing ambulances as an illustration of the Nationalists' brutal approach to the war. Hospitals were commonly attacked, while drivers covered up the crosses on their ambulances to avoid being targeted.[102]

When enemy planes struck, the trucks made so much noise that drivers could not hear them approaching – or even firing. "The saving thing," Ibing explained in one interview, "was that the roads were mostly gravel." This meant that "you could see – if . . . they missed you – you could see the gravel and the little dust springing up on the road, and . . . you jammed on the brakes and took a dive out of the truck."[103] Much of the landscape around Spain was barren, even more so during the war, and it offered little natural cover from the strafing. Ibing would often crawl under the truck, hearing bullets hitting the ground around him or clanking against the truck, and wait out the attack.

When cover was available, diving right in brought new dangers. On one occasion, Ibing was injured after jumping into a ditch to escape strafing from overhead. When the plane passed and he climbed out, he noticed that he was bleeding from his right leg. He thought he had been hit or, more likely, landed on something, "a piece of root, a stick, you know, sticking out of the ground."[104] He drove on to a first aid station and got stitched up, but he felt pain deeper in the leg for weeks afterward. After the war, a doctor told him that there was a tear or cut in the muscle, which, because it had not been sewn back together right away, became deformed when it healed.

Ibing insisted the leg did not give him "any trouble at all" later in life – indeed, he usually downplayed the incident as "an accident more than anything."[105]

Strafing from the air could be especially deadly when the trucks were in a larger convoy. And Ibing recalled that Republican commanding officers showed a "lack of precaution" about how convoys could be sitting ducks. Sometimes the trucks were delayed on the road, or forced to sit on the roadside – usually out in the open – and await orders. Ibing recalled these problems mostly occurring on a smaller scale, but dangers were greater during the Great Retreats in early 1938. He recalled one frightening incident in March 1938 when trucks from the Regiment de Tren were ordered to pick up a unit of retreating troops. They sat and waited – thankfully this time in "a small woods" where there was a bit of cover. Ibing recounted, thousands of other retreating soldiers "were streaming by us on the road . . . in a large swath and there were Franco's planes diving on that mass, circling and diving again and again. With thousands of rifles there, not one was turned on those planes to scare them off." When the unit that Ibing was ordered to carry finally arrived, they wisely decided to stay in the woods until the planes were gone before joining the retreat.[106]

While the enemy attacks on the trucks presented great danger, what seemed to haunt many drivers in the Regiment de Tren the most was the chance that they might get lost driving around in a foreign country, in the middle of a war zone. The Regiment got precious little help in steering clear of dangers. With the artillery and warplanes blasting everything that had been standing to pieces, there were fewer reliable landmarks left as the war went on. And Ibing noted that "in all this time" in Spain, he "never once saw a roadmap."[107] This was another example of disorganization on the Republican side; according to Beevor, many officers in combat units in the International Brigades were not supplied with maps and some tried to draw their own.[108] But Orwell wrote that deeper issues, including Spain's basic underdevelopment, also played a significant role. He claimed that parts of Spain had never been properly surveyed when the war started, and the useful maps that did exist were made for the military; once the war started they fell into the hands of Franco's generals.[109]

There were supposed to be sentries posted along the routes to warn soldiers and trucks away from danger spots. But in his recollections of the war, Ibing described them as "lax," "lazy," "not disciplined," and "sometimes negligent or nonexistent." He noted that some sentries failed to appreciate the importance of their jobs: "If a guard falls asleep . . . to him it's nothing," but for drivers the results could be catastrophic.[110]

The lack of direction served to amplify the obvious risks involved in driving on small, broken roads. This was another reason Ibing especially dreaded driving at night.[111] One brush with disaster stood out in his memory, when he was sent to Barcelona to pick up a load of supplies. He had the unusual luxury of a second driver with him, and Ibing took advantage to catch a little sleep during the night. He was awoken when the truck came to a sudden stop. In the pitch black of the night, he looked outside and saw what he thought was "the most beautiful moon low in the sky." When Ibing asked what was happening, the other driver said that he had seen the waving light of a sentry. The truck had stalled when the driver hit the brakes and now he seemed uncertain how to proceed. Still groggy, Ibing looked out at the moon again. "It was like no moon I had ever seen before," he told Grenke, "almost within grasp." But as Ibing's eyes focused, he realized that the moon was "the big eye of a locomotive moving slowly up" on them. He looked forward and saw that the truck's front end was in the path of the train. Ibing told the driver to hit the truck's starter and get it into reverse, but "he did not get the idea fast enough." The engine stalled again. The train hit the truck in a slow-motion collision and "shoved [them] into a ditch." It turned out that there was indeed a sentry there, but somehow he did not notice that the light from his oil lamp was so dim that the truck drivers would barely be able to see it. The conductor of the train, meanwhile, either failed to see the truck sitting on the tracks or decided against sounding his horn to alert the drivers for fear that the noise would draw enemy fire. Ibing knew he was lucky to escape uninjured, except for a few "blue marks" that swelled up later on.[112]

Perhaps the drivers' greatest fear, as Ibing noted with a nervous chuckle in one interview, was that they would get lost near the front, "cross into no man's land . . . and wind up on the other side. And that's what happened sometimes."[113] Indeed, Ibing recounted many ways that drivers could have been captured by the Nationalists, and historians of the war have noted more. Even if the drivers knew where they were, they also had to know where the front lines were – and the lines were hardly stable. Losing track of the enemy's movements was a serious risk for retreating combat units, let alone transport drivers. During the Great Retreats, regiments would flee and still the Nationalists would overtake them on their flanks; groups of soldiers would settle in what they thought was a safe spot to rest overnight and awaken to find themselves surrounded by the enemy.[114] Small wonder, then, that so many trucks were lost when armies fell back.

Even during the rare moments when the Republicans were advancing, transport units could be misdirected. Indeed, Beevor contends that some Republican commanders would lie brazenly about their progress in battle. Most did this due to the massive pressure they felt to reach a target; Communist political officials could be unforgiving if goals were not met.[115] Apparently other commanders exaggerated their gains simply out of vanity.[116] It is thus quite probable that drivers in the Regiment de Tren might have found their way to their assigned destination, only to end up captured behind enemy lines.

What took a still greater toll on Ibing's morale were the wretched physical conditions he and his comrades had to endure. Ibing frequently emphasized how cold it could get in Spain's mountains in the winter. He spent much of his time "chilled to the bone and feeling blue," and fighting off exhaustion.[117] Between the endless hours on the road or sitting nearby awaiting instructions, he did not sleep in a bed during his entire time in Spain.[118] He was often left scrounging for food as well. Since he was not part of the regular army units he was transporting, usually he did not get fed when they did.[119] He was often an afterthought when it came to getting provisions, and if he did not happen to be on the spot where the food was, he was "just out of luck."[120]

On many trips – heading to the front or getting clear of advancing enemy forces – there was no time to eat anyway. In general, the supplies of food grew more meagre as the war went on, and the food was almost always cold. The only meat that was left was mule, and Ibing mostly had to get by on beans or rice. For the rest of his life, Ibing would refuse to eat garbanzo beans, as they reminded him too much of desolate times in Spain. Another Canadian veteran remembered the beans were often "rotten and stinking" and "plumb full of bugs."[121] Ibing insisted, however, that the constant physical strains had at least one benefit in wartime: "It seems that the more miserable, cold and hungry one feels, the less does danger or death make an impression, especially when one is busy at the same time."[122]

But there were times when danger and death clearly did leave an impression on Ibing. He was haunted by one incident in early 1938 when all of these depressing features of the war – the physical hardships, the meagre provisions, and the deepening sense of doom – hit him at once. It did not involve him witnessing any fighting and there were no emotional outbursts involved; in fact, it was the profound silences that struck him most deeply. He was assigned to transport a small unit of German troops to the front. When they disembarked, they fell in line without a word. Ibing described them as "worn out and underfed," and wearing "rags and some [were] in bandages." In one interview, he wept when recalling "the misery in their eyes. They felt lost . . . you could see it. . . . They were going up into the trenches and they knew they were not coming back."[123] In writing his reminiscences for the Mackenzie-Papineau Battalion history, he clearly took time to evoke the emotion of the moment: "They marched off without waiting or command, single file they disappeared behind the next bend. I never saw such a moving sight as these lost souls, most of their comrades killed, the war looking hopeless, no country to offer them a home, no future awaiting them at all."[124]

Ibing was also deeply affected by the suffering of the Spanish people. While Ibing and his comrades in the International Brigades had signed up to fight knowing the risks, it was different for civilians because "they suffered innocently."[125] He remembered the times when he would rest for the night near the front and see civilians displaced by the war. "They were between the lines and they did not know where to go" or how they could move to safety with no transport, since they were forced to flee on foot. "They had lost all their earthly belongings," he remembered. "They couldn't take anything with them. [And] the poor children . . ."[126]

Spending so much time on the road before, during, and after battles, Ibing got much more exposure to the anguish of Spanish civilians than other volunteers. The bombed-out civilian homes that Ibing and his comrades had first seen on leave in Madrid became "a sight that followed [them] everywhere [they] went in Spain,"[127] and injured and desperate civilians often descended on the Republican hospitals where he served. Doctors and support staff recalled instances when, after waves of Nationalist bombing, masses of civilians would arrive at the hospital carrying injured relatives and children.[128] One of Norman Bethune's best-known pamphlets about the war recounted how he found himself in a sea of refugees while trying to get his mobile transfusion unit to the port city of Málaga, which was under assault by Franco's armies. On the road he saw 150,000 refugees, including "thousands of children"; they "counted five thousand under ten years of age, and at least one thousand of them barefoot." Eventually he and his drivers decided to turn the truck around "and start transporting the worst cases to safety." But they quickly found their vehicle "besieged by a mob of frantic mothers and fathers who with tired outstretched arms [handed up] their children. . . . 'Take this one.' 'See this child.' 'This one is wounded.'"[129]

The depth of fear and despair on the Republican side was compounded by Franco's insistence on waging a "war of annihilation." This meant not only targeting civilians in aerial bombing raids and maximizing attrition in the military campaign, but also seeking and destroying Republican supporters once an area had been conquered. This policy was announced at the outset of the war, and it would continue, indeed be expanded, to the bitter end. Paul Preston shows in his seminal study *The Spanish Holocaust* that while there continued to be outbreaks of violence by the Republican forces, the

Nationalists' butchery was systematic, merciless, and massive in scale. In village after village and town after town, conquest by Nationalist forces was followed by mass executions, rapes, beatings, and torture. A favourite tactic was to make victims watch as soldiers brutalized their family members – and then attack them in turn.[130] Franco and his generals constantly reiterated that the violence was crucial to "cleanse the country of all of the putrefaction that had poisoned it."[131] Once they were in control of a region, they would never be open to reconciliation with former enemies or tolerant of the slightest dissent. As Franco once declared: "Our regime is based on bayonets and blood, not on hypocritical elections."[132]

As Preston highlights, brutalizing everyone on the Republican side was also part of Franco's "policy of institutionalized revenge," and a way to reward his soldiers after a victory with "an orgy of rape, looting, killing and alcohol."[133] Right-wing militias, particularly the Carlists and the Falangists, also played major roles in the atrocities. Nationalist leaders were convinced that there was a psychological advantage in spreading terror as they advanced, as a way to "paralyze the enemy."[134] The Republicans' resolve to fight remained remarkably strong even as the war turned against them; nevertheless, civilians in Republican territory had little doubt about what awaited them if they were captured.

As Ibing understood, prisoners from the International Brigades would face a grim fate at the hands of Nationalist forces. Franco called members of the Brigades "the scum of the earth," and most of those captured were executed. Franco reportedly liked to tell officials from Western governments that they should be grateful that he killed thousands of them, because otherwise they would be causing unrest back in their homelands.[135] Carl Geiser – himself a prisoner of war and a former commissar of the Mackenzie-Papineau Battalion – did a careful study of records of captured American volunteers. He contends that of the 287 Americans known to have been taken prisoner, 173 were killed. Of those who survived, most were lucky enough to be captured during short periods (such as the Great Retreats) when Franco put a temporary stop to the policy of shooting POWs from the International Brigades. At these times

Franco saw international prisoners as valuable commodities to be swapped with the Republicans for his own captured soldiers, or traded to Western democracies in exchange for diplomatic recognition of the Nationalist side.[136] But even if their lives were spared by Franco's army, POWs suffered greatly in Nationalist camps, facing regular beatings, hunger, and appalling living conditions. One historian describes in detail the horrific conditions international POWs faced, kept on the move from one camp to another, "erratically fed, endlessly photographed [for use in propaganda or 'scientific' studies], repeatedly threatened with execution, they had been paraded like Roman slaves through the streets of a dozen towns in their bloodstained rags and had been forced to salute with flat palm the Nationalist flag."[137]

For soldiers in the infantry, a key to keeping up morale in these circumstances were the bonds forged within their ranks during the long hours together, especially during combat. Many veterans of the Mackenzie-Papineau Battalion, for instance, noted the sense of "brotherhood" that developed in the battalion. Soldiers described how at times they would fight for each other as much as for the larger cause that brought them to Spain. According to Petrou, one Canadian veteran, future novelist Hugh Garner, felt that "the soldiers came to love each other, and this was reason enough to fight."[138]

In Ibing's accounts of the war, it is evident how much he missed this solidarity with fellow soldiers; he missed the chance for "comradeship and mutual sharing of dangers." Ibing knew that dangers were greater for combat soldiers in the line of fire – still, without the support of comrades in arms, the misery of the war sank even more deeply into him. As the war ground on, "most missions became single truck operations and the lot of the driver was isolation and loneliness," at least for Ibing.[139] It was a terrible combination: Ibing saw more of the misery inflicted by the war while on the road, and he had fewer chances to share the experience with comrades. Most of the officers who rode in his cab were Spanish; they knew little English and, in any case, had little to say. Ibing believed they were usually too exhausted or distracted to talk. According to Beevor, officers were being carefully watched by Communist political commissars and would have been reluctant to say anything to a driver they did not know.[140] Ibing said he learned barely enough Spanish to get by during the war; he often claimed that he had learned more French from speaking with comrades in the Regiment de Tren from France.[141]

The isolation did have its benefits, although Ibing was hardly in a position to appreciate them during the war. Precisely because he was alone and on the move, Ibing had relatively little exposure to the indoctrination and coercion from Communist commissars. For many veterans, this repressive weight of Communist authority was one of the most demoralizing and dangerous aspects of their experience in Spain. Officers could be tyrants, and expressing frustration with superiors could get volunteers reported to political commissars. Dissenting from Communist party policy also invited the commissars' attention. Stalin's Great Terror – the mass purges of suspected subversive elements – was at its peak in the Soviet Union during this time, and his murderous paranoia spilled over into Spain. Stalin's notorious secret police force, the NKVD, became increasingly active in policing the International Brigades. Punishments could include being sent to a "labour company" or a "prevention house," and an uncertain number of volunteers were executed.[142]

But in Ibing's recollections, the military and political leaders in the Regiment de Tren were mostly benign characters. He described little party coercion or harsh discipline against drivers. Indoctrination sessions were rare, and most of the volunteers "weren't interested that much."[143] At first glance, Ibing's upbeat assessment of discipline in the Regiment may seem unlikely, given the scale of repression in the International Brigades. However, the Communists' file on Ibing from the war was only a few lines long and it did not suggest that he had been subjected to rigorous scrutiny. It noted that he had "been on all fronts" with the Regiment de Tren and that he had a "very good record of service." It also added a general comment – "Will develop" – possibly about his long-term future as a Communist.[144]

Looking broadly across the Brigades, discipline was not as severe in some units as it was in others. Moscow was especially paranoid about "subversion" by dissident Communists from Eastern European countries, so their battalions often bore the brunt of the NKVD's activities.[145] In the Regiment de Tren, the volunteers seem to have created an unusually democratic and non-doctrinaire culture. This, too, was likely connected to the independent nature of their work. There were cases of units in the International Brigades making their political commissars somewhat accountable, but the experience of Bill Sennett, a political commissar in the Regiment, was remarkable. Sennett was in charge of the mostly American first company, not Ibing's, but his story is instructive about the Regiment's culture.

In his first months as commissar, Sennett tried to impose strict discipline, even carrying out the commissariat's orders to put limits on socializing within the ranks. In response, the members of the company organized a meeting, aired their grievances, and voted to dismiss him. Sennett joined a combat unit to salvage his reputation, but then returned to the Regiment later on, apparently with a better attitude – he was re-elected to the commissar's post. "It was a case of the men making the decision," Sennett stated.[146] According to Ibing, the political commissar in his company was another American, and a "nice guy, easy to talk to. He did not try to strong-arm anyone."[147] Even more noteworthy, the companies of the Regiment de Tren elected their regular military officers as well. For at least part of the war, one of the elected commanding officers was a member of the American Socialist party named Durward Clark. It was a rare case of a non-Communist holding a high-ranking position.[148]

By the end of the Great Retreats in late April 1938, the International Brigades were in a desperate state. Many of its battalions had lost well over half of their soldiers. According to Petrou, it is unlikely that more than sixty members of the Canadian Mackenzie-Papineau Battalion were able to make the retreat across the Ebro River back into Republican territory. The Abraham-Lincolns were down to about 120 soldiers – having lost over 250 in the previous two weeks of fighting alone. Provisions were as bad as ever. Volunteers remained short of weapons and ammunition, and many wore rags around their feet because they could not find shoes that fit.[149]

Ibing (third from left, with his hands around his knee) with other members of the International Brigades and a Spanish boy. Date unknown.

For Ibing, the strain of the war had worn his body down to a dangerous level. His digestive system was the biggest problem. The stress of keeping the truck on the bending roads, the pounding from the potholes, and the long stretches of hunger all combined to wreak havoc on it. In addition, as did many soldiers in the Brigades, Ibing suffered from dysentery from the food he did manage to eat; it had become as a steady, chronic ailment by late spring 1938.[150] He also had a serious case of tonsillitis – the swelling was so bad that eating and even drinking water brought almost unbearable pain. In eighteen months in Spain, Ibing had lost twenty pounds from his already lean frame.

But he had survived – and although he could hardly know it, his work in the direct line of fire was about to start winding down. Some dangers remained, as Franco's air force continued bombing and strafing missions. There was also still much work to do. In the weeks after the retreat, trucks from the Regiment went up and down the roads along the Ebro, looking for more Republican soldiers who were belatedly finishing the retreat across the river. There were many more supply runs to perform, as the army's needs were urgent and imports were allowed over the French border between March and June.[151]

However, for the International Brigades, there was a break in the fighting. Franco turned his attention toward the southern sector of Republican territory (where only a few internationals were stationed) and launched a new offensive toward the capital in Valencia. Rumours spread that the internationals would be pulled out of the Republic's army and sent home. This talk of repatriation raised a whole new set of questions about how volunteers could get back to their countries of origin. For many, including Ibing, this was not simply a practical matter of arranging transport – it became another matter of life and death.[152]

4 The Long Trek Home

From Chaos to Limbo

THROUGH THE LATE SPRING AND EARLY SUMMER OF 1938, morale in the International Brigades in Spain continued to sag. There were increasing reports of volunteers from the U.S., Canada, and Britain being openly insubordinate to superior officers.[1] Meanwhile, Communist leaders in Spain and Moscow were angry about the outcome of the recent battles, and their repression and paranoia reached new heights. Suspicion and mutual recrimination spread everywhere, and top commissars demanded official reports from military leaders explaining the failures of the offensives of 1937 and the routs inflicted by Franco's drive toward the Mediterranean. Commissars hunted for deserters, traitors – anyone to blame for the losses.[2]

It was in this context that rumours of the repatriation of volunteers spread. The rumours created new problems and new potential dangers. The rules about when internationals could leave Spain had always been unclear and inconsistent. Certain units (including many in the Abraham Lincoln Battalion) had a policy that volunteers could return home after six months, although they did not always honour it; other regiments were not as open to repatriation. There were many cases throughout the war of internationals expressing a desire to leave – often assuming they could do so, since after all they were volunteers – and then being punished severely as cowards, or worse, as deserters. These inconsistencies became even more pronounced after the Great Retreats. In many units, the Communist political commissars were slow to dispel rumours of repatriation. Yet at the same time, they were facing pressure not only to find "subversives" to blame for recent defeats, but also to bolster their depleted ranks. Many commissars thus initially let talk of repatriation flourish, only to emphatically slam the door to it later.[3]

Ibing, for his part, showed no interest in repatriation – he was determined to stay on the job as long as the Brigades were active.[4] But the confusion about repatriation caused serious problems for units in the Regiment de Tren. In a cruel irony, a main cause of the problems was the Regiment's democratic culture, which had usually shielded the drivers from the worst of the Communists' repressive practices. Many Regiment members were excited by the possibility of early repatriation, and, given the open culture of the Regiment, seemed confident that they would be allowed to leave. One officer even circulated a list for drivers and mechanics to sign if they wanted to depart right away. The list circulated around the American company, and perhaps other companies in the Regiment as well. But when the Communist commissars moved to stamp out any talk of repatriation, those who had signed up to leave instead were denounced for breaking their "oaths" to keep fighting, and were reassigned to front-line infantry units.[5]

Ibing was not caught up in these upheavals (he never mentioned them in his memoirs), but he was among the large contingent of volunteers for whom the talk of repatriation raised a different concern: If the war was lost, how could they get out of Spain and find a safe haven?[6] About half of the total contingent of internationals actually had no home to go to, as they came from Italy or Germany, or fascist-allied dictatorships in Eastern Europe. Other countries, in another manifestation of the non-intervention policy, had deemed participation in the Spanish Civil War illegal. Canada was among them, having passed the Foreign Enlistment Act in April 1937, a few months after Ibing left for Spain.[7] It was uncertain whether these laws could also prohibit volunteers from returning or lead to them being prosecuted if they were allowed back. Still another concern for many volunteers was where their passports had gone. Communist officials forced volunteers to surrender their passports upon arrival in Albacete and often never returned them. Thousands of volunteers' passports were sent to Moscow for Soviet spies to use on international missions.[8] In the most notorious example, the Soviet agent who assassinated Leon Trotsky in Mexico City in 1940 allegedly entered North America using the modified passport of a Canadian volunteer who had died in Spain.[9]

Ibing was not much concerned about getting his passport back, however, because he did not think it was valid for international travel – at least not to Canada. Ibing was not a Canadian citizen at the time; he had travelled on a German passport with a Canadian visa, which remained valid for twelve months after departure.[10] Ibing was never quite clear in his recollections about exactly what instructions he had been given about his papers and how long they would be valid. He consistently maintained, however, that he thought little about it for most of the war. In one interview, he recalled with a laugh his feeling that "you are young and you are going there and you are going to win the war singlehanded."[11] By the time talk of repatriation became serious, it was too late – the expiration date on his papers had long passed.[12]

Ibing took his problem to his captain, who – typically for the Regiment's commanders – was responsive to his needs and set up a meeting in Barcelona for Ibing to get new papers. Ibing travelled there in late July 1938, just before the Republican forces crossed the Ebro and started their final desperate offensive. He got some overdue medical treatment, and the doctors decided he should stay in Barcelona for several weeks. Thanks to medicine, some much needed rest, and decent food, his stomach and tonsils both improved a little (they would continue to trouble him throughout his remaining time in Europe). As for Ibing's travel papers, the Spanish authorities could only provide what he called "a passport for stateless people." The pass's limited value was all too evident, as it was little more than "a piece of paper with [his] picture on it" and full of errors; the date of issue was wrong and his name was spelled "Ybing."[13]

While Ibing was in Barcelona, the Republican army's Ebro offensive was decisively defeated. By September 1938, fewer than fifteen thousand members of the International Brigades were left in Spain. On the international stage, the last glimmers of hope were dying out that Britain or France would assist the Republic or put diplomatic pressure on Hitler and Mussolini to limit their intervention. The British and French governments' commitment to appeasement was reaching its peak at the negotiating table in Munich, as they sacrificed Czechoslovakia in order to avoid war with Germany and Italy.[14] Soon afterward, Stalin brought home most of the Soviet officials engaged in Spain.[15] Ibing recalled that growing numbers of international volunteers were also pulled out of Spain, and he quickly found himself among them: the army discharged him and sent him north to France. He never mentioned having a chance to say goodbye to his comrades in the Regiment de Tren. There would not have been many remaining from the original group who were with Ibing at the formation of the Regiment: he recalled that by the time he left, at least half of the Regiment was made up of Spanish replacements.[16]

He was sent by train to the town of Portbou on the border with France, along with a couple of other German volunteers who had similar problems with their passports. As the French border guards would not accept their papers, another trek through the wilderness across the frontier awaited. Again they needed to rely on a guide to keep clear of French authorities and find a safe passage. This hike would prove less arduous, however; Ibing did not have to go over the mountains again, but instead snuck through vineyards and orchards, while having to "avoid all villages." Once across the border they were directed to a main road and told to wait for a bus that would take them to the town of Perpignan. The bus never appeared, and Ibing and his companions had to make the fifty-kilometre journey to the town on foot. But a well-organized support network in Perpignan provided food, shelter, and a ticket for the next day's train to Paris. In Paris, Ibing stayed at a safe house whose address he always remembered, 20 bis Rue Louis Blanc (in the tenth arrondissement), unsure of what would happen next.[17]

Ibing's participation in the war thus ended unceremoniously. He was likely just entering France when Spanish prime minister Juan Negrín López announced a complete withdrawal of the International Brigades on September 21, 1938. In a fitting encapsulation of the isolation that characterized his experience in Spain, Ibing was gone before *La Despedida* (the farewell) for the International Brigades in Barcelona on October 28, where citizens turned out in the tens of thousands to thank the members of the Brigades and say goodbye. Volunteers were showered with flowers and kisses from young women running out from the crowd as they marched through the centre of the city. They remembered hearing the speech by Communist leader Dolores Ibárruri, "La Pasionaria," whose words are inscribed on the Ottawa monument to the Canadians in the International Brigades: "You are history. You are legend. You are the heroic example of the solidarity and the universality of democracy. . . . We will not forget you; and, when the olive tree of peace puts forth its leaves, entwined with the laurels of the Spanish Republic's victory, come back!"[18]

But the timing of Ibing's departure brought some benefits – at least in the short term. He missed the Ebro offensive, which Preston described as "the most hard-fought battle of the entire war" and which saw the Brigades suffer heavy casualties.[19] Moreover, because Ibing left Spain in a very small group, he was also able to clear the first hurdle of the journey – getting out of Spain – much more easily than other Canadians. By this time, the Popular Front was out of power in France, and the new government became increasingly rigorous about guarding the border and rounding up members of the Brigades through 1938; large groups of decommissioned veterans therefore had to stay in Spain.[20] Thousands of the volunteers – including most of the Canadians – were collected in the northern Spanish town of Ripoll, and remained stuck there for weeks as diplomats wrangled over where their passports had gone and whether they could travel without them, and Communist parties in most Western democracies collected and forwarded the funds to bring their volunteers back.[21] For exhausted and war-weary survivors of the Brigades, spending weeks in the dreary, broken town was almost unbearable. In his study of American volunteers, Cecil Eby claims that in Ripoll "food reached an all-time low," firewood was scarce, and volunteers shivered in thin blankets as winter approached.[22] Beeching recounted that each day "the cooks boiled bones until they were white and then split them to remove the nourishing marrow." It made for paltry meals, but at least the volunteers were better off than the starving locals who picked up the bleached bones and brought them home.[23] Meanwhile, a few Canadian volunteers were trapped in the Republic's Southern Zone, most of whom would keep fighting to the end of the war. The least fortunate of all were those held prisoner in Franco's camps.[24]

By comparison, Ibing enjoyed relatively comfortable conditions in Paris through much of late 1938. He was finally able to sleep in a warm bed. Different organizations – Ibing believed it was a combination of Communist groups and French unions – raised money to support him and other veterans staying in the city. A number of local restaurants provided meals. There were even sightseeing trips and a few weekend picnics.[25] Nevertheless, as the autumn wore on, Ibing's anxiety about his future grew. Paris was a transit hub for veterans heading out of Spain, although not to the same extent as it had been earlier for volunteers heading into the fight. Still, Ibing had to watch as other international volunteers passed through on their way home. When the largest group of French volunteers arrived at the Gare d'Austerlitz, the streets were cleared for them to parade from the station to the steelworkers' union hall. But for Ibing, weeks passed by "without anybody doing anything about [his] status."[26]

Ibing was worried that as a German national, he might be deported to Germany – and to a grim fate. The Nazis had been hunting German Communists and other leftists since they'd seized power in 1933. During the Spanish Civil War, the Nazis were particularly eager to capture German members of the International Brigades. In the spring of 1938, when the Nationalists clearly had the upper hand, the head of the Nazi SS, Heinrich Himmler, initiated talks with Franco to secure the turnover of all Germans captured while fighting for the Republic. After the deal was finalized on July 31, Nazi agents went to Spain to "interrogate" (that is, torture) German prisoners and repatriate them.[27] Ibing would not have known in detail the intensity of the Nazis' pursuit of German internationals in Spain, but his sense that his life was in danger was extremely well founded. As a refugee in

France, without money or a clear path out of the country, Ibing's relatively comfortable exile in Paris could not last long.

Expulsion

In the late fall of 1938, Ibing and roughly twenty-five other veterans of the International Brigades were caught in a sweep by the Paris police. They were photographed, fingerprinted, and shipped by bus to an internment camp in the countryside near Limoges, which was about halfway back to Spain. The reasons for the raids were unclear, although they were likely related to the French authorities' expanding security measures against internationals coming out of Spain.[28] Through late 1938, the French grew unwilling to allow internationals to enter France unless their passage to their homelands was arranged, paid for, and cleared by officials from home governments; in some cases, the French insisted that internationals be transported in sealed trains.[29] For those who were still crossing the border without permission or a plan to leave, the French set up large concentration camps, where conditions were atrocious and prisoners were hardly fed.[30]

The conditions of Ibing's internment near Limoges were not nearly as severe. Ibing and his comrades were given three meals a day and at least a bit of freedom to move around the town, as long as they reported back to the police at night. Long after the war, Ibing was able to remember the location of his internment because he had got to see the porcelain manufacturing for which the region is famous.[31] After a few weeks, a local Communist party official came to speak with the internees about their situation. As Limoges had been known for decades as the "Red City" for its long-standing support for leftist organizations, it is not surprising that local Communists started to advocate for the internationals interned in the area.[32]

Ibing recalled that the official's primary concern was how they were being treated. As Ibing was one of the only internees able to communicate in French, he did a lot of the talking for the group. He did not spend much time complaining about the conditions, but rather told him that they "wanted to get out of there." Soon after, the Communist official was able to secure the prisoners' release and get them returned to Paris. Ibing's internment lasted only about a month.[33]

On his return to Paris, however, the police handed Ibing an "expulsion order": he had forty-eight hours to get out of France or face deportation. The French authorities did not specify where Ibing would be sent – but Germany seemed the most likely destination. Ibing pleaded with the police that he had lived in Canada and needed papers that would allow him to get back there. Clearly eager to get rid of him, the police told him that if he was still a German citizen, he should go to their embassy.[34]

Ibing now faced a desperate scramble to save his life. He raced over to the German embassy. Ibing recalled that a "Frenchman" went with him, likely from one of the organizations supporting the volunteers; the man waited outside the embassy to make sure Ibing came back out again. The precaution was understandable: as soon as he entered the German embassy, Ibing knew that he had stepped onto the terrain of the fascist enemy he had been fighting for almost two years. Zuehlke writes that the entryways and uniforms were all covered in swastikas, while "everywhere Ibing looked men and women sternly traded the straight-armed salute of the Nazi Party, loudly exchanged Heil Hitlers, and clicked heels together so sharply it sounded as if guns were constantly being fired in the consulate halls."[35]

Amid all of these forceful expressions of Nazism, there was Ibing in his ragged clothes and his beret, which he described as "the pickings" from a pile of civilian clothing available for volunteers as they rushed out of Spain. He looked exactly like a veteran of the bedraggled International Brigades, and he knew it. In a serious understatement, he told one interviewer that at that moment, he "felt kind of worried."[36]

Hope that he might be able to fool anyone at the embassy faded more when he was sent to the office of one consular functionary. He walked in and said: "Good morning." The German official's reply was "Heil Hitler." Ibing knew that he had given himself away by not using the mandatory salute for a German to a Nazi government official. But the "Hitler salute" was something he "hated worse than anything else." Even with his life at stake, he would not utter those words.[37]

Ibing told the official a story he had concocted on the way to the embassy: he was a German citizen living in Canada and had been visiting an uncle in Alsace-Lorraine, in eastern France. (That region is by the border and much of its population was German, and Ibing did in fact have an uncle there.) He claimed that he had lost his passport on his trip and needed another one to get back to Canada. The German official looked at him and said, "You were in Spain."[38]

Ibing persisted with his story that he was a German citizen living in Canada and on a visit to France. The official told him that Ibing could only get a passport valid for travel to Germany. Ibing insisted that he wanted to go to Canada, but his pleas were brushed aside. He asked them to draw up the new German passport, which was clearly marked with the travel restrictions. He still had no doubt about the fate that awaited him if he went to Germany, but Ibing hoped the passport would help his cause with the French police. If he could show that he had followed their advice and tried to get travel papers from the German authorities, the police might be more helpful.[39]

He left the German embassy, "glad to get out of there," and headed back to the police station. The police, still unmoved, took Ibing and some other veterans from Spain to a French government office (likely an office of the French Foreign Ministry). Through it all the Parisian police officers "were just as tough as you could imagine," Ibing recalled. Waiting at the ministerial office, with hours and minutes ticking away before his expulsion, Ibing "was lined up on the bench" with other veterans from Spain, with the police watching over them, and ordered "to shut up." "And [the police] said well, if we persisted then they were going to lock us up in solitary if we keep on talking."[40]

The French government officials were no help. They issued Ibing another stateless person's pass, or Nansen passport – another piece of paper with his photograph on it, like the one he'd received in Spain. Ibing now had a small collection of useless papers. And the French officials made sure to attach his expulsion order to his new Nansen passport.[41]

Ibing went back to the organization that was looking after veterans in Spain, but they offered no help regarding his papers. With little more than twenty-four hours left to get out of France, Ibing was running out of options. The Soviet Union made scant effort to offer a new home to the veterans. Stalin's paranoia made him suspicious of soldiers from other countries, although eventually he did accept several thousand Spanish refugees. But about 270 of these refugees, along with hundreds of Soviet officials who served in Spain, would end up in Stalin's Gulag labour camps; anyone who had been "contaminated" by exposure to outside ideas, or to the world in general beyond the Soviet Union, was targeted in his purges.[42] The only country that was publicizing its openness to refugees was Mexico.[43] Ibing considered the possibility of going to Mexico a few times; the Nansen passport he received in Spain named Mexico as his intended destination, although it was possible this was only a default answer to that part of the form.

But Ibing's heart was set on returning to Canada. The French organization supporting the volunteers reached out to a connection in the Paris travel office of the Canadian Pacific Railway, one of the main companies running passenger ships between Canada and Europe. They went to the CPR offices, where an agent gave Ibing a ticket for a boat leaving the next day from Le Havre for Halifax. The CPR agent accompanied him on the train to Le Havre early the next morning. On the train ride (about three hours), the agent had time to explain his plan to have Ibing wait behind the freight shed until the very last second, then dash onto the boat, hopefully without having to show his papers.

The first part of the gambit worked: one of the sailors spotted Ibing with his suitcase, and held the gangplank for him. Ibing remembered, "The two sailors of course thought I was a belated passenger, and let me on." As he hoped, there was no time to check papers. "I rushed up that gangplank and they pulled it in and I was aboard."[44] Ibing was on his way back to Canada.

But not yet safe. There was still the matter of getting into the country.

Later in the day, as the ship moved out to sea, the purser asked all of the passengers to turn in their travel papers for processing. Ibing handed in his Nansen passport – and was called back to the purser's office in a matter of minutes. The purser was apoplectic and railed at him for coming on board with a "piece of scrap" for travel papers. Ibing recalled, "[He] gave me a lecture on how I never would have got on board his ship if he'd seen my papers before boarding."[45] But it was a direct trip to Halifax, and they could not turn the ship or throw him overboard – although the purser seemed tempted. Ibing believed that the ship's crew had previous experience with veterans of the International Brigades travelling home from Spain, and that the purser in particular "was not sympathetic" with their cause. "Even though he didn't say it," Ibing recalled, "he was quite hostile."[46]

The purser told Ibing that he would not be allowed to disembark when the ship landed in Halifax; an immigration officer would be brought on board to interrogate him. He would remain in limbo throughout the trip across the Atlantic. When the ship docked, Ibing was kept on board as the rest of the passengers departed. He waited for several hours, thinking to himself, "Well this ship, it was already being prepared for the return voyage, and I was still on it . . . so if I went back to Paris or to France, it meant that I would be deported to Germany."[47] Then he was called up into the ship's first-class lounge – which he had not yet seen – where a Canadian immigration officer "in uniform" was waiting for him. The official subjected him to a long lecture on the rules regarding admission, and a lengthy interrogation about his life in Canada. Ibing answered all sorts of questions about where he had lived and what he had done in Winnipeg – even providing street addresses of his residences and workplaces.[48]

The officer left and Ibing had to endure another wait. He sat in the first-class lounge, guessing that the official was communicating back to shore, checking on his story.[49] By the time he returned, Ibing was at his wits' end from the suspense. Yet the officer made Ibing sit and listen while he weighed several considerations regarding the case: he was satisfied that Ibing had indeed lived in Winnipeg, but nevertheless he was coming back to Canada illegally and did not meet the requirements for readmission. In the end, the officer said that the idea of Ibing being deported to Germany weighed heavily on his conscience, so he would overlook these problems and allow Ibing back into Canada. He issued him a landing pass; shortly thereafter, Ibing was on a train back to Winnipeg.[50] Zuehlke writes that "Ibing knew he would never be able to adequately thank either the [immigration officer] or his adopted nation enough for this act of mercy and kindness."[51] Through the rest of his life, Ibing would frequently note that because the officer that day was French Canadian, he was "ever grateful to the Frenchmen in Canada."[52]

Ibing never learned that much of this gratitude was almost certainly misplaced: the official's conscience may have been a factor in Ibing's readmission into Canada, but only a minor one. The fate of returning veterans had been decided in the corridors of power in Ottawa a few weeks earlier. The immigration official's handling of Ibing's case in Halifax conformed entirely to the policy that the Canadian government had already established.

The Gates Quietly Reopen

After the International Brigades were withdrawn in September 1938, there was intense discussion among senior government officials regarding returning Canadian veterans.[53] The debate had been simmering for almost a year and a half since the passage of the Foreign Enlistment Act in April 1937. The RCMP consistently advocated an expansive reading and rigorous enforcement of the act, which meant prosecuting volunteers or at least the Communist groups that recruited them and assisted their passage to Spain.[54] The RCMP's stance was hardly surprising: by far the majority of its efforts at this time were aimed at monitoring, prosecuting, and generally harassing leftist organizations.[55] Moreover, in 1938 the RCMP was readying for what Reg Whitaker and Gregory Kealey, who have extensively studied the RCMP's activities against the left, call a "nation-wide assault on the Communist Party of Canada," including arresting CPC leaders for contravening the Foreign

Enlistment Act.[56] But through 1937 and into 1938, all of the RCMP's plans to attack the CPC faced resistance from officials in the Ministry of External Affairs and other branches and leaders of the Liberal government. They worried that charging veterans and their supporters could further energize Communist organizations and generate public sympathy for them. In general, Prime Minister King's political success was built on finding ways to evade divisive issues; as Petrou argues, by early 1938 the prime minister rightly saw the Spanish Civil War as just such a thorny subject that was best avoided. The RCMP's plans for a wave of prosecutions were ultimately rejected.[57]

The debate about the specific question of veterans of the International Brigades returning from Spain unfolded along the same lines. Here, too, the decisive factor was the decision by the Ministry of External Affairs and other departments that a gentler policy was the most politically expedient. An External Affairs memo stated that veterans would be allowed to return and would not face prosecution.[58] Crucially, the government also decided to allow the readmission of immigrants, such as Ibing, who had been out of the country for an extended period.

Officials were fully aware of the rules regarding immigrants who had left the country for more than twelve months. As one memo put it, in these cases "there would be a presumption of loss of domicile under the Immigration Act with a corresponding presumption of loss of the right of return to Canada."[59] Again the RCMP pushed for a tough approach, insisting that these veterans should be kept out of Canada for violating the Immigration Act, the Foreign Enlistment Act, and other laws. Since the war had started, the RCMP had argued that volunteers were going to Spain in order to "gain experience in practical revolutionary work and [they] will return to this country to form the nucleus of a training corps" for Communist organizations.[60] In response, External Affairs again focused on public relations, arguing that readmitting the veterans, including immigrants who had been away for extended periods, "would arouse no serious objections anywhere in Canada, while any other policy would evoke immediate and widespread criticism of the government."[61]

Officials also worried that excluding veterans from Spain would create embarrassing problems in international relations. External Affairs voiced concerns about alienating countries that would end up bearing the costs of providing refuge to Canada's veterans. The government also felt compelled to follow the example of the U.S. and Britain, which were already repatriating their veterans. "In such circumstances," an External Affairs memo noted, "it would be difficult for this country to stand alone in refusing help in settling the Spanish mess."[62]

In this context, the Immigration Branch decided to be remarkably flexible when it came to returning veterans; this was a significant break from its usual approach through the 1930s of strictly interpreting the regulations on the books in order to keep the gates to Canada shut. It opposed the RCMP's hard line regarding immigrants who had been absent from Canada for more than a year, and contended that a "presumption of loss of domicile could be rebutted" by some unspecified amount of "satisfactory evidence." It also argued that for "most if not all" volunteers to fight in Spain, "the nature of the absence from Canada would be inconsistent with an intention of settlement abroad."[63]

The government also decided to overlook the returning veterans' lack of travel papers. Indeed, probably the majority of Canadian volunteers returned from Spain without valid papers; they were either ineligible for them or their passports were still in Albacete or in the hands of Soviet spies. Ottawa did not drop all security precautions regarding the re-entry of the Canadian volunteers. Officials were preoccupied with the chance that foreign agitators, or veterans who had never lived in Canada, would be among those seeking repatriation, and they made a concerted effort to weed them out. They were instructed to ask the veterans about where they had lived in Canada, where they worked, and the main cities and cultural events in their area.[64]

Ibing had no idea that Ottawa had adopted such an open policy on repatriation. Canadian officials were hardly going to broadcast the policy far and wide: it is evident in their policy discussions that they did not intend to make things easy for the veterans, and the government's overall priority was to avoid publicity related to Spain as much as possible. In October 1938, Ottawa briefly weighed the possibility of getting more active in repatriating volunteers and even devoting some money to fund their return. Again, senior bureaucrats were worried that Canada might stick out in the international community for being unwilling to "pay the petty price of repatriation." But the government – which was miserly in all things through the Depression – decided to wait and thus keep the pressure on "the Canadian friends of the volunteers who have sent the volunteers to Spain and should pay their return."[65]

All Ottawa proved willing to do was to assign some officials in November to start processing veterans waiting to get home. The officials appear to have gone only to the main group of veterans in Ripoll – not to Paris or the camps in France where other Canadian veterans might have been held.[66] But an even deeper layer of problems affected the Canadian volunteers: the Canadian party was even more caught out by the end of the war than Communists in other countries. Tim Buck, the leader of the CPC, claimed that the party continued to expect the Republic to win (showing an astonishing lack of foresight, especially by 1938), and hence they had not made any preparations to rush volunteers home.[67] The Friends of the Mackenzie-Papineau Battalion (FMPB) and the CPC mounted a new fundraising effort, and in the end the party had to mortgage property to pay for veterans' return trips. For weeks in late 1938, the Communists' efforts continued to be bogged down in confusion regarding paperwork, travel arrangements, and money transfers.[68]

Canadian Communists also had to scramble to get someone to Europe to advocate for the veterans. They gave the job to A.A. MacLeod, an influential figure in the party, especially regarding foreign affairs.[69] MacLeod appears to have gone directly to Ripoll to help the largest contingent of veterans, before racing around Spain trying to find other Canadians; he did not go to Paris while Ibing was there.[70] The behaviour of both the federal government and the CPC ensured that most Canadians veterans faced longer waits to get home than other internationals.[71]

Another problem that had an impact on Ibing was lack of communication between the CPC and other organizations supporting veterans, including

Communist organizations in France. This reduced any chance that information about the Canadian policy that was quietly being implemented would be relayed to him. One confidential RCMP memo suggested the FMPB knew about the policy by October 18, 1938, and through November it was being executed for the large group of Canadians in Ripoll.[72] Yet no one in Paris knew about it, and no one trying to help Ibing appears to have considered sending him to the Canadian embassy. Ibing and everyone working with him seemed convinced that his lack of citizenship and lack of valid papers eliminated any chance that Canadian officials would allow him to return.[73]

If he had gone to the Canadian embassy, would the consular officials have helped him get back? It is impossible to know for certain. But what *is* certain is that while he was interned in France and then rushing around Paris trying to get travel papers, government officials were, however slowly, screening Canadians in Ripoll and approving them to return.[74] It is also certain that officials at the Canadian embassy in Paris would have known about this process. According to one confidential RCMP memo, once returning veterans without passports in the main group were approved to return, they were "supplied with Identification Documents by the Canadian authorities in Paris."[75]

When interviewing veterans in Ripoll, the officer in charge, Colonel Andrew O'Kelly, asked the same security questions that the immigration officer in Halifax asked Ibing. According to Zuehlke, O'Kelly was concerned that foreign agents would be lurking among the recent immigrants to Canada, so he subjected these "ethnic" veterans to especially extensive questioning.[76] But if the recent immigrants could give satisfactory answers to the questions – just as Ibing would do in desperate circumstances on the boat in Halifax, and as he most likely could have done at a Canadian consular office in Paris – they were accepted for repatriation. Petrou recounts the story of one veteran, Frank Hadesbeck, who was approved for re-entry after he gave O'Kelly an adequate description of the Calgary Stampede.[77] Those approved in Ripoll could not leave immediately, as transport to Canada was still not secured and funded. Still, it appears that only a few Canadian veterans were rejected after undergoing examinations by Canadian officials.[78] Indeed, in an internal report to the Comintern, Canadian Communist leaders themselves acknowledged that "when the question was finally settled, the government permitted many men to enter that it could have easily denied."[79]

Considering the Canadian government's policies and the experience of other volunteers leaving Spain, it is evident that at least part of Ibing's ordeal in France could have been avoided – including his forty-eight-hour race to get out and his nerve-breaking trip to Halifax. However, Ibing was fortunate in other ways: few veterans separated from the main group of Canadians in Ripoll would find as quick a passage to Paris. Most got stuck in French concentration camps on the Mediterranean (particularly if they left in early 1939) and became engulfed in the flood of refugees fleeing the collapsing Republic. Some of those left in the French camps were forced to sleep outside for several months, received no attention for their wounds or illnesses, and got food only in the form of bread thrown over barbed wire fences. According to Beeching, a number of veterans died in the camps before Ottawa sent officials to deal with their readmission.[80]

A number of members of the Brigades were still held prisoner in Spain, where they were moved from camp to camp, paraded through towns by Franco's guards, and kept in the most wretched conditions. A large group of internationals, including thirty Canadians, was not released by Franco until early April 1939. Among them was Jules Paivio, who was in Ibing's group that trekked into Spain through the mountains in February 1937; he left Spain so malnourished that he suffered from bone rheumatism and scurvy sores.[81] This group of veterans also suffered a rocky journey out of France through Le Havre.[82] Still another group was stuck in Le Havre for longer as the CPC implored the rank and file again for help in the late summer of 1939.[83]

Several thousand internationals with backgrounds in fascist countries remained in France through 1939. Not having been forced to find a way out as Ibing had been, or having become stuck in some camp or hiding spot, these internationals were captured when France fell to the Nazis in June

1940 (about a year and a half after Ibing left). Most of them would perish in Nazi death camps.[84]

The largest group of Canadian veterans were welcomed by a crowd of supporters when they landed at the port in Halifax on February 3, 1939. When about 270 of them arrived in Toronto two days later, they got a raucous reception from about ten thousand people gathered to cheer them at Union Station.[85] There were similar events in cities across the country that month, all drawing several thousand supporters.[86] But since Ibing returned to Canada on his own and before the others, he arrived to no fanfare at all.

Ibing may not have minded that much. To him, a triumphant rally would not have been an appropriate way to end his time in Spain; it would not have been true to his experience there. Indeed, Ibing would probably have agreed with the great French writer Albert Camus, who described Franco's victory as "like an evil wound" to the supporters of the Republic. "It was in Spain," observed Camus, "that men learnt that one can be right and yet be beaten, that force can vanquish spirit, that there are times where courage finds no reward. It is this without a doubt that explains why so many men, the world over, regard the Spanish drama as a personal tragedy."[87] Perhaps these sentiments help explain why Ibing always insisted that from the moment he got back to Canada, he wanted to put the war in Spain behind him. However, he did not give up his determination to keep fighting fascism. He would find new ways to continue that fight on the home front in World War II.

5 Settling Down

Back to Square One

HAVING RETURNED TO WINNIPEG, Ibing's first priority was recovering his health. At long last, he received sustained medical treatment for injuries to his leg and for his ailing stomach. Most pressing were his tonsils; they were seriously inflamed throughout his struggle to get home, and it would require a stay in the hospital to have them removed.[1] Ibing never recounted who covered his medical expenses (and they would have been substantial, as Canada remained a long way from creating a generous social welfare system, let alone public medical insurance); it was almost certainly local Communist organizations. According to the National Committee of Friends of the Mackenzie-Papineau Battalion, it was supporting fifty-six veterans from the International Brigades in Winnipeg alone, including eleven who required visits to the hospital. Veterans also needed aid to cover their most basic needs, including clothes, rent, and medicine.[2] CPC officials complained to Moscow that since the federal government's approach to the veterans remained icily indifferent, "a heavy burden" for supporting them was falling on Communist organizations. They claimed that the fundraising drive on behalf of the veterans was a major success, raising almost $4,400 in Winnipeg alone by early 1939; but party officials also reported that due to the "conditions of [the veterans'] return," the costs of helping them put the CPC in "a financial crisis" that forced a "retrenchment of other activity."[3]

Canadian Communist leaders also saw the returning anti-fascist fighters as political assets. Local branches of the FMPB were ordered to make every effort to keep in touch with the veterans, evaluate their potential for the party, and engage them in local Communist activities. One top CPC official declared that "their importance in Canada was far greater than their work overseas" because they commanded such respect as heroes in the war against fascism and their presence could be used to boost turnout at public events.[4] In both Toronto and Vancouver, veterans were given leading places in the 1939 May Day marches.[5]

Ibing obliged the party to a limited extent, returning to the fold of the German-Canadian League (a new iteration of the German Workers and Farmers Association).[6] He also gave a few speeches about his service in the International Brigades to local Communist groups. But his heart was not in giving speeches about the war. He remained averse to revisiting his experiences in Spain, let alone putting a positive face on them.[7] Many of the Communist activities he did join were more social than political, as community events organized by the German-Canadian League were a needed chance to enjoy himself. In a way, Ibing went back to the sort of "hall socialism" he'd engaged in when he'd first joined the GWFA in 1934.

Many returning veterans wanted even less to do with Communist organizations than Ibing did. Indeed, in early 1939 Communist officials reported that a number of veterans "attacked the CPC" when approached about getting active in the party. The RCMP claimed that the "truculent attitude" taken by "not a few" of the veterans was "causing considerable anxiety in Communist Party circles."[8] Communist officials usually expressed confidence that most veterans remained loyal to the cause. But one report of the FMPB worried that the "demoralized element" was sufficiently large that, even though it was "geographically separated," it would likely "have a detrimental effect on the whole." The Manitoba branch of the FMPB was concerned that veterans could be recruited by leftist splinter groups; its report urged that "the bad, demoralized element" be watched carefully and "dealt with coolly and without such methods which would push them into the arms of our enemies."[9] Motivated by both solidarity and suspicion, the FMPB tracked Spanish veterans carefully in the following months, each branch keeping detailed lists of veterans in their area.[10]

At the same time, there was no easing of the RCMP's obsession with leftists – and its particular determination to lock up Spanish Civil War veterans and their Communist sponsors. The RCMP made another push for arrests in early 1939, but again senior government officials followed the lead of the major Western powers. A memo from Canadian Undersecretary of State for Foreign Affairs O.D. Skelton in February 1939 noted that authorities in the United States and Britain still declined to take action against returning veterans, so Canadian authorities should continue to stand down, too.[11]

As these political forces swirled around him, Ibing put his head down and focused on carving out a new life for himself in Canada. As for getting work, once he was healthy Ibing was dispirited to find conditions in Winnipeg had changed very little while he was gone. He had departed in 1936 full of hope of defeating fascism and maybe even starting a new life in a socialist Spain; after the Republic was defeated, he returned to the same dreary, depressed capitalist economy he had left.[12]

Local Communist organizations, led by the FMPB, tried to help, but their resources were extremely limited. And their support for veterans in Canada was scaled back in early 1939 in order to devote all funds to emergency efforts to bring home those still stuck in France.[13] After a few weeks, Ibing ended up in the place he least expected (or wanted) to be: back at the butcher shop. He remembered that the shop's owner "sort of liked [him]. . . . He was sympathetic."[14] As in the early 1930s, Ibing was grateful to have a job, but he had to survive the grind of driving the truck twelve hours a day, six days a week. One benefit of the old routine was renewing acquaintance with the people who worked at the restaurants he served on his route. Many were surprised but happy to see him again after an absence of more than two years. Ibing took a particular shine to a young woman named Sarah Kasow, who worked at her family's restaurant on Main Street, near Winnipeg's train station.[15]

Ibing had known the family from his first weeks in Canada in 1930, as the restaurant was near the boarding house where he had initially stayed. In fact, Kasow was the young waitress Ibing had greeted so awkwardly just days after arriving in Winnipeg. Her father had started the restaurant when he first came to Canada around 1912. He was caught out by the start of the war and was unable to return to the family in Russia until it had become the Soviet Union. Kasow's mother and her sister, Bessie, lived through the war and the 1917 revolutions on their own in Belorussia. Despite the upheaval, for Sarah Kasow it was a far from difficult experience: she was a strong supporter of the Communist regime and remained a Soviet patriot for the rest of her life. After the family was reunited after the revolution, they migrated to Canada and worked together at the restaurant.[16]

When Ibing had returned to Winnipeg from farm labour in Stornaway in 1930 and stayed again at the rooming house, he had eaten at the restaurant frequently. It served mostly Ukrainian food, although Ibing recalled there were also "Russian, Slavic, and Canadian" dishes on the menu.[17] It offered entertainment, too. There was a piano in the back, and on weekends he and others would sometimes come to hear music and sing along. Ibing stopped dining there regularly after he moved out of the rooming house, but he still saw the family when he made deliveries from the butcher shop. He also saw Kasow at local socialist events. She was a member of the Canadian Workers' Circle, a Communist-allied organization that would later be one of the founding groups of the United Jewish People's Order (UJPO). Ibing recalled having seen her at a few speaker's events, discussion groups, and social events at the organization's hall through the early 1930s.[18]

After Ibing returned to Winnipeg from Spain, he spent increasing amounts of his spare time at the restaurant with Kasow, her sister, and her mother. (Her father had died in 1937.) In addition to personal chemistry, he and Kasow were drawn together by shared political convictions. They had in common a commitment to socialism, and a faith that the Soviet Union showed a path toward a better future. As with so many leftists at the time, they centred their social lives around their politics, including the socialist halls that immigrant communities supported around the city.

This common ground was essential, because the broader political climate created obvious barriers for a match between a man born and raised in Germany and a Jewish woman from Eastern Europe. It would be a couple more years before the Nazis started killing Jews on a massive scale. But by 1939, no one could have any doubts that anti-Semitism was at the core of Hitler's ideology, and the Nazis had already committed numerous atrocities against German and Austrian Jews. In November 1938 – a few weeks before Ibing returned to Canada – there was the massive *Kristallnacht* (Night of Broken Glass) pogrom in which more than a thousand synagogues were destroyed, dozens of Jews were killed, and more than thirty thousand were arrested and placed in concentration camps.[19] The plight of German Jews fleeing Hitler was one of the most pressing political issues in the Jewish community in Winnipeg (and elsewhere) throughout the 1930s.[20]

In this context, it was significant that Ibing had recently returned from Spain – from serving in the struggle that united the left in the fight against fascism. Indeed, even though Ibing was German, no one could have been more unmistakably committed to fighting Hitler than he was. It is also significant that Ibing's main Communist organization, the German-Canadian League, had a strong record of speaking out against Nazi anti-Semitism. Since the mid-1930s, its predecessor, the GWFA, had continually portrayed anti-Semitism as a key part of the Nazi's regressive, right-wing ideology that German Canadians and indeed all progressive Canadians had to resist. In the late 1930s, moreover, the German-Canadian League agitated in favour of the admission of Jewish refugees into Canada, monitored and reported on the activities of Nazi sympathizers in Canada, and organized rallies protesting Nazi anti-Semitism in a number of cities, including Calgary and Kitchener.[21]

In pursuing these activities, the German-Canadian League worked in co-operation with a number of Jewish organizations, including prominent ones such as the Canadian Jewish Congress. The league was building upon connections established by the GWFA, whose public meetings about Nazi anti-Semitism were well attended by local Jews. For instance, when the GWFA organized an event featuring two German Jewish exiles in Montreal in 1936, the RCMP noted (in crude status-conscious language) that "the hall was packed, there being approximately 1,000 people, principally Jews of the better class, present."[22] In some cities, the league also signed up members of the German-Canadian Jewish community, many of whom were middle-class professionals rather than part of the working class. Forging such broad-based alliances was consistent with the Popular Front strategy of the era, although the emphasis on combatting Nazi anti-Semitism did diverge somewhat from Moscow's official position on fascism. The Soviets tended to portray Nazism as indistinguishable from fascism, and thus tended to downplay the essential role of racism and anti-Semitism in Nazi ideology.[23] Yet the league's approach helped its efforts to mobilize anti-Nazi protests; for instance, the largest rally against Hitler's persecution of the Jews, held in Toronto in December 1938, drew about two thousand people.[24]

More Bad Times

This social spark of light in Ibing's personal life was certainly needed. His long days driving the butcher's truck were hardly uplifting, and in his political world, the news coming from Europe was deeply dispiriting. Hitler was becoming ever more aggressive and confident as war clouds gathered. Then on August 23, 1939, came the announcement that the Soviet Union signed a Non-aggression Pact with Nazi Germany. After years of presenting itself as the leader of the struggle against fascism, Moscow agreed that it would launch no hostilities against Germany, nor ally itself with any of its enemies. In exchange, Germany made the same commitment to the Soviets.[25] The deal was met with shock almost everywhere, and caused much soul searching for Communist supporters. The RCMP's well informed but biased assessment was that the pact had "the effect of a bomb exploding in the midst of the Communist Party, leaving . . . dark consternation and bewilderment. . . . Profound confusion and embarrassment was manifest in every language section of the Party."[26]

At first Ibing saw the pact as a strategic move by Stalin. He held on to the belief that Stalin had given up hope that Britain and France would confront Nazi Germany. They would continue to delay until Hitler invaded the Soviet Union; hence, Stalin made the pact in order to buy time to build up his forces for the inevitable war.[27] This was a common view among Communists in many countries, and it had particular appeal to those – such as Ibing – who remained bitter about how Western democracies had abandoned the Spanish Republic.[28] Many Communist parties – including Canada's – thus argued that Moscow's security calculations should not stand in the way of their continuing fight against fascism. Communists' sincerity in holding this position – tenuous as it may have been – was evident enough. Days after Hitler invaded Poland on September 1, 1939, Tim Buck declared: "This is our war." Other prominent Communists such as Joe Salsberg in Toronto and Fred Rose in Montreal declared they wanted to see a "complete defeat" of the Nazis.[29] The CPC in Winnipeg produced a leaflet that urged Canadians: "Unite in this Hour of Grave Test! SMASH HITLER!" Former commissars of the Mackenzie-Papineau Battalion Edward Cecil-Smith and Bill Kardash offered their services as experienced wartime leaders to the government.[30]

But it soon became apparent that even this uneasy accommodation with the Non-aggression Pact was unsustainable, that the Popular Front was dead, and that Stalin had turned his back on the struggle against fascism. On September 14, Soviet official media outlets called the war "an imperialist and predatory war for a new redivision of the world, a robber war kindled from all sides by the two imperialist groups of powers."[31] At the start of October, Moscow ordered Communist parties in Western democracies to support the new policy and demand that their countries stay out of the conflict. After a few weeks' delay, the leaders of the CPC duly fell into line, adopting the slogan "Withdraw Canada from this Imperialist War." The *Toronto Clarion* urged the public to speak up and "make it abundantly clear to the King Government that the Canadian people are more interested in an early peace than in the prosecution of the war."[32]

Ibing was hit hard by the betrayal of the cause that meant most to him.

Just when Western democracies had been moved to declare war against fascism, the Communists were declaring themselves (as the *Toronto Clarion* also put it) "opposed to victory of either side in this imperialist war."[33] Ibing recalled, "Here I came from Spain fighting Hitler and [now] here is Hitler fighting Canada," but the Communist party declared "it was an imperialist war, and ... keep out of it."[34] More galling still was the propaganda coming out of official Communist sources in Canada, much of which was deeply cynical and patently absurd. For instance, Tim Buck declared, while in hiding in the United States, that refusing to join in this "criminal" war was a way for Canada to assert its independence from Britain.[35] The *Toronto Clarion* even tried to argue: "For us in Canada the principal danger of fascism comes not from Germany but from the war policies of the King government."[36]

Ibing could not bring himself to leave the party in 1939, as many who had joined during the Popular Front period did. But like many who remained, he refused to support Moscow's policy. Resistance from Ibing's German-Canadian League was particularly strong; a number of its leaders rejected demands from the CPC that they speak out in favour of Canada staying neutral.[37] Among returned veterans from the Spanish Civil War, contempt for the accord with Hitler and for Communists' anti-war rhetoric ran deep. "Well Christ almighty," one veteran put it to Michael Petrou, "we had just fought the son of a bitch and now [Stalin] was trying to make friends with him."[38] Many Canadian veterans enlisted to fight in the armed forces – in defiance of Communist policy. Even Cecil-Smith, the Mackenzie-Papineau Battalion's former commissar and still a prominent figure in the CPC, noted supportively that many veterans from Spain had enlisted.[39]

Ibing was among those who tried to enlist, heading to the recruiting office of the Royal Canadian Air Force. He saw it as both another chance to fight Hitler, and a chance to gain new skills "and learn something different."[40] But Ibing was immediately rejected; he recalled that the official in charge "turned his back" on him and said that Canada was fighting Germany, so they wouldn't "take any Germans."[41] Ibing was stung by being turned away; he knew that the armed forces were hardly being selective in their recruitment. He recalled that once the war broke out, most of the soup kitchens in Winnipeg closed – but at one of the few that remained open, there was a table right at the entrance "with three Mounties there and a clerk sitting at the table. And everyone who wanted to enter had to register for the Canadian army."[42]

Less than a year after returning from his service in a war against fascism, Ibing was now officially seen an "enemy alien." This made him part of a large group held in suspicion by the state – and rejection for military service was far from the worst thing the state could do to those it deemed suspicious. Even before Parliament formally declared war, it passed the Defence of Canada Regulations (DOCR) – sixty-four in all – which gave the government sweeping powers to supress any potential subversive activity. Arrests without warrants, internments, press censorship, and confiscation of property were all made permissible with no judicial or parliamentary review. Regulation 21 allowed authorities to detain "any particular person" they deemed to be "acting in any manner prejudicial to the public safety of the State."[43]

The DOCR named the commissioner of the RCMP as the registrar general of enemy aliens, tasked with tracking immigrants from countries Canada was fighting. The RCMP created a special branch to do this work, and by early 1940, it had registered sixteen thousand German immigrants.[44] Ibing was one of them; throughout the war he would have to report monthly to his local RCMP office.[45] He was not at much risk, however, of being among the German immigrants who were put into internment camps by the government. According to Whitaker and Kealey, the RCMP focused its efforts on arresting prominent Nazi sympathizers in the German community, and generally had good intelligence about who were such people were.[46]

But Ibing was doubly suspect in the eyes of the Canadian state – for his German origins *and* for his membership in the Communist party. Even after the war began, the authorities continued to view Communists as the state's primary enemies. It did not seem to matter that Canada was at war with fascist states in Germany and Italy and not the Soviet Union, or that rank-and-file Communists had just been fighting fascism in Spain: the RCMP remained convinced that "there is more to fear from acts of espionage and sabotage on the part of the Communist Party than from Nazi or Fascist organizations and adherents."[47] In the weeks and days before the war, the commissioner of the RCMP was planning yet again for mass arrests and incarcerations, primarily of Communist agitators; he asked for seven hundred officers to carry out the sweep.[48]

As soon as the war started, the leaders of the German-Canadian League hid their records so that the RCMP could not find them and use them to arrest their members. Many members of the other Communist-allied "foreign language associations" were interned, including some from the Ukrainian Labour-Farmer Temple Association and the Finnish Organization of Canada. The leaders of the German-Canadian League were waiting for the RCMP to round up their group, too. Indeed, that was the RCMP's plan: it had tabbed the league as another Communist group whose members should be arrested.[49]

Ibing and his comrades were saved from potential internment partly by the general limits the government put on the scale of the RCMP's sweep – only a few dozen Communists supporters were detained in late 1939. But more important was the support that the German-Canadian League had built up among respectable middle-class figures – especially Jewish ones – during its campaigns against Nazism in the two years before the war. Norman Robertson – a leading diplomat and adviser to Prime Minister King – had come to know a number of the league's middle-class Jewish activists who had been lobbying Ottawa before the war. Robertson insisted that the league was a firmly pro-war organization intent on fighting against the Nazis, and therefore should not be prosecuted. Robertson's stance carried the day, despite the RCMP's continued objections. In the context of World War II, this was a truly extraordinary turn of events: ethnic Germans were saved from prosecution and internment by their connections to prominent Jews.[50]

Ibing himself never complained much about the Canadian state's security measures during the war. He found reporting to local RCMP offices little more than an annoyance. Although he had been spared the worst of the internal repression in the International Brigades, he knew that much more drastic security measures had been taken in Spain, such as after the May Days uprising in Catalonia. He also knew that at least a few ethnic Germans in Canada did indeed support fascism. He had little sympathy for CPC leaders such as Buck at most times, and none at all when they started speaking out against the war.

Ibing remained primarily concerned not with politics but with finding new opportunities in Canada. He wanted very much to find a way out of his truck-driving job. In the spring of 1940, a couple of acquaintances in the local German-Canadian League told him they were heading to Ontario to look for work. Ibing did not know these men well – they were skilled carpenters and migrants from Yugoslavia who spoke a particular dialect of German he sometimes struggled to understand – but, enticed by their confidence that there were jobs in Ontario, he joined them.[51]

The move brought brighter economic prospects, as Ibing quickly found work in Toronto and then a steadier job at a meat-packing plant in Barrie. But there was no escaping what he remembered as "all the pressure . . . because of the war effort."[52] A wave of panic gripped the Dominion (and all Western democracies) as the Nazis successfully executed their Spring Offensives of 1940, conquering first Denmark and Norway, and then sweeping through the Netherlands and Belgium on their way into France. After the Netherlands fell in May and France in June, there was a deepening sense among the public that internal subversives, or Fifth Columnists, had played a crucial role in undermining resistance to the Nazi offensives. As the hysteria spread, much of the public became convinced that Canada was similarly vulnerable to internal subversion. Enemy aliens and Communists were especially held in suspicion. Prominent political figures fanned the flames. For instance, Sir William Mulock, a long-time prominent Liberal known as "the Grand Old Man of Canada," claimed to the government that "Communism and disloyalty are rampant in Ontario, and doubtless elsewhere, amongst the alien classes particularly."[53] Predictably, the RCMP's paranoia about the Communists reached new heights, with the most outlandish scenarios being taken seriously; one RCMP bulletin claimed that veterans of the Mackenzie-Papineau Battalion had been ordered to Mexico in support of a planned Communist insurrection there.[54] Around the country vigilante groups were formed to target subversives, and members of Parliament and the Prime Minister's Office were flooded with demands for mass arrests and detentions of suspected Fifth Columnists.[55]

In response, Ottawa took new security measures, formally banning the Communist party and a number of affiliated organizations (most of them ethnic), and conducting a new wave of internments. Although the total number of internments remained small, many people were arrested on the basis of flimsy evidence.[56] Indeed, in internal communications, the RCMP readily acknowledged that its aim was to be seen as responding to the widespread anxiety, as "the effect of periodic internments is very beneficial in stabilizing public feeling."[57] Many of those arrested were simply told that "representations had been made" that they were Communists or engaged in subversion; at times the authorities appealed to citizens to confidentially denounce their neighbours and co-workers.[58]

Ibing was not high on the RCMP's list of suspicious figures to monitor or detain. One RCMP list of veterans from the war in Spain claimed he was living in Winnipeg almost a year after he had left the city.[59] But he still found himself in danger around May or June 1940. Ibing recounted that there had been some labour unrest at the Barrie plant where he was working, "with which [he] had nothing to do at all." Indeed, he knew little about it except what he had heard over a beer with some co-workers after his shift. Nevertheless, fingers had been pointed at him. "This crony reported me to the police," he explained, "and he said to them that I was the guy who stirred up all the trouble there."[60] Ibing suspected he was denounced for his German background rather than his politics, although he was never certain. Whatever the case, the local police met him when he arrived at work one day and told him get out of Barrie immediately.[61] He was lucky that he was only "run out of town" – the local police did not contact the RCMP and he faced no charges.

Ibing described this incident as the only time he faced serious anti-German discrimination in Canada. Even in recollections of losing his job and having to leave Barrie, he said little about the political climate of the time beyond the general tension in the air as the war turned against the Allies. Overall, he remained focused on getting established somewhere in Canada. He quickly gathered his belongings and returned to Toronto.

Settling in Toronto

Ibing used his driving experience to get another job delivering meat for a butcher shop – an Italian wholesaler on St. Clair Avenue. He remained there for a few months and got involved in Toronto's chapter of the German-Canadian League, perhaps the only Communist-affiliated group that Ottawa had not banned.[62] This allowed him to lay down some roots in the German and leftist community, although the league's activities were severely hampered by the political climate. The CPC leadership continued to demand that Canada stay out the "imperialist war" in Europe; through 1940 and early 1941, many members of the league gradually toned down efforts to rally support for the war. Some members insisted that whatever the official CPC policy, fighting Hitler was the league's raison d'être – but their efforts to launch new pro-war campaigns quickly faltered. Popular suspicion of "enemy aliens" was running high, the government was unwilling to give resources to a German-Canadian organization, and the RCMP remained implacably hostile. The RCMP continued to tell the government that the league was not only a Communist front but also generally a group that was "running in various directions on alarms of all kinds, the majority of them being without foundation."[63] Ibing never recounted in interviews how much he supported the league's pro-war campaigns; in any case, it was not long before the league was barely active.

Yet Ibing's engagement with Communist groups in Toronto did pay off in one crucial way in the fall of 1940. An opening came up in the Communists' main print shop, Eveready Printers, and an acquaintance from the German-Canadian League asked Ibing if he was interested in the job. This was his chance to get established doing manual tradeswork. It was what he had been seeking since he had left Germany in 1930, and once at Eveready he eagerly developed his skills. Ibing recalled that he found it awkward to be "starting as an apprentice" at over thirty years old, but he quickly found that he had a knack for working with the press machines. "I must have had some natural ability or something like that," he recalled, likely because he "had a background in the printing industry." His father, Gustav, had been a master craftsman in the trade. Over the following months, Ibing took a series of "correspondence courses" through his union and eventually worked his way up to the status of journeyman pressman. This gave him, for the first time, a secure job and a solid footing in a union, the International Printing Pressmen and Assistants' Union, which was affiliated with the American Federation of Labor and the Trades and Labor Congress of Canada.[64]

Ibing enjoyed not only the work but also the shop-floor culture at the press, where all the employees were Communists. The atmosphere was brightened by a sense of common cause among employees, and by the presence of interesting co-workers such as Percy Saltzman, who would become the main weather forecaster on the CBC and later a host of public affairs programs.[65] But when it came to getting active in distributing some of the Communist propaganda at this time, Ibing balked. Eveready printed Communist leaflets that persisted in denouncing Ottawa's wartime policies and in general condemned the war as "imperialist." Ibing recounted in one interview, with a laugh, "I could never bring myself . . . to support anything like that."[66]

Hitler's attack on the Soviet Union on June 22, 1941, changed the situation entirely, and brought another radical shift in Moscow's policies. Communists everywhere now sought to rally support behind "a just war, a people's war," against Hitler, and once again cast the Soviet Union as the leading force in the struggle to defeat fascism. Communist leaders in Canada immediately became champions of the war effort, demanding unity from Canadians in the fight. After insisting since September 1939 that Canada assert its independence by staying out of the "imperialist war," Communists now declared their full support for "a people's war of national freedom and liberation." Indeed, Communist publications declared that not only the Soviet Union, but Canada too, was "in mortal danger."[67]

Although it was the second complete policy reversal in less than two years, Canadian Communists adopted the new position with enthusiasm – and in many cases, not a little relief that they were freed from the obligation to oppose the war and downplay the threat that Hitler posed. Communist leaders became fervent patriots, telling their members that "if you are not engaged in vital war production, get into uniform" – and a wave of new enlistments by members followed.[68] Communists also led efforts to unify workers behind the war effort and maintain harmonious industrial relations in order to maximize wartime production.[69]

Ibing, however, did not immediately drop his reservations or regain his faith in the Communist leadership. He remained unhappy about Moscow's endless policy reversals, and while the betrayal of the struggle against the Nazis in 1939 continued to anger him most, he complained about the new switch in 1941 every time he was interviewed and in his written reminiscences for the history of the Mackenzie-Papineau Battalion. For instance, he told Michael Petrou, "They said it was an imperialist war. And then when Russia was invaded it became a people's war. . . . I was an anti-fascist. Hitler was the enemy. And I got tired of all their political somersaults."[70]

Ibing put his focus on his work rather than on politics – but while he was on the job, he made a quiet but notable contribution to both Eveready press and local Communist groups. He continued to absorb all the information he could find about his trade and showed considerable initiative in taking on new challenges. For example, Ibing noticed a large, old machine sitting idle at the back of the shop. It was a rotogravure machine, which Ibing sometimes described as having a cylinder like "a big rolling pin" for printing large runs of material. The machine had not been used for a long time and no one seemed to know what was wrong with it, but after much exploration of its inner workings, consulting with trades material he received in the mail and making a few improvised repairs, Ibing got it running. And thanks to the additional machine, Eveready press was able to reduce its production costs and expand its output.[71]

Business was thriving for the press at this time. Although the authorities stubbornly refused to lift the ban on Communist organizations and kept some leaders interned for many months, the restrictions on Communist activity – and the Communist press – were eased. Through the war years, Eveready printed leaflets, brochures, manifestos, and journals for a host of left-wing organizations. Ibing remembered producing literature for Communist-affiliated organizations in languages such as Ukrainian, Finnish, Yiddish, and Hungarian. Even as he approached a hundred years old, he could readily recall titles of journals Eveready produced, such as the *Vochenblatt* (*Canadian Jewish Weekly*, published in Yiddish) and the *Kanadai Magyar Munkás* (*Canadian Hungarian Worker*). Eveready also produced a large amount of pulp fiction for members of the armed forces – mostly westerns and crime novels. Ibing often enjoyed the irony that even while the Communist party remained outlawed officially, perhaps the largest source of revenue for this Communist press was Canadian government contracts.[72]

Ibing had stayed in touch with Sarah Kasow since he had left for Ontario, and in 1941 she joined him in Toronto. They got married the following year, with Salem Bland, a United Church minister, presiding. Bland did not share the religion of either Ibing, who was Lutheran, or Kasow, who was Jewish. But neither of the newlyweds were much concerned about that; what mattered more was that Bland was a committed leftist, though mostly on the social democratic side, and a staunch supporter of the Republic in the Spanish Civil War. Bland had been one of the official Chairs of the Committee to Aid Spanish Democracy, and received major accolades after the civil war from the Friends of the Mackenzie-Papineau Battalion for his work in support of the International Brigades.[73]

In December 1943, Hans and Sarah's daughter, Irma, was born. Meanwhile, Sarah's mother and her sister, Bessie, sold their restaurant in Winnipeg and moved to Toronto. They used the proceeds of the sale and a bit of Ibing's savings to make a down payment on a house for the five of them on Glen Morris Street, on the edge of the University of Toronto campus. Although the population on the campus itself was mostly white and British, the areas to the west and south were extremely diverse, full of immigrants to Canada like the Ibings and Kasows. The location was good fit for his wife and in-laws, as Toronto's Jewish community was just to the south, along College Street and down Spadina Avenue.

The German-Canadian Federation

While Ibing was putting down roots in Toronto, he slowly became re-engaged in political activity. The German-Canadian League had remained dormant though most of 1941, but in 1942 a new Communist-allied organization was launched, the German-Canadian Federation. The appeal of the organization to Ibing was evident from the outset, as the ambiguities that marked the final months of the league were gone; the new federation affirmed that anti-fascism was its core principle, and that meant supporting the war against Hitler and fighting against Nazi sympathizers in Canada.[74]

Ibing was involved in the Toronto unit from the beginning and was part of a group of activists who usually made up the executive, often serving as secretary. In 1943, they started a journal entitled the *Volksstimme* (*People's Voice* – also printed by Eveready). Ibing claimed that only a few members of the group had enough education and practice writing in German to contribute to the journal, so it fell to about ten of them to produce an edition each month.[75] True to its mandate, the journal was full of warnings about the fascist threat and exhortations of German Canadians to mobilize against it. It also reported on the progress of the war, focusing especially on the Soviets' efforts on the Eastern Front.[76] But articles in the *Volksstimme* could also venture into domestic politics and world affairs beyond the main theatres of the war; Ibing had an article in one issue on the fortunes of the Communists in China. The federation's continuing connections to the Jewish community were evident in articles denouncing anti-Semitism, announcements about Jewish cultural events in the area, and advertisements for the *Vochenblatt*. One of the journal's regular contributors, Bernd Weinberg, was himself Jewish.[77]

The federation published a number of pamphlets and small books, most of them reproductions of works by Communist-affiliated anti-fascist groups in other countries. Ibing clearly played a large role in producing this literature; he wrote the foreword to one of the larger ones, entitled *The Nazi Scourge*. The foreword – and the book itself – attacked the notion that the Nazis were legitimate representatives of German culture or the German people's interests, and exhorted people of German extraction everywhere to join the anti-fascist struggle. This was a frequent argument of the Free Germany Movement, the anti-fascist group with which the federation had the strongest ties. The movement was led primarily by German refugees, most of them Communists, who had fled the Nazis and continued the struggle to free their homeland from Hitler's grip. Horst Döhler, the main figure in the German-Canadian Federation and editor of the *Volksstimme*, relied on guidance from the Free Germany Movement's unit in Mexico (which took in leftist refugees from Germany and many other countries, including Spain after the Republic fell). The federation also collected publications from chapters of the Free Germany Movement in Britain, the United States, Mexico, and the Soviet Union. It reprinted much of this material, either in its pamphlets or as articles on overseas anti-fascist activity in the *Volksstimme*.[78]

The German-Canadian Federation's loyalty to Communism was evident in all of its work. Döhler was an extremely committed Communist and usually a faithful adherent to directives handed down from Moscow or the Canadian politburo.[79] For Ibing, this internal discipline remained a source of frustration. When discussing his activity in the federation in interviews, he recounted that his independent nature continued to make him uneasy with the culture of Communist organizations. Like other Communist activists at the time, he found the grip of the central command especially tight in Toronto, where the party national headquarters was located and where the leaders took direction straight from the Soviet Union. "I didn't agree with the policy that everything was run from Moscow," he said. "Whatever was announced by Moscow was adopted here. Whatever came out of Stalin's mouth was the gospel."[80]

A still greater disappointment was the federation's inability to gain much traction in the German-Canadian community. In Ibing's opinion the main problem was that as long as Canada was at war with the Nazis, German Canadians did not want attention drawn to them as a distinct community.[81] After the Fifth Column hysteria of 1940, there was also fear that any kind of mobilizing as a community might arouse public suspicions or attract the RCMP's attention. As Ibing put it in one interview, "Germans didn't come to us because they wanted to remain mostly anonymous. They didn't want to be known to the authorities during the war. . . . They always used the excuse that it wasn't a nice thing to do, it would be misunderstood or something like that."[82] They were particularly uncomfortable with the federation's claims that there were Nazi sympathizers in the German-Canadian community, and that at least some members of the community might be drawn in by Nazi propaganda. This nervousness reinforced Ibing's sense that there were at least a few German Canadians who did quietly support Hitler.[83]

The struggles of the federation became more apparent as the war went on. The circulation of the *Volksstimme* remained small and it continued to rely on the same core of contributors to keep it going through the war years. Ibing recalled that publishing the journal and other pamphlets "became a great sacrifice to us, financially. . . . You couldn't go anywhere to raise money for a [German journal or pamphlet], except to other Germans. And the Germans, they were not very much in favour of it anyway."[84]

While Ibing tended to emphasize the problems he encountered in Communist organizations during the latter parts of the war, there were undeniably positive aspects to his participation. While the Communists' disciplinarian culture grated on him, he never recalled facing a great deal of pressure to toe the official Communist line. The fealty of Döhler and others in the federation to the party was evident to him, yet he did not feel the watchful eyes of the Communist hierarchy on his activity. He recalled that his group would have its discussions about policy and organizing priorities; in the end, he "didn't always feel like supporting causes [he] didn't believe in" and on such occasions, he would simply put his energies elsewhere.[85]

Although the federation's impact was limited, Ibing felt assured that it was a worthy cause. He felt it was important that there be a voice within the German community speaking out loudly against fascism and in support of the war. And even if the reception was lukewarm, the federation did get the message out, through the *Volksstimme*, the steady production of pamphlets, as well as a number of speakers' events and film nights.[86]

Policy disagreements did not keep members from forming a strong social circle. Ibing recalled that all of the main activists in the federation – and their families – spent much time together during the war. Although his commitments to work, family, and activism left him little spare time, he regularly attended socials and community events organized by other Communist ethnic clubs in Toronto. His wife, Sarah, also became immersed in Toronto's Jewish Communist circles, and would be a member of the United Jewish People's Order from its foundation in 1945. Both of them came to know a number of prominent Communists in Toronto, particularly Joe Salsberg, who was a ubiquitous presence in their neighbourhood. Although Ibing never discussed Salsberg's politics in detail, he must have been drawn to Salsberg's propensity to frame issues in terms of basic social justice, to approach policy matters "from a human point of view."[87]

It also helped Ibing feel at ease in Communist circles that he agreed with the party's main agenda in these years. While he was frustrated with the party's insistence that the Soviet Union's interests always came first, after June 1941 all of the Communists' energies were devoted to defeating Hitler. And in Europe it was the Red Army that played the leading role in achieving this goal. The importance of the Soviet Union as an ally in the war became widely noticed in Canada, particularly after its victory in the Battle of Stalingrad in early 1943. Pro-Soviet sentiment grew among the public and the media through 1943 and early 1944 when the majority of the fighting was on the Eastern Front; and as Communists never tired of highlighting, even when the other Allies finally created a Western Front in June 1944, it remained smaller than the eastern one.[88] The Canadian government organized pro-Soviet rallies; Prime Minister King attended the largest one in September 1943, which filled Toronto's Maple Leaf Gardens and featured delegates from Moscow's Jewish Anti-fascist Committee.[89]

Thanks to these favourable conditions, Canadian Communists enjoyed an upturn in fortunes in the latter years of the war. To be sure there was no letting up of the Canadian security apparatus's determination to keep them in check. The party remained officially banned throughout the war, Communists who had been interned would not be freed until mid-1942, and the authorities pursued a nasty campaign against the largest Communist-allied ethnic organization, the Ukrainian Labour-Farmer Temple Association.[90] Yet Communist activists took leadership roles in the rapidly expanding industrial unions, and the party reformed itself under a different name, the Labour Progressive Party (LPP), in 1943. After launching a policy of encouraging members to form clubs under the umbrella of the larger party, the LPP soon counted scores of new allied organizations. Once again the ethnic organizations led the way in mobilizing and in turn driving a surge in the new party's membership roles.[91] In this regard the German-Canadian Federation, although it had limited success in gathering members, was a precursor of the wave of organizations that followed.

These clubs proved instrumental in supporting the 1943 provincial election campaigns of LPP candidates, such as those of A.A. MacLeod (whom the party had sent to Spain to help returning veterans in late 1938) in the highly diverse Toronto riding of Bellwoods, and of Salsberg in the neighbouring (and even more diverse) riding of St. Andrew. As Ibing would have wanted, anti-fascism was the primary theme of the Communist-allied organizations' campaigns. This was an effective approach in St. Andrew, which had a large Jewish population. Both LPP candidates prevailed in 1943, thus becoming the first Communists to sit in the Ontario legislature. When Salsberg's victory was announced, a spontaneous parade broke out a few hundred metres from Ibing's home, heading from the corner of College Street and Brunswick Avenue to Spadina Avenue, and then south toward Dundas Street.[92] By the end of the war, LPP politicians held four seats on Toronto's city council and another on its board of control, while MacLeod and Salsberg were on the verge of being resoundingly re-elected to the Ontario legislature.

Indeed, Ibing had much to be pleased about in his personal and family life, as well as in his work, in local politics, and of course in the defeat of fascism. Yet by mid-1945 there was also widespread doubt that wartime unity and sympathy toward Communism could last. New tensions were emerging that would test Ibing's political allegiances.

Gradual Disillusionment

The Cold War came to Canada as quickly as it did anywhere. In September 1945, a cipher clerk working in the Soviet embassy in Ottawa named Igor Gouzenko defected; to strengthen his request for asylum, he brought with him documents showing that there was a large spy ring operating in Canada. An investigation revealed there was indeed extensive Soviet espionage in Canada, and when the Gouzenko affair became public in February 1946 it caused an immediate revival in anti-Communist sentiment.[93] In the post–World War II Red Scare, and amid the broader geopolitical conflict between the Soviet Union and Western powers, being Communist once again meant being associated with Canada's enemies. There would be additional problems in many of the Communist-allied ethnic organizations. Stalin's brutal treatment of the Ukraine would erode the large base of support for Communism in the Ukrainian community. Similarly, growing evidence of anti-Semitism in the Soviet Union alienated Jewish Communists; Sarah Ibing's UJPO eventually broke its association with Communism in 1956, after a series of fractious debates over the treatment of Jews in the Soviet Union and Eastern Europe.[94]

Problems for the German-Canadian Federation started early – as soon as the war ended. The federation took up one of the major (if often forgotten) causes of the postwar period: stamping out lingering sympathies to the Nazis not only in Germany but in German populations everywhere. The federation continued to produce anti-Nazi literature and hold educational events through the late 1940s. However, it turned most of its attention toward diplomatic affairs in Europe, as the structure of postwar Germany was one of the most pressing issues to be settled between the Soviet Union and the Western Allies. The federation faithfully followed Moscow's lead on every aspect of this complex issue: it blamed the West for the division of Germany into separate parts, claimed that the Soviets were trying to keep Germany together, and attacked the Marshall Plan as an attempt to reduce Germany to a permanently dependent client state of the United States.[95]

Ibing was deeply depressed by this new turn in Communist policy. He opposed "the splitting up of a country" and the eventual creation of East Germany. As he stressed in interviews, he was no "German patriot" – but he did want to see a Germany that was united, free, and socialist, not one carved into two separate states. He saw such separation as having "the seed of trouble in it," the seed of long-running antagonism and possibly war.[96] He bitterly dismissed the Communist propaganda blaming the U.S. and its allies for the break-up of Germany. He increasingly saw the split as a product of "Communist influence," imposed through "Soviet force."[97] He also had growing doubts that the Soviets had a legitimate mandate for the rule they exercised in their occupied zone, and it seemed in general they were acting as imperialists in asserting control throughout Eastern Europe. For Ibing, this was not only a national and ideological question but also a personal one: his family was in the Soviet-controlled part of Germany. He'd had only irregular contact with them since the Nazis had taken power in 1933, and he did not want to see them stuck in a separate and closed country after the war ended.[98]

Ibing gradually stopped participating in the German-Canadian Federation, although he did remain a member of the Communist party. He was hardly alone in the German-Canadian community in rejecting the pro-

Soviet rhetoric of the federation in the late 1940s. What little support the federation had during the war rapidly eroded – yet it stuck doggedly to its defence of Moscow's policies. Döhler himself admitted that the federation's unfailing loyalty to Moscow led to its sinking fortunes and eventual demise in 1949.[99]

As Ibing disengaged from Communist organizations in the late 1940s, he also sought to get out of his job at Eveready press. He wanted to stop printing the material of organizations from which he felt increasingly estranged, but his greatest motivation was simpler: he wanted a better job at a larger shop and a chance to further enhance his skills. Having tenure in the pressmen's union, Ibing was in a good position to take advantage when the postwar economy started to gather steam and positions became available. He recalled that it was "through the union" that he got a position at the *Globe and Mail* in 1946. It was the kind of job at a major press that he wanted, but his work was mostly on the night shift, which left him little time or energy for his family. In 1948, he found a new position as a pressman on a rotogravure machine (his speciality) at the *Toronto Star*, where he settled in quickly.[100]

Meanwhile Ibing's disenchantment with Communism continued to grow. In 1949, the East German state (formally the German Democratic Republic, or DDR) was formed, and Ibing's former comrades in the federation promptly launched a new organization, the Friends of the DDR. This group made its allegiances clear from the outset, and Döhler was once again the central figure.[101] Not surprisingly, Ibing wanted nothing to do with the new organization or with its continued support for Moscow as it took an iron grip on all of Eastern Europe. The outbreak of the Korean War the following year deepened his conviction that splitting countries would only lead to "trouble." Again, he was scornful of the Communist propaganda that tried to blame the war on U.S. aggression: "I knew that it wasn't entirely a thing that was done by South Korea and by American Imperialists."[102] Before long, Ibing would have a chance to visit East Germany and experience for himself a Soviet-controlled society.

Behind the Iron Curtain

By the early 1950s, Ibing was able to maintain regular contact with his family in East Germany. All of the members of the immediate family had survived the 1930s and the 1940s, and his parents were now in Rudolstadt, about a hundred kilometres south of Bad Frankenhausen and less than fifty kilometres from the border with West Germany. Not surprisingly, Ibing knew little about how they survived and how they were faring: when writing letters from authoritarian states like Nazi Germany or the German Democratic Republic to other countries, one had to exercise the utmost caution, especially about political matters. Ibing became increasingly intent on visiting them after a twenty-year separation, and he finally got a chance in 1952.[103]

Ibing arrived first in West Germany and was heartened to see that it was being "put back in order": buildings and infrastructure destroyed in the war had been rebuilt, and there seemed to be optimism about the economy. He found members of his extended family who had stayed in this area doing well. He visited an uncle who was prospering as a machinist, and another, named August Ibing, who had become a painter of some note and taught art at the prestigious Düsseldorf State Academy of Art.[104]

But Ibing recalled that when he entered East Germany, "it was like day and night." He saw rubble left by the war "all over the place" – cars could barely negotiate the wreckage that remained strewn over the streets. East German soldiers "were still strutting around in the Nazi black uniforms" because the new regime had not given them new ones.[105] And the soldiers were everywhere: what bothered Ibing most was the extent to which the society was militarized, and everyone lived under the thumb of the Ministry of State Security, or Stasi. Indeed, perhaps no society in history was as comprehensively controlled by its security apparatus as East Germany under the Stasi. Although the Stasi spilled less blood than other Soviet-controlled security systems, East Germans could never escape the reach of its massive system of officers, informants, and functionaries. Hobsbawm (who personally knew many East German Communists) writes that it was "a monstrous all-embracing bureaucracy which did not terrorize but rather constantly chivvied, rewarded and punished its citizens."[106] As a visitor from a Western capitalist state, Ibing had no doubt that he was being watched constantly, and his movements were severely restricted. He could not travel further than twenty-five kilometres from Rudolstadt, and he had to report to the local police every other day.[107]

Signs of the Soviet Union's grip on East Germany were everywhere. Once they had some privacy, everyone Ibing spoke to was eager to share stories of how much Soviets had pillaged the economy, seizing vast chunks of the agricultural produce (much of Germany's most fertile land is in the east) and controlling the factories. People in town complained about how the Soviets controlled and benefited from all of the production at the local mines. Ibing did not necessarily believe everything he heard, but he was deeply affected by the overwhelming evidence that East Germany was a "so-called Russian colony" where the material conditions – indeed the spiritual conditions – were unrelentingly miserable.[108]

The family was much less forthcoming about their experiences since he had left Germany in 1930. This was in part because more than two tumultuous decades had passed; Ibing had left when he was twenty-one and he was now forty-three. Moreover, what happened while the Nazis were in power was a taboo subject for the family at this time, as it would largely remain for them and most Germans – East or West – for many decades. Ibing was told little more than that when the Nazis consolidated their hold on power in early 1933, they fired Gustav Ibing and evicted the family from the mayor's house. Fifty-five years old, unemployed, and desperate to feed his family, Gustav decided he had to join the Nazi party in order to get work; he held "a minor office job" in the civil service through the 1930s and the war years.[109]

This account was consistent with what was known to occur around Germany: after the Nazis formed the government, social democratic offices were ransacked by the SA, while many SPD politicians were purged from political positions. Thousands were detained and tortured in concentration camps. But as the Nazis made Germany a one-party state, they also knew they needed people to keep the government and public services running. They offered politicians from other parties with requisite skills and experience a stark choice: sign up with the Nazi party and stay employed, or become pariahs and look for work at a time when unemployment was about 35 per cent.[110]

Ibing (third from left) visiting his relatives in what was then East Germany, 1953. His father is seated at the centre.

Ibing was given a few more details about the postwar period. He was told that the family held out hope that the new regime would at least be less authoritarian and brutal than the Nazis had been, and might offer positions to officials of leftist parties from the Weimar era. Historians have noted that the Communists initially made encouraging moves in this direction. Starting in 1945, the Soviets removed top-level Nazi officials in East Germany (over a half million were fired by April 1948). Since the Soviets were aware they did not have popular support to govern their occupied territories in Eastern Europe, they also employed a version of their old Popular Front tactic and formed new coalitions with other "anti-fascist" parties. The first in Eastern

Europe was the Socialist Unity Party in East Germany, which was keen to draw in members of the old SPD. But the "coalition" proved to be a means by which Communists forcibly consumed the much more popular SPD. All of the powerful government positions went to German Communist officials who arrived from Moscow "in the baggage train of the Red Army," as Judt puts it.[111] The Soviets also found, much like the Nazis had in 1933, that they needed people with experience to keep the public administration running. Around East Germany they retained millions of officials from the former regime, as long as their reputations were not too tainted by association with the Nazis.[112] Ibing was told that the Soviets "trusted only those who were part of an autocratic regime." Gustav Ibing was given no role in the new government, and ended up working as a night watchman immediately after the war.[113]

This was the version of his father's life that Hans Ibing knew when he returned to Canada. And to the end of his life, he spoke in admiring terms about his father's skills and his principles.[114] But as did many Germans after the war, Gustav Ibing seems to have sanitized the story of his experiences during the Nazi regime. According to a master's thesis about a prominent academic in this part of Germany by archivist Ulrich Hahnemann, Gustav Ibing lost his role of Bürgermeister of Bad Frankenhausen in 1931, when a budget crisis forced the city council to eliminate the position.[115] He also appears to have overstated the extent of his suffering at the hands of the Nazis after they took power, and his resistance to joining the party in 1933. His Nazi membership card at the Bundesarchiv in Berlin shows that he joined the party on February 2, 1933, only a few days after Hitler was appointed chancellor on January 30.[116] The exact position he took in the party or in the government in 1933, let alone his reasons for joining, remain unclear. Through the early 1930s, large numbers of people across Germany were joining the Nazi party. The defections accelerated still more after the Nazis took power; Nazi party membership grew by about 1.6 million from February to the end of April 1933 alone.[117]

According to Hahnemann, after 1935 Gustav Ibing held the position of "welfare administrator," which meant there was a grain of truth in his claim that he had a minor office job for the Nazis. He was also a member of the SA, as was common for civil servants in the early years the Nazi regime.[118] It is unclear when he first joined the SA, and in terms of his involvement with the Nazis, the timing matters. By 1935 the SA had been stripped of its paramilitary role and hollowed out as an organization, after its leaders were purged in the Night of the Long Knives in 1934. More than a million members left the SA in the following months, and in a 1935 restructuring, the remaining young members were reassigned to the regular army and those under forty-five to the reserves.[119] Thereafter the SA was essentially a repository for aging figures in the party. The International Military Tribunal at Nuremberg ruled that although it regularly produced anti-Semitic material and certain detachments participated in Nazi atrocities, notably the 1938 *Kristallnacht* pogrom, on the whole the SA was too marginal within the Nazi structure for its members to be subject to prosecution for war crimes. The tribunal noted that "after the purge the SA was reduced to the status of unimportant Nazi hangers-on."[120]

By 1941 Gustav Ibing had moved to the larger town of Rudolstadt, still working in welfare administration in the Nazis' regional office. In the SA's hierarchy, which was based on a military model even for administrators, his position gave him the rank of Oberscharführer, or senior squad leader. This was roughly the equivalent of a field sergeant, a position that was prominent enough for him to be among those purged by the Soviets and "retired" from politics in East Germany in 1946.[121]

There is some uncertainty about whether – or for how long – Gustav Ibing remained marginalized in East Germany.[122] Hans (and some of his family) suggested that his father eventually did take a better position in the regime. By the early 1950s, he seems to have had enough influence – official or unofficial – to help his son visit East Germany. This was a rare privilege at the time, especially for a family visit, and Hans was sure it was only possible because his father "had some pull" within the Communist government. Even if he had regained some stature, Gustav seemed a bitter and broken man when Hans visited. He died suddenly of a heart attack in 1953, just a few months later.[123]

Ibing's trip to Germany had a major impact on him. Although his attachment to Communism had been weakening since the announcement of the Nazi-Soviet pact of 1939, he stressed in interviews the importance of "seeing with [his] own eyes" what life was like under a Communist regime.[124]

If Soviet claims to be leading a workers' revolutionary government in East Germany had an ounce of credibility left, it dissolved in the Berlin Uprising of 1953. In mid-June about 400,000 workers went on strike in the capital and across East Germany in response to deteriorating conditions at their jobs. With the help of the Red Army, German authorities suppressed the strike in brutal fashion, killing almost 300 in street fighting, handing long prison sentences to 1,400, and executing 200 alleged protest leaders. The uprising and the government response gave the whole of the Eastern Bloc an international black eye. Even the playwright Bertolt Brecht, usually a committed supporter of the Communist regime, was moved to ask in a poem whether it would be "simpler under these circumstances for the government to dissolve the people and elect another one."[125]

Ibing did return to Communist party meetings in Canada, as he still had friends in the movement and he wanted to tell them about what he saw in East Germany. He tried to argue that Communists in the West should speak out, in the name of workers' rights, about the dismal conditions behind the Iron Curtain. But he was hardly surprised when these last pleas went unheeded, and not long after the Berlin Uprising he dropped out of the Communist party entirely. Sarah remained in the UJPO, and through her Hans followed developments in socialist circles in Toronto. But while he continued to identify as a socialist, he would remain inactive politically after leaving the party.[126]

When looking back on his decision to leave, Ibing focused on his many "disagreements" over policy, but he often returned to a broader issue, one that was crucial in his decision to join the Communists in the first place: humanitarianism. "I can only support something that has . . . some kind of human aspect to it," he explained in one interview, and by the early 1950s he understood this was something "the Communist parties haven't got."[127] In other words, he understood that his faith in the Soviet system in the 1930s as the new hope for humanity had been misplaced. Visiting East Germany brought home to him just how dehumanizing the Communist regime was, how much the system left its people wrecked and defeated. To consume media reports about the plight of people under Communist rule was one thing (and such reports were always dismissed by Canadian Communists as Western propaganda), but it was quite another to talk with his own family and with people from his hometown, to sense the despair and frustration in their voices and their body language.

As difficult as it was to leave the party after almost twenty years, and to lose many friends in the process, Ibing did not fall into a bitter sense of defeat, as his father had. Indeed, outside of politics, Ibing was quite content with his lot in life. He was living in prosperous times in Canada, and for once the labouring classes – particularly white working men – were reaping the benefits. He continued to enjoy a stable, secure job, doing work that he found rewarding for pay that, thanks to his union, rose with every collective agreement. Hans, Sarah, and Irma moved into their own home in Don Mills, Canada's first planned community on the edge of Toronto, in 1954. It was a brand-new home in a fledgling suburban neighbourhood – indeed, when Ibing bought it, there was nothing more than a design on paper and a few stakes in the ground. In moving there, the family felt a bit like pioneers who were breaking the land in a new way. Don Mills was on the fringes of the city at this time, and Ibing often joked that the experience was "a bit rustic." Travelling to work at the *Star*'s presses downtown involved taking a gravel road (Eglinton Avenue) or a path along the Don River that would later be expanded into the Don Valley Parkway. Irma sometimes rode to and from school on the back of a local farmer's trailer. The family were also pioneers in another sense, as they were part of the early waves of working-class people moving into middle-class suburban developments that depended on having at least one car per family.[128]

In the decade after the war, Ibing grew profoundly attached to Canada; he became a citizen in 1954 and would remain a fervent patriot for the rest of his life. He was no jingoistic flag-waver, and he generally laughed off conservative nationalist clowns he saw in the media. He remained critical of the inequities that he still saw in Canadian society, and he certainly never pretended that his start in Canada had been easy. He also tended to giggle at Canadians' tendency to be self-conscious and sensitive to any perceived slight. But Ibing knew that as terrible as its economy had been and as mean as its social programs were in the 1930s, as inhospitable as it was toward a German Communist in the early 1940s, it was Canada that gave him his chance to build the prosperous life he had always wanted. He also knew – he had seen and heard for himself – that the hard years of the 1930s and 1940s had been even harder in many other places in the world, such as in Spain or Germany. Indeed, he understood how much postwar Canada offered working people like him, and he developed a deep sense of gratitude to his country.

6 Rarely Looking Back

ONE EVENING IN THE EARLY 1970S, a local television news show in Toronto reported on an event for Canadian veterans of the International Brigades in the Spanish Civil War. Ibing was in attendance and he was mentioned briefly in the story. When Ibing came to work the next morning at the *Toronto Star* press, one of his colleagues told him that he had listened to the broadcast and wanted to ask Ibing about his experience in the war. But above all, his colleague wanted to express his astonishment: he had worked with Ibing almost every day for years and had no idea he had played a role in the war in Spain. In all those hours working side by side, Ibing had never said a word about it.[1]

Indeed, Ibing had moved on from the war and his time as a Communist. He always said that his approach to life was to look forward, not back. Nostalgia was utterly foreign to him. However, he did not break all his connections to his history in Spain. He became friends with his old comrade Jules Paivio, who lived not far from him in suburban Toronto; the two met a few times a year until they were well into their nineties. Ibing also joined the Veterans of the Mackenzie-Papineau Battalion (VMPB) and participated in some of their meetings and social events. These gatherings gave him the chance to spend time with people who had experienced the same journey as he had, but he was not a deeply committed member of the organization and he was weary of the political agenda of some of its members. As during the war itself, most were not ardent Communists, but some were. For instance, William Beeching, a long-time leader of the Communist party in Saskatchewan, would write the official history of the Canadian volunteers for the VMPB.

Ibing gave only tepid support to the group's campaigns to get recognition from the Canadian government for their service in Spain. While he believed that the veterans deserved acknowledgement from a government that had been hostile to them for many years, in general he would have preferred the veterans to stop engaging in political struggles over the past. He sometimes urged the VMPB to mount its own major event to celebrate the efforts of the veterans – and then disband the organization and move on. He was also left cold by the nostalgic tone of many of the organization's events; he was bewildered when the veterans organized a trip in 1979 to Spain to revisit wartime battlegrounds.[2] He once joked that reliving the terror and misery of the war was the worst vacation plan he could possibly imagine.

Ibing was also uneasy with the triumphalist tone some members of the group could strike when discussing Spain in meetings and newsletters.[3] He never forgot that it was an ugly war that Franco and his fascist allies won. He also remembered that while most internationals volunteered for admirable reasons and fought for the right side, many Communist officials in Spain behaved less commendably. Even though Ibing was not exposed to the worst Communists abuses, he would have had reservations when he heard speakers such as Beeching declare at one meeting, "We knew we represented the truth of history. We stood for what's right, decent and honest in life; and didn't worry about being popular. . . . We were partisans of a noble cause, the success of which meant the victory of the people, the victory of truth, justice, peace and social progress."[4]

It was probably as a corrective to such sentiments that Ibing expressed his most serious reservations about serving in the International Brigades in his reminiscences for the official history of the Mackenzie-Papineau Battalion. It was well known that Beeching was writing the history, and there could be little doubt that its tone would be exultant. Near the conclusion of his reminiscences, Ibing wrote:

> In retrospect I do wonder, if the Spanish Republic would have been victorious over Franco, whether the civil war would have ended there, or whether the Communist Party would have fought on to its political victory over all the other elements in the Spanish spectrum. That feeling first occurred to me when we went to Barcelona in the Spring of

1937 and I suppose at that time I would have gone along with that, blindly perhaps, because in those days Stalin was still a saint and not a word about his and [the head of his secret police] Berias' doings had come out of the Soviet Union until Khrushchev's revelations much later. However, I believe that at the time in 1937, I did the right thing, and I have never regretted it.[5]

In other discussions about the war, Ibing was not nearly as uncertain as this about the Republicans' cause, or the role he would have played if they had won. When recounting his motivations for volunteering, what was most important was fighting fascism, defending the Republic, and generally sticking up for the underdog. He was not driven by a desire to advance Moscow's agenda. "We didn't really fight for Communist policy," he declared in one interview. "We fought in defense of the democracy."[6]

Despite having been caught in the middle of the fighting for so long, Ibing consistently offered a clear-eyed analysis of the forces shaping the outcome of the war. In particular, he recognized that Franco could never have been defeated without major assistance from Britain, France, or other Western democracies. In other words, what Ibing wanted above all was for the Soviets *not* to be the only major foreign power aiding the Republican side (and thus in a position to supress rival interests in Spain), but for Britain and France to take up the fight against fascism. He wanted the Popular Front strategy that was fundamental in drawing him to Communism to succeed, with different nations and interests within Spain uniting to defeat fascism.

Serving in the Regiment de Tren deepened Ibing's appreciation of the extent to which the Republic was abandoned and left at a material disadvantage. Every day in Spain he had to grapple with the shortcomings of the supplies and equipment – the unsuitable trucks, the huge and ungainly cannon – that the Republic did receive. It is telling that upon leaving Spain, the Regiment de Tren published a parting statement that included a pointed comment that it "felt the shame of the infamous embargo."[7] If Ibing had one continual source of regret, it was how little chance the Republicans ultimately had during the war, due to decisions that were mostly out of their control. As he noted in one interview: "It's not the fighting spirit that was lacking, but it was the equipment . . . [we had] nothing to match what the other side had." He added bitterly that if the Republic had received better equipment and support from Western democracies, "it would have been even-Steven [and] we would have defeated them . . . even with the German and Italian help" that Franco received.[8] His strong feelings were also not surprising in another sense: he was always most incensed by instances when an underdog was denied a chance to defend itself.

Ibing's basic sense of justice and his concern for the oppressed are the greatest reasons why he need not have wondered too much about whether he would have "gone along" with Communist aggression against others if the Republicans had won the war. Throughout his life, Ibing's decisions came down to a question of what he thought was right – even if doing the right thing brought terrible risks. As he also noted in his reminiscences, he was always confident that he was right to join the International Brigades. And at other points in his life, such as the day he walked into the German embassy in Paris, he would not bow to authority and salute a cause he knew was wrong even if his survival was in doubt. Of course, he was neither perfect nor omniscient in making his decisions: he understood that he was grappling with extraordinary conditions in the years of constant crisis in the 1930s and 1940s. His comments at the end of his reminiscences about what might have happened in Spain reflect his regret that he did not see the truth about the Soviet Union under Stalin earlier.[9] Moscow's foreign policy decisions, in 1939 and after World War II, caused him to struggle seriously with his conscience. But when confronted with clear evidence of an unjust, failed system that oppressed its people, as he was in East Germany in 1952, he saw reality and left the movement he had been part of for almost twenty years. As he put it in his reminiscences, "I thought it was much more important to be an honest anti-fascist than to be a Charlie McCarthy to any political party, right or left or center. I am still a socialist."[10]

Indeed, Ibing maintained his leftist convictions for the rest of his life. He usually supported the New Democratic Party (NDP), although he frequently wished that it would act more unambiguously as a workers' party than it did. He remained uninterested in returning to political activism. Hence, he was a little uneasy when, in the early 1960s, his daughter started dating a Trotskyist radical named Clifford Orchard. But he quickly came to accept him and was happy when Irma and Clifford married in 1963.

In general, Ibing focused on continuing to reap the fruits of what historians call the Golden Age of capitalism for workers, from the postwar years to the mid-1970s, when prosperity and a growing welfare state allowed millions of working families to enjoy steady increases in their standard of living. He often spoke about how lucky he was to hold a secure job for almost twenty-five years doing work he enjoyed, for an employer he could respect. In publishing the *Toronto Star* every day, he still felt connected in his own way to current events; he not only printed the news but also followed it carefully. When he retired in 1974, there was a large party for him at the *Star*'s presses that showed how much his colleagues respected and valued his work; he kept a photo from the party at his desk for the rest of his life. In retirement, he devoted much of his time to long walks at nearby Edwards Gardens, tending his own gardens at home, and hobbies such as painting. Though it was too late for him to become a serious artist like his uncle August, he showed similar talent. For years, a number of his favourite paintings hung around his house. Hans and Sarah also enjoyed having their family nearby.[11]

Following Sarah's death in 1988 (after forty-six years of marriage), Ibing sold the house to Irma and Clifford Orchard, but he did not go far, moving to an apartment around the corner. In 1997, he moved back into the house after they converted their basement into a flat for him. By then, their daughter, Lisa, had fallen for yet another leftist, an academic interested in labour history. In the years that I knew Ibing, he was a contented man who was always keeping himself busy and could be relied upon to bring his sense of humour and sharp wit into any conversation. He was pleased that both his grandchildren, Lisa and Mark, stayed in Toronto so that he could visit with them regularly and hear how they were doing. During family visits, one of his first questions was always, "What's happening in the big city?"

Last day at work: Ibing (centre) with his coworkers at the *Toronto Star*'s rotogravure press at his retirement, 1974.

Indeed, Ibing especially liked to talk about how his adopted hometown had grown into a real urban centre. He loved to poke fun at the dour, "puritanical" character of Toronto when he first arrived in the 1940s. "The only thing that was open on the weekend was the Church," he once recalled. "You couldn't go anywhere except the park. You couldn't have a bottle of beer in the open; women weren't allowed in the beer parlors. . . . Everything was closed tight so that nobody sinned on the weekends." He credited the waves of immigration from Europe after World War II for bringing a "new fresh breath of air" to the city, giving it life it badly needed. In general, he felt that immigration helped create not just a better Toronto but also "a different Canada," a better Canada that was more open and vibrant.[12]

Ibing settled comfortably into the feeling he adopted in the early 1950s that for all its faults, Canada and Western democracies offered a much better life for their people than a Communist system could. He remained a socialist, and maintained his belief that the masses only got a share in the wealth that capitalism created because of movements that organized workers and engaged them politically. He always insisted that mainstream politicians and big business would keep the profits in the hands of the elites unless they felt pressure from the public – and especially from organized labour. But radical transformation of society no longer enticed him as it did in the 1930s, when the economy had broken down. He felt there was no escaping the truth that "Canada has achieved more in the form of industrialization without dehumanizing people than the Soviet Union has."[13]

Eventually, Canada did give Ibing and other Canadian veterans of the Spanish Civil War some – but only some – recognition. When Bob Rae's Ontario NDP government created a plaque for the veterans in 1995, Ibing went to Queen's Park for the unveiling.[14] In the fall of 2001, a long campaign by the Mackenzie-Papineau veterans' association was rewarded when a national monument to the Canadian volunteers was unveiled in Ottawa.[15] The monument was funded entirely by private contributions, as the federal government continued its long-standing tradition of giving nothing to the veterans. Still, the National Capital Commission and Governor General Adrienne Clarkson endorsed the creation of the monument, and Clarkson and her husband, John Ralston Saul, were enthusiastic participants at its unveiling.[16] Only about a dozen veterans were still alive at the time, and only three attended the ceremony, including Jules Paivio, who was president of the veterans' association.[17] Ibing contributed to the campaign to build the monument, but at ninety-two, he did not feel up to the trip to Ottawa for the event.

In general, Ibing stayed close to home and kept to his routine, which allowed him to stay in remarkably good health in his later years. He remained strong enough to enjoy family outings for dinner on special occasions, including a joyous feast at a downtown restaurant to mark his hundredth birthday. Only in his last couple of years did he suffer serious health problems; as he approached his 101st birthday, he was still able to do yardwork around his house. He died in late 2009.[18]

To the end of his life, Ibing was a kind-hearted source of optimism. If he had one abiding sense about his own life, it was that he had seen things get

No slowing down: Ibing shovelling snow at his home in Don Mills in 2008 – at age 99.

better. He never forgot the "depression times" of the 1930s or driving around Spain in constant danger, but for him those grim years served as a touchstone that helped him to appreciate the better times that followed. He also took great heart in seeing how his country had matured from the first time he landed in Halifax in the 1930s. In fact, if there was one thing that he wanted me to note in my interview with him, or indeed from other conversations about his life, it was that he knew that "the best thing [he] ever did was to decide to come to Canada."[19]

Altogether, the list of great events that Ibing experienced is impressive – but he was not just a witness to these points of history. On the contrary, his life also stands as a prime example of that key theme in social history: agency. Ibing's story is marked by a continual effort not only to shape his own life and strike out in his own direction, but also, once he became an adult, to help the broader fight for social justice. Indeed, Ibing's life was shaped by his actions and especially by careful, thoughtful consideration about what was the right thing to do and what would help create a better world. This was plainly evident from his refusal in his youth to join in the street violence between paramilitary groups that was spreading throughout Germany, through his decision to fight in Spain, to his break from the Communist party in the early 1950s.

Ibing also learned throughout his life that choosing to be on the right side did not guarantee good fortune. He certainly would have appreciated Marx's famous observation that people "make their own history, but they do not make it as they please; they do not make it under self-selected circumstances, but under circumstances existing already, given and transmitted from the past."[20] Ibing escaped Germany before the Nazis took power but arrived in Canada just as the despair of the Great Depression was setting in. Regarding his time in Spain, Ibing did not hesitate to call it "the most miserable experience" of his life – one that he put to the back of his mind once he was back in Canada. Throughout his time as a Communist, he struggled against the party's authoritarian and instrumentalist culture, and when he left he lost not only his political causes but also a cherished circle of friends.

Yet Ibing's is not a story that ends mired in bitterness or a sense of defeat. The greatest cause of his life – wiping out fascism – was achieved, and Ibing could certainly say that he played his part in the effort. Moreover, in the 1940s Ibing reached that goal that so many industrial workers pursued: to find good work in a trade, as a pressman in the newspaper printing business. He got married and started a family during the war, and in the postwar period gradually settled into a peaceful and secure life that would have been unimaginable in earlier times.

Acknowledgements

Although this is not a long book, putting it together was a very long process. Along the way, I received the support of many people. The staff at Library and Archives Canada deserve recognition for their help during my many visits to examine their holdings on key organizations and people. I should also thank the staff at Between the Lines, especially Amanda Crocker, for their efforts in seeing the project through to publication; Tilman Lewis deserves special credit for his work in editing the manuscript.

Research for this book was supported by grants from the Social Sciences and Humanities Research Council of Canada and McMaster University's Arts Research Board. Thanks to these bodies for their support.

My colleagues and students at McMaster University also provided much help along the way. I am especially indebted to Ian McKay, the L.R. Wilson Chair in Canadian History, for giving the manuscript such a careful reading and providing invaluable feedback. Pamela Swett, Professor at McMaster's History Department, was generous with her time in helping me contextualize some German sources. Abigail Puttock and Lindsay Blackman did very good work as Research Assistants, tracking down material on German Canadians and Communist organizations, respectively.

I am also grateful to David McElroy, who put great skill and care into making the maps. Christian Russau gave up some of his precious spare time from his heroic work as an activist in Berlin to help find some important German sources. David Messenger, a Professor at the University of South Alabama, provided some valuable and very timely help with some of the Spanish context. Of course, any errors to be found in this book are solely my responsibility.

Above all, I want to thank everyone in my family. In particular, the Orchards helped me understand many parts of Ibing's life; they were also encouraging and patient through the years I worked on this project. Special thanks to my wife, Lisa, for her support and love, and for being a skilful editor and source of sage advice, and to our children, Maddie and Max, for being themselves – and for moving me to make sure they knew the story of their Opa's life. The last note of thanks should be to Hans Ibing himself, for his warmth and generosity of spirit, and for being such a source of inspiration.

Notes

Introduction

1. Hans Ibing, Interview with Arthur Grenke, 1980, Library and Archives Canada (LAC) German Workers and Farmers Association Fonds R11667-0-6-E, formerly MG28-V112 (hereafter Ibing, interview with Grenke, LAC R11667-0-6-E); Mark Zuehlke, *The Gallant Cause: Canadians in the Spanish Civil War* (Mississauga: John Wiley & Sons, 1996), 277–78.
2. Hans Ibing, "Reminiscences of Members of the Mackenzie-Papineau Battalion of the Spanish Civil War," LAC Mackenzie-Papineau Battalion Collection, MG 30 E173 Vol. 4, 84–85.
3. Ibing, interview with Grenke, LAC R11667-0-6-E; Ibing, "Reminiscences," LAC MG 30 E173 Vol. 4, 84; Zuehlke, *Gallant Cause*, 278.
4. Ibing, interview with Grenke, LAC R11667-0-6-E.
5. Ibing, interview with Grenke, LAC R11667-0-6-E.
6. In addition to his concerns about returning to hard times in his past, he seemed uneasy with his grandson-in-law conducting formal interviews with him; I did not ask again for years.
7. Ibing, interview with Reynolds, "Canadian Broadcasting Corporation, Radio: Spanish Civil War Oral History Tapes," LAC 1979-0081 MISA. According to archivist Ernest J. Dick, Reynolds was among a group of researchers at the CBC who became interested in oral history, and they conducted interviews on many subjects "for their own sake, or on speculation that they might prove useful for a future CBC documentary." Many of Reynolds's interviews were used in Victor Hoar's book on Canadian volunteers in Spain, although the one with Ibing was not. Dick claims that this was "perhaps one of the first Canadian examples of such oral history interviews being used for a published history." See Ernest J. Dick, "Oral History as a Process: The CBC Experience," *Oral History Forum – Forum D'Histoire Orale* 16–17 (1996–1997), 71–83. The CBC did not produce a documentary using these interviews in the 1960s and the tapes went missing for years. But they were recovered in 2012 and turned into a documentary, "The Spanish Crucible," which featured in two parts on the CBC radio program Living Out Loud (www.cbc.ca/radio/livingoutloud). Hoar's book was first published in 1969 (Toronto: Copp, Clark), then republished in 1986 under the name Victor Howard; the latter will be cited here. See Victor Howard with Mac Reynolds, *The Mackenzie-Papineau Battalion: The Canadian Contingent in the Spanish Civil War* (Ottawa: Carleton University Press, 1986).
8. The transcript of Grenke's interview is almost 26,000 words; Ibing, interview with Grenke, LAC R11667-0-6-E.
9. Michael Petrou, *Renegades* (Vancouver: University of British Columbia Press, 2008). In 2010 Petrou kindly agreed to share his notes from the interview as well.
10. Ibing, "Reminiscences," LAC MG 30 E173 Vol. 4; William Beeching, *Canadian Volunteers in Spain, 1936–1939* (Regina: Canadian Plains Research Center, 1989). Ibing's experience as a truck driver did not fit Beeching's focus on combat units, especially the Mac-Paps themselves.

11 Indeed, scholars do not often get the opportunity to engage literature on subjects as diverse as Weimar Germany, the rise of the Nazis, Canadian immigration policy, the impact of the Depression in Canada and the government's response, the international Communist movement, the left in Canada in the 1930s and 1940s, the Spanish Civil War and the International Brigades, the plight of veterans from the war, the experience of enemy aliens in Canada during World War II, the impact of the Cold War, life behind the Iron Curtain in East Germany, and the Golden Age of welfare capitalism in the mid-twentieth-century – all for one book.

1: Turbulent Times

1 Hans Ibing, personal notes left to his family.
2 By 1914 the SPD counted more members (at over a million) than any other political party in a Western democracy. The party also overcame an electoral system slanted in favour of conservative rural areas to win more seats in the Reichstag than any other party. Still, in general, the imperial German political system was far from democratic: the power of elected assemblies remained quite limited up to and through World War I. (Eric Hobsbawm, *Age of Empire, 1875–1914* [London: Abacus, 1987], 116–18.)
3 Ibing, "Reminiscences," LAC MG 30 E173 Vol. 4, 73.
4 Ibing, personal note.
5 Ibing, personal note.
6 Ibing, personal note; Ibing, interview with the author.
7 Richard Evans, *The Coming of the Third Reich: How the Nazis Destroyed Democracy and Seized Power in Germany* (London: Penguin, 2003), 74–81; Ian Kershaw, *To Hell and Back: Europe 1914–1949* (London: Penguin, 2015), 85–86; Geoff Ely, *Forging Democracy: The History of the Left in Europe, 1850–2000* (New York: Oxford, 2002), 165–69.
8 Evans, *Coming of the Third Reich*, 118–19.
9 Evans, *Coming of the Third Reich*, 78.
10 Ibing, "Reminiscences," LAC MG 30 E173 Vol. 4, 73.
11 Evans, *Coming of the Third Reich*, 62–65; Eberhard Kolb, *The Weimar Republic*, trans. P.S. Falla (London: Unwin Hyman, 1988), 5–9. Soviet Russia would become the Soviet Union in 1922.
12 Evans, *Coming of the Third Reich*, 60–61; Kolb, *Weimar Republic*, 29–32. The Allies saw these as appropriate terms, far less punitive than those the Germans had imposed on the Soviet Union at Brest-Litovsk in early 1918, and consistent with the Germans' culpability as established in the war guilt clause. France and Belgium especially wanted compensation after more than four years of bitter fighting on their soil, not to mention the toll the Germans took upon land they occupied for most of the war. (Kershaw, *To Hell and Back*, 188–89.)
13 Hans Mommsen, *The Rise and Fall of Weimar Democracy*, trans. Elborg Forster and Larry Eugene Jones (Charlotte: University of North Carolina, 1996), 91.
14 Kolb, *Weimar Republic*, 35–36.
15 Kershaw, *To Hell and Back*, 86–87. Indeed, most Germans on the political right only saw – or only wanted to see – the alleged treason of the left's "November criminals" as the cause of Germany's humiliation. (Evans, *Coming of the Third Reich*, 74–75.)
16 Evans, *Coming of the Third Reich*, 186–87.
17 Kershaw, *To Hell and Back*, 144; Mommsen, *Rise and Fall of Weimar*, 91–92.

18 Ibing, interview with the author.
19 Kolb, *Weimar Republic*, 46; Frederick Taylor, *The Downfall of Money: Germany's Hyperinflation and the Destruction of the Middle Class* (New York: Bloomsbury, 2013), 238.
20 Ibing, interview with the author.
21 Kolb, *Weimar Republic*, 48–50.
22 Kolb, *Weimar Republic*, 46–47; Evans, *Coming of the Third Reich*, 104–5.
23 Evans, *Coming of the Third Reich*, 110–11.
24 Taylor, *Downfall of Money*, 240–41.
25 Ibing, interview with the author.
26 Ibing, personal note to his family.
27 Kolb, *Weimar Republic*, 68–69.
28 Ibing, interview with the author.
29 Ibing, interview with the author.
30 Ibing, interview with Petrou.
31 Evans, *Coming of the Third Reich*, 72–73.
32 Evans, *Coming of the Third Reich*, 72–73, 183, 269–70; Kershaw, *To Hell and Back*, 104–5.
33 Ibing, "Reminiscences," LAC MG 30 E173 Vol. 4, 73.
34 Ibing, interview with Grenke, LAC R11667-0-6-E.
35 Ibing, interview with Petrou.
36 Richard Evans, *The Third Reich in Power* (London: Penguin, 2005), 13–15.
37 Ibing, interview with Grenke, LAC R11667-0-6-E; Ibing, personal communications with the author.
38 Ibing, interview with Grenke, LAC R11667-0-6-E.
39 Emigration from Germany itself grew to the point that by 1923, the annual rates of departures (at 115,000) exceeded those from the last "great wave" of emigration in the early 1880s. The outflow fell off somewhat through the mid and late 1920s, after German political leaders took measures to discourage emigration; they became concerned that the country should retain its population in order to weather its time of crisis. Nevertheless, emigration rates remained steady at 50,000 to 60,000 annually through to the end of the decade. Ibing came right at the tail end of this wave of migration. (Jonathan Wagner, *A History of Migration from Germany to Canada, 1850–1939* [Vancouver: University of British Columbia Press, 2005], 172–73.)
40 Arthur Grenke, "From Dreams of the Worker State to Fighting Hitler," *Labour/Le Travail* 35 (Spring 1995), 66–67.
41 Men were two to three times more likely to emigrate than women; single men were twice as likely to emigrate as men who were married. In previous periods, Canada had lagged behind South American countries Argentina and Brazil and even further behind the United States in its ability to attract German immigrants. Indeed, the United States consistently received no less than three-quarters of all German emigrants, and this included a large portion of migrants who first landed in Canada but immediately moved on to the U.S. Yet from 1927 to 1930, Canada climbed to second among preferred places to settle, attracting an unusually large proportion – about one-eighth – of all German migrants. (Wagner, *Migration from Germany*, 168–69.)
42 The quoted terms are ones that Ibing frequently used in conversation about his impression of Canada at the time.
43 Although a government-led building program eased the housing crisis (and helped the

emergence of the modernist style of architecture for which Weimar became famous), the appeal of unsettled lands in Canada remained strong. (On housing policy, see Kolb, *Weimar Germany*, 89–90; on the sense that Germany was overcrowded and Canada was more open, see Wagner, *Migration from Germany*, 173–76.)

44 Ibing, interview with Grenke, LAC R11667-0-6-E.
45 Wagner, *Migration from Germany*, 173–75, 186–88.
46 See, for instance, James Daschuk, *Clearing the Plains: Disease, Politics of Starvation, and the Loss of Aboriginal Life* (Regina: University of Regina Press, 2013).
47 Middle-class reformers, organized labour, the popular press, and other voices complained constantly about "unassimilative" and "uncivilized" Eastern European immigrants posing a great "threat" to Canadian communities and standard of living. And Asians were vilified to an event greater extent. See, for instance, Ninette Kelley and Michael Trebilcock, *The Making of the Mosaic: A History and Canadian Immigration Policy* (Toronto: University of Toronto Press, 1998), 132–61; David Goutor, *Guarding the Gates: The Canadian Labour Movement and Immigration, 1872–1934* (Vancouver: University of British Columbia Press, 2007), 22–25.
48 The population grew by 34 per cent between 1901 and 1911 alone, and still greater influxes occurred in the early 1910s before the war started. (Donald Avery, *Reluctant Host: Canada's Response to Immigrant Workers, 1896–1994* [Toronto: McClelland and Stewart, 1995], 20, 24–25; David J. Hall, "Room to Spare," *Horizon Canada* 76 [1986], 1803.)
49 Wagner, *Migration from Germany*, 127–28.
50 Avery, *Reluctant Host*, 72; Desmond Morton, "Sir William Otter and Internment Operations in Canada during the First World War," *Canadian Historical Review* 55 (1974), 32–58; David J. Otter, *Behind Canadian Barbed Wire: Alien, Refuge and Prisoner of War Camps, 1914–1916* (Calgary: Tumbleweed, 1980).
51 To be sure, the hostility in Canada did not reach the levels seen in Britain, South Africa, or Australia, where there were a number of outbreaks of street violence against Germans during the war. Although the United States stayed out of the war until 1917, once it entered the fight, vigilante groups and mobs targeted Germans in the street; more than thirty were killed and hundreds were injured. (Stephen Heathorn, *Haig and Kitchener in Twentieth-Century Britain: Remembrance, Representation and Appropriation* [Farnham: Ashgate, 2013], 34–40; Eric Kirschbaum, "Whatever Happened to German America," *New York Times*, opinion/editorial page, Sept. 23, 2015, www.nytimes.com.)
52 Altogether, most Central and Eastern Europeans in Canada, whatever their actual ethnic background or political allegiances, faced discrimination and suspicion that they were from Germany, the Austro-Hungarian Empire, or some country full of dangerous ideas or revolutionaries. (Goutor, *Guarding the Gates*, 25–26.)
53 Avery, *Reluctant Host*, 83–84; see also Kelley and Trebilcock, *Making of the Mosaic*, 164–82.
54 The economy, contrary to the popular image of the era today, was mired in a wretched slump through the early 1920s.
55 Under the Railway Agreement, around 185,000 immigrants came to Canada from 1925 to 1930, and overall immigration averaged about 145,000 annually. In reopening its gates to large-scale immigration, Canada stood out from many other countries, especially the United States, which kept most of its restrictions in place through the 1920s. (Goutor, *Guarding the Gates*, 25–27; David Scott FitzGerald and David Cook-Martin, *Culling the Masses: The Democratic Origins of Racist Immigration Policy in the Americas* [Cambridge: Harvard University Press, 2014], 98–107, 163–66.)

56 Wagner, *Migration from Germany*, 166–67, 183–84.
57 Wagner, *Migration from Germany*, 175–76, 203–4.
58 The Canadian Lutheran Immigration Society sent 567 migrants to Canada in the first seven months of 1930 alone, an impressive total for a single religious organization. (Wagner, *Migration from Germany*, 189–90.)
59 Wagner, *Migration from Germany*, 197–98; Avery, *Reluctant Host*, 97–98.
60 Ibing, interview with Grenke, LAC R11667-0-6-E.
61 LAC RG76, C-1-b (Records for Port of Halifax) Vol. 11, 117.
62 Wagner, *Migration from Germany*, 171.
63 LAC RG76, C-1-b Vol. 11, 113–121; Ibing, interview with the author. Ibing's recollections of the trip were remarkably clear for the rest of his life. In casual conversation about the trip more than sixty years later, he remembered that there were about a half-dozen Swiss on the boat.
64 Wagner, *Migration from Germany*, 212.
65 Ibing, interview with Grenke, LAC R11667-0-6-E.
66 Ibing, "Reminiscences," LAC MG 30 E173 Vol. 4, 73; LAC RG 76 C-1-b Vol. 11, 113–21.
67 Ibing, interview with Grenke, LAC R11667-0-6-E.
68 Ibing, interview with the author; on the role of Lutheran Immigration Board in placing immigrants in Canada, see Wagner, *Migration from Germany*, 197–99.
69 Ibing, interview with the author.
70 On the LIB's promises, see Wagner, *Migration from Germany*, 197.
71 Ibing, interview with Grenke, LAC R11667-0-6-E; Ibing, interview with the author.
72 Ibing, interview with Grenke, LAC R11667-0-6-E.
73 Ibing, interview with Grenke, LAC R11667-0-6-E; Ibing, interview with the author.
74 The relief budget grew from around $32,000 in 1927–28 to $1,684,000 in 1930–31. (Barbara Roberts, "Shovelling Out the Unemployed," *Manitoba History* 5 [Spring 1983], www.mhs.mb.ca/docs/mb_history.)
75 Avery, *Reluctant Host*, 109.
76 In Winnipeg, it was already "a regular practice" by the fall of 1930 for municipal relief officials "to report to the local Immigration office the names of any immigrants (of less than 5 years) who received relief"; in such cases, deportation was usually automatic. (Roberts, "Shovelling Out the Unemployed"; see also Valerie Knowles, *Strangers at Our Gates: Canadian Immigration and Immigration Policy, 1540–1997*, rev. ed. [Toronto: Dundurn Press, 1997], 117.)
77 Avery, *Reluctant Host*, 110.
78 Ibing, interview with Grenke, LAC R11667-0-6-E; Ibing, interview with the author.
79 Ibing, interview with Grenke, LAC R11667-0-6-E.
80 Ibing, interview with Grenke, LAC R11667-0-6-E.
81 Ibing, interview with Grenke, LAC R11667-0-6-E.
82 Ibing, interview with the author.
83 Ibing, interview with Grenke, LAC R11667-0-6-E.
84 *Rowell-Sirois Commission Report*, Book 1: Canada 1867–1939, 150. In Manitoba, Saskatchewan, and Alberta, net farm income fell from $363 million in 1929 to *negative* $3.1 million in 1932. (Kenneth Norrie, Douglas Owram, and J.C. Herbert Emery, *A History of the Canadian Economy*, 3rd ed. [Toronto: Thompson, 2002], 323.)
85 Avery, *Reluctant Host*, 110; Knowles, *Strangers at Our Gates*, 115.

86 Kelley and Trebilcock, *Making of the Mosaic*, 229.
87 Eric Strikwerda, *The Wages of Relief: Cities and the Unemployed in Prairie Canada, 1929–1939* (Edmonton: Athabasca University Press, 2013), 54.
88 Strikwerda, *Wages of Relief*, 59–61.
89 Ibing, interview with Grenke, LAC R11667-0-6-E.
90 Strikwerda, *Wages of Relief*, 138; James Struthers, *No Fault of Their Own: Unemployment and the Canadian Welfare States, 1914–1941* (Toronto: University of Toronto Press, 1983), 81–82; Bill Waiser, *All Hell Can't Stop Us: The On-to-Ottawa Trek and the Regina Riot* (Winnipeg: Fifth House, 2003), 25–40.
91 Ibing, interview with the author.
92 Overall, Canada deported around 30,000 immigrants in the early 1930s, most of them for being "public charges." (Knowles, *Strangers at Our Gates*, 116.)
93 Roberts, "Shovelling Out the Unemployed."
94 In September 1934, Winnipeg cut off 500 families and 1,600 single men who had arrived in Canada in 1929 and 1930 from relief programs. According to Avery, the clear majority of those affected by the cuts were Central Europeans. (Avery, *Reluctant Host*, 110–11.)
95 Ibing, interview with the author.
96 Ibing, interview with the author.
97 Ibing, interview with Grenke, LAC R11667-0-6-E; Ibing, interview with the author.
98 Ibing, interview with the author.
99 Ibing, personal communication with family.
100 Ibing, interview with the author.
101 Ibing, interview with Grenke, LAC R11667-0-6-E.
102 Ibing, interview with Grenke, LAC R11667-0-6-E.

2: *Turning Left*

1 Ibing, interview with Grenke, LAC R11667-0-6-E.
2 Ibing, interview with Grenke, LAC R11667-0-6-E.
3 Ibing, "Reminiscences," LAC MG 30 E173 Vol. 4, 74.
4 Ibing, interview with Grenke, LAC R11667-0-6-E.
5 Evans, *Coming of the Third Reich*, 56–58, 74–75.
6 Eley, *Forging Democracy*, 251–2.
7 Kershaw, *To Hell and Back*, 210–12; Evans, *Coming of the Third Reich*, 237–43.
8 As James Naylor notes, even when their rivalry was at its worst, the two sides could find ways to co-operate, especially on the grassroots level where "there was relatively broad interest in preserving working class unity and sympathy for what the Communists described as a 'united front from below.'" (James Naylor, *The Fate of Labour Socialism: The Co-operative Commonwealth Federation and the Dream of a Working-Class Future* [Toronto: University of Toronto Press, 2016], 180.)
9 Bryan Palmer, *Working Class Experience: Rethinking the History of Canadian Labour, 1800–1991*, 2nd ed. (Toronto: McClelland and Stewart, 1992), 196–205 ; Tom Mitchel and James Naylor, "The Prairies: In the Eye of the Storm," in *The Workers' Revolt in Canada, 1917–1925*, ed. Craig Heron (Toronto: University of Toronto Press, 1998), 176–230. For an overview of the labour unrest in the period, see Craig Heron, "National Contours: Solidarity and Fragmentation," in *Workers' Revolt in Canada*, ed. Heron, 268–304.
10 Stephan Epp-Koop, *We're Going to Run This City: Winnipeg's Political Left after the Gener-*

al Strike (Winnipeg: University of Manitoba Press, 2015), 42–43, 56–57, 85, 116–18, 143.
11 Naylor (*Fate of Labour Socialism*, 3–16) contends that "labour socialists" is a better term for these activists, but this book will keep the more common term "social democrats." A particularly significant difference between the Canadian ILP and the German SPD was the former's connection to British democratic and union traditions.
12 Henry Trachtenburg, "The Jewish Community of Winnipeg and the Federal Election of 1935 in Winnipeg North," *Manitoba History* 61 (Fall 2009), www.mhs.mb.ca/docs/mb_history.
13 Epp-Coop, *We're Going to Run This City*, 117–18.
14 Communists held only two council seats, while the ILP held six seats and the mayor's office; there was also one independent socialist alderman. (Epp-Coop, *We're Going to Run This City*, 117–18.)
15 Trachtenburg, "The Jewish Community of Winnipeg."
16 Woodsworth and Heaps held two of only seven seats in Parliament that the CCF managed to win in its first election in 1935, and the party would have little organizational strength at the grassroots level in most of the country until the end of the decade. (Ian McKay, "Joe Salsberg, Depression-Era Communism, and the Limits of Moscow's Rule," *Canadian Jewish Studies* 21 [2013], 130–42. See also Walter Young, *Anatomy of a Party: The National CCF, 1932–61* [Toronto: University of Toronto Press, 1969].) Although the Communist Party of Canada was smaller than its counterparts in Europe, since being launched in 1921 it was an energetic force, often working through affiliated groups such as the Workers Party of Canada. (See also David Ackers, "Rebel or Revolutionary?: Jack Kavanagh and the Early Years of the Communist Movement in Vancouver, 1920–1925," *Labour/Le Travail* 30 [Fall 1992], 9–44.) In fact, Ian McKay calls the CPC "the first attempt in Canada to organize a modern, powerful, left-wing *party* in a contemporary sense – that is, a stable organization with a discernible membership and leadership structure, capable of intervening from coast to coast, with a program, regular conventions, and elected representatives in various political bodies and ultimately in Parliament." Hence in this period, the CPC was "in essence *the* major party of the left in Canada." (McKay, "Joe Salsberg," 136.)
17 Ibing, interview with Grenke, LAC R11667-0-6-E.
18 John Manley, "'Communists Love Canada!': The Communist Party of Canada, the 'People' and the Popular Front, 1933–1939," *Journal of Canadian Studies* 36,4 (Winter 2002), 4. See also Stephen Endicott, *Raising the Workers' Flag: The Workers' Unity League of Canada, 1930–1936* (Toronto: University of Toronto Press, 2012). As Naylor notes (*Fate of Labour Socialism*, 182), labour socialists and ILP supporters were not as well prepared to mobilize workplace protests at this time, and thus tended to be "on the outside looking in at this activity."
19 Manley, "'Starve, Be Damned!': Communists and Canada's Urban Unemployed, 1929–1939," *Canadian Historical Review* 79,3 (Sept. 1998), 478.
20 Waiser, *All Hell Can't Stop Us*, especially ch. 6 and 10.
21 Naylor, *Fate of Labour Socialism*, 182–83.
22 Tony Judt and Timothy Snyder, *Thinking the 20th Century* (New York, Penguin, 2012), 169.
23 Ibing, interview with Grenke, LAC R11667-0-6-E.
24 Ibing, interview with Grenke, LAC R11667-0-6-E.
25 Eric Hobsbawm, *How to Change the World: Tales of Marx and Marxism* (London: Little, Brown, 2011), 285–86.

26 Manley, "'Communists Love Canada!,'" 62–63.
27 Hobsbawm, *How to Change the World*, 299.
28 Naylor, *Fate of Labour Socialism*, 168–69.
29 See, for instance, Manley, "'Starve, Be Damned!,'" 479–80; Ian Avakumovic, *The Communist Party in Canada: A History* (Toronto: McClelland and Stewart, 1975), 9–10, 35–39. On the Communists' relationship to European immigrant communities in Winnipeg in particular, see Epp-Coop, *We're Going to Run This City*, 68–72, 87.
30 Other "language affiliates," like the Finnish and Ukrainian affiliates, were large in comparison. (Grenke, "From Dreams of the Worker State to Fighting Hitler," 66.)
31 Grenke, "From Dreams of the Worker State to Fighting Hitler," 66–69.
32 Ibing, interview with Grenke, LAC R11667-0-6-E. On "hall socialism," see Ian Radforth, "Finnish Radicalism and Labour Activism in the Northern Ontario Woods," in *A Nation of Immigrants*, ed. Franca Iacovetta, Paula Draper, and Robert Ventresca (Toronto: University of Toronto Press, 1998), 293–316. The term is usually used to describe the experience of Finnish immigrants, though it applies to other communities such as the German one, as well.
33 Manley, "'Communists Love Canada!,'" 61–62.
34 "Documents on Volunteers of the International Brigades, Participants of the National-Revolutionary War in Spain, 1936–1939" (Comintern Records), Ibing, Hans J, LAC MG 10 K2, Mackenzie-Papineau Fonds 545, File List 6, Microfilm Reel K 263.
35 Ibing, interview with Grenke, LAC R11667-0-6-E.
36 Ibing, interview with Grenke, LAC R11667-0-6-E.
37 Ibing, interview with Grenke, LAC R11667-0-6-E.
38 Jack Scott, *A Communist Life: Jack Scott and the Canadian Workers Movement, 1927–1985*, ed. Bryan Palmer (St. John's: Committee on Canadian Labour History, 1988), 49.
39 Ibing, interview with the author.
40 Paul Preston, *The Spanish Civil War: Reaction, Revolution and Revenge* (New York: W.W. Norton, 2006), 146–47. Manley depicts the change as starting at the formal July 1935 announcement, although he also notes that in late 1934 the party was already changing, looking for "new blood and new members," and launching some initiatives that are discussed here. (Manley, "'Communists Love Canada!,'" 63.) I would argue that these changes reflect the influence of the May 1934 signals from the Comintern in favour of the Popular Front.
41 Manley, "'Communists Love Canada!,'" 60–62.
42 Ibing, interview with Grenke, LAC R11667-0-6-E.
43 Hobsbawm, *Age of Extremes: The Short Twentieth Century* (London: Abacus, 1994), 154.
44 See, for instance, Nigel Copsey, "Communists and the Inter-war Anti-fascist Struggle in the United States and Britain," *Labour History Review* 76,3 (2011), 184–206.
45 Kershaw, *To Hell and Back*, 249, 264–65, 449–50; Judt and Snyder, *Thinking the 20th Century*, 169–70; Timothy Snyder, *Bloodlands: Europe Between Hitler and Stalin* (New York: Basic Books, 2010), 15–16, 60–62.
46 Waiser, *All Hell Can't Stop Us*, 18–20; CBC, "Communist Canada," *Canada: A People's History*, www.cbc.ca/history.
47 Eley, *Forging Democracy*, ch. 9; Kershaw, *To Hell and Back*, ch. 3.
48 Preston, *Spanish Civil War*, 135–36.
49 Hobsbawm, *How to Change the World*, 267; Pierre Birnbaum, *Léon Blum: Prime Minister*,

Socialist, Zionist, trans. Arthur Goldhammer (New Haven: Yale University Press, 2015), 116–17. That Blum was Jewish only deepened the right's hostility toward him.
50 Ibing, interview with Petrou.
51 Manley, "'Communists Love Canada!,'" 61.
52 In addition to the 17,000 supporters inside, there was a crowd of 8,000 more outside. (Zuehlke, *Gallant Cause*, 37–38.)
53 Manley, "'Communists Love Canada!,'" 61–62.
54 Ibing, interview with Grenke, LAC R11667-0-6-E.
55 Manley, "'Communists Love Canada!,'" 63.
56 Manley, "'Communists Love Canada!,'" 63–65.
57 Ibing, interview with Grenke, LAC R11667-0-6-E; Ibing, interview with the author. The Comintern's (very brief) records on Ibing from his service in Spain are confusing on this point. They note that he was a unit secretary – which is consistent with his description of his role in the GWFA – but suggest that he had this role with the Communist Party of Canada itself. This was either a case of imprecision and ambiguity in the note-taking (which would not be surprising, as the record seems to be a hastily assembled list of details and comments), or simply a mistake. Ibing never spoke of having such a role. "Documents on Volunteers of the International Brigades," LAC MG 10 K2, Mackenzie-Papineau Fonds 545, File List 6, Microfilm Reel K 263.
58 Ibing, interview with Petrou. On the persistence of Stalinism, see Manley, "'Communists Love Canada!,'" 59–62.
59 Ibing, interview with Grenke, LAC R11667-0-6-E.
60 Ibing, interview with Petrou.
61 Judt and Snyder, *Thinking the 20th Century*, 219.
62 Ibing, interview with Petrou.
63 Ibing, interview with Grenke, LAC R11667-0-6-E.
64 Kershaw, *To Hell and Back*, 254–55; Adam Hochschild, *Spain in Our Hearts: Americans in the Spanish Civil War* (Boston: Houghton Mifflin Harcourt, 2016), 25.
65 Preston, *Spanish Civil War*, 136.
66 Ibing, personal communications.
67 Hochschild, *Spain in Our Hearts*, 69.
68 Preston, *Spanish Civil War*, 189.
69 Preston, *Spanish Civil War*, 154.
70 See Preston, *Spanish Civil War*, ch. 5, "Behind the Gentleman's Agreement: The Great Powers Betray Spain," 135–62; Hochschild, *Spain in Our Hearts*, 43–46; David Wingeate Pike, *France Divided: The French and the Civil War in Spain* (Eastbourne: Sussex Academic Press, 2011), ch. 3, "The Appeal of Giral," 18–28; Jacques Danos and Marcel Gibelin, *June '36: Class Struggles and the Popular Front in Spain*, trans. Peter Fysh and Christine Bourry (London and Chicago: Bookmarks, 1986), 220–22.
71 Eric Hobsbawm, *Revolutionaries*, 2nd ed. (London: Abacus, 2007), 126.
72 H.V. Nelles, *A Little History of Canada* (Toronto: Oxford University Press, 2004), 179.
73 Zuehlke, *Gallant Cause*, 140–41.
74 Hochschild, *Spain in Our Hearts*, 22.
75 Preston, *Spanish Civil War*, 139.
76 This reached the point that by early 1937 there were more than 100,000 Italian troops fighting on Franco's side. (Preston, *Spanish Civil War*, 140–45.)

77 Ibing, "Reminiscences," LAC MG 30 E173 Vol. 4, 73.
78 Ibing, interview with Grenke, LAC R11667-0-6-E.
79 Ibing, "Reminiscences," LAC MG 30 E173 Vol. 4, 73; Ibing, interview with Grenke, LAC R11667-0-6-E.
80 Zuehlke, *Gallant Cause*, 59–60; Ibing, interview with Grenke, LAC R11667-0-6-E.
81 Ibing, interview with Grenke, LAC R11667-0-6-E.
82 Helen Graham, *The Spanish Civil War: A Very Short Introduction* (Oxford: Oxford University Press, 2005), 33. General Mola, another leading military figure on the Nationalist side, declared the same month: "It is necessary to spread terror. We have to create the impression of mastery, eliminating without scruples or hesitation all those who do not think as we do. There can be no cowardice." (Preston, *Spanish Civil War*, 103.) See also Paul Preston, "Franco as a Military Leader," *Transactions of the Royal Historical Society* 6,4 (1994), 21–41.
83 Preston, *Spanish Civil War*, 121.
84 Eley, *Forging Democracy*, 276.
85 Ibing, interview with Grenke, LAC R11667-0-6-E.
86 Ibing, interview with Grenke, LAC R11667-0-6-E.
87 Hobsbawm, *Age of Extremes*, 159.
88 Petrou, *Renegades*, 39; Hochschild, *Spain in Our Hearts*, 46–47.
89 Zuehlke, *Gallant Cause*, ch. 2. See also G. Scott Waterman, "The Common Cause of All Advanced and Progressive Mankind: Proletarian Internationalism, Spain, and the American Communist Press, 1936–1937," unpublished MA thesis, University of Vermont, 2015; Hochschild, *Spain in Our Hearts*, 46–49.
90 Antony Beevor, *The Battle for Spain: The Spanish Civil War, 1936–1939* (London: Phoenix, 2006), 176. On activities in Canada, see Petrou, R*enegades*, 18–19, 27, 38–45; Manley, "'Communists Love Canada!,'" 70–72; Zuehlke, *Gallant Cause*, 37–40.
91 Ibing, interview with Grenke, LAC R11667-0-6-E.
92 Ibing, "Reminiscences," LAC MG 30 E173 Vol. 4, 74.
93 Zuehlke, *Gallant Cause*, 60–61.
94 Ibing, interview with Grenke, LAC R11667-0-6-E; Ibing, interview with the author.
95 Beevor, *Battle for Spain*, 176–77.
96 Ibing, interview with Grenke, LAC R11667-0-6-E; Ibing, interview with Petrou; Ibing, interview with the author.
97 Preston, *Spanish Civil War*, 171.
98 There were 1,700 according to Petrou, based on his collection of names; Beeching's figure is 1,448 based on materials from the Friends of the Mackenzie-Papineau Battalion, and some supplementary research by Lee Burke, a veteran of the Mac-Paps. But after the Russian archives were opened to researchers, Petrou found some new names in them of Canadian veterans – many of them not in the Mac-Paps but part of other units. See Petrou, *Renegades*, 11–12; and Beeching, *Canadian Volunteers*, 7, 13n.8.
99 Ibing, interview with Petrou.
100 Beeching, *Canadian Volunteers*, 7–8; Petrou, *Renegades*, 31–33; Zuehlke, *Gallant Cause*, 135.
101 Petrou, *Renegades*, 18–19, 26–27, 33–35. Like Ibing, many of the European immigrants who volunteered were involved with Communist-allied organizations in their communities. Ibing never recounted being recruited by the GWFA, but in general the CPC did much of its

recruiting through ethnic organizations such as the Ukrainian Labour-Farmer Temple Association. See also Myron Momryk, "Ukrainian Volunteers from Canada in the International Brigades, Spain, 1936–39: A Profile," *Journal of Ukrainian Studies* 16,1–2 (Summer–Winter 1991), 181–94.
102 Ibing, interview with Petrou.
103 Petrou, *Renegades*, 33.
104 Ibing, interview with Grenke, LAC R11667-0-6-E.
105 Petrou illustrates this point with the fact that "once in Spain, few complaints made by Canadian soldiers were about their pay." (*Renegades*, 32.)
106 Beeching, *Canadian Volunteers*, 8.
107 Surveys by the CPC showed that "to fight fascism" was the most common reason Canadian volunteers cited for going to Spain. Ibing did not participate in these surveys, but as noted, in interviews he identified fighting fascism as his main motivation for volunteering.
108 Petrou, *Renegades*, 43.
109 Ibing, interview with Petrou.

3: *The International Brigades*

1 Ibing, "Reminiscences," LAC MG 30 E173 Vol. 4, 82.
2 Ibing, interview with Reynolds, LAC 1979-0081 MISA. Most volunteers took ships to Le Havre, but in interviews and written testimony, Ibing recalled landing in France at Cherbourg. In his interview with Grenke (LAC R11667-0-6-E), however, Ibing did seem a little uncertain.
3 Petrou, *Renegades*, 56.
4 Ibing, "Reminiscences," LAC MG 30 E173 Vol. 4, 74.
5 Peter Carroll, *Odyssey of the Abraham-Lincoln Brigade: Americans in the Spanish Civil War* (Stanford: Stanford University Press, 1994), 66–67; Beeching, *Canadian Volunteers*, 15; Petrou, *Renegades*, 56.
6 "Ile de France Ocean Liner," Ile de France French cheese website, http://iledefrancecheese.com.
7 Ibing, "Reminiscences," LAC MG 30 E173 Vol. 4, 74.
8 Beevor, *Battle for Spain*, 177–79.
9 Hochschild, *Spain in Our Hearts*, 88–89.
10 Cecil Eby, *Comrades and Commissars: The Lincoln Battalion in the Spanish Civil War* (University Park: Pennsylvania University Press, 2007), 17–18.
11 Petrou, *Renegades*, 56–57; Howard, *Mackenzie-Papineau Battalion*, 45–46.
12 Beeching, *Canadian Volunteers*, 18–28; Petrou, *Renegades*, 57–58, Carroll, *Odyssey of the Abraham-Lincoln Brigade*, 124–26.
13 Edward Cecil-Smith, draft history of the Mackenzie-Papineau Battalion, LAC MG 30 E173 Vol. 1, File 14.
14 Ibing, interview with Grenke, LAC R11667-0-6-E.
15 Hochschild, *Spain in Our Hearts*, 132–33.
16 Ibing, "Reminiscences," LAC MG 30 E173 Vol. 4, 75.
17 Ibing, "Reminiscences," LAC MG 30 E173 Vol. 4, 75.
18 Beeching, *Canadian Volunteers*, 20.
19 Ibing, "Reminiscences," LAC MG 30 E173 Vol. 4; Petrou, *Renegades*, 57; Carroll, *Odyssey of the Abraham-Lincoln Brigade*, 125.

Notes to pages 68–74

20 Beeching, *Canadian Volunteers*, 20. See also Hochschild, *Spain in Our Hearts*, 133–34.
21 Carroll, *Odyssey of the Abraham-Lincoln Brigade*, 125.
22 Ibing, interview with Grenke, LAC R11667-0-6-E; Ibing, "Reminiscences," LAC MG 30 E173 Vol. 4, 75.
23 Zuehlke, *Gallant Cause*, 112–13.
24 Zuehlke, *Gallant Cause*, 112.
25 Zuehlke, *Gallant Cause*, 113.
26 Zuehlke, *Gallant Cause*, 112–13.
27 Ibing, "Reminiscences," LAC MG 30 E173 Vol. 4, 75.
28 Zuehlke, *Gallant Cause*, 113.
29 Ibing, "Reminiscences," LAC MG 30 E173 Vol. 4, 75; Ibing, interview with Grenke, LAC R11667-0-6-E.
30 George Orwell, *Homage to Catalonia* (London: Penguin, 2000 [1938]), 93–96; Sid Lowe, *Fear and Loathing in La Liga: Barcelona vs. Real Madrid* (London: Yellow Jersey Press, 2013), 48–49.
31 Preston, *Spanish Civil War*, 235–43.
32 Lowe, *Fear and Loathing in La Liga*, 31.
33 George Orwell, *Homage to Catalonia*, 3.
34 Preston, *Spanish Civil War*, 239–41.
35 Orwell, *Homage to Catalonia*, 93–96; Lowe, *Fear and Loathing in La Liga*, 48–49.
36 Preston, *Spanish Civil War*, 250–52.
37 Ibing, "Reminiscences," LAC MG 30 E173 Vol. 4, 76.
38 To add to the confusion, in his reminiscences Ibing identified it as the office of the POUM, but he described the POUM not as the Trotskyist party, but as "the military arm of the anarchists in Spain." (Ibing, "Reminiscences," LAC MG 30 E173 Vol. 4, 76.)
39 Ibing, "Reminiscences," LAC MG 30 E173 Vol. 4, 74.
40 Ibing, interview with Petrou; Ibing also made this claim a number of times during informal conversation.
41 See, for instance, Beevor, *Battle for Spain*, 345. Ibing was likely exposed to less propaganda than other volunteers. Since they were constantly on the road, the members of Ibing's transport regiment were often isolated from the rest of the Brigades and their political commissars.
42 Ibing, "Reminiscences," LAC MG 30 E173 Vol. 4, 74.
43 Hochschild, *Spain in Our Hearts*, 112; Howard, *Mackenzie-Papineau Battalion*, 120–21; Eby, *Comrades and Commissars*, 24–25.
44 Beevor, *Battle for Spain*, 180–81.
45 In fact, the Mackenzie-Papineau Battalion would first be formed as a unit within the Abraham Lincoln Battalion.
46 Some continued to do so after the Mac-Paps were formed.
47 Petrou, *Renegades*, 59; see also Beevor, *Battle for Spain*, 182, 235.
48 In his reminiscences for the Mackenzie-Papineau Battalion (LAC MG 30 E173 Vol. 4), Ibing did not mention his initial placement in the Thaelmann Battalion – but he did note it in his interviews with Petrou and Grenke.
49 Ibing, "Reminiscences," LAC MG 30 E173 Vol. 4, 76.
50 Ibing, "Reminiscences," LAC MG 30 E173 Vol. 4, 76–77.
51 Ibing, "Reminiscences," LAC MG 30 E173 Vol. 4, 77.

52 Ibing, "Reminiscences," LAC MG 30 E173 Vol. 4, 77.
53 Ibing, interview with Petrou, Ibing, interview with Grenke, LAC R11667-0-6-E.
54 Ibing, "Reminiscences," LAC MG 30 E173 Vol. 4, 80.
55 Eby, *Comrades and Commissars*, 208–9.
56 Ibing, interview with Reynolds, LAC 1979–0081 MISA.
57 Ibing, interview with Grenke, LAC R11667-0-6-E.
58 Preston, *Spanish Civil War*, 194–95.
59 Ibing, "Reminiscences," LAC MG 30 E173 Vol. 4, 80.
60 Ibing, "Reminiscences," LAC MG 30 E173 Vol. 4, 80.
61 See, for instance, Rhodes, *Hell and Good Company*, ch. 8 and 9.
62 Preston, *Spanish Civil War*, 196–98.
63 Ibing, interview with Grenke, LAC R11667-0-6-E.
64 Ibing, "Reminiscences," LAC MG 30 E173 Vol. 4, 80.
65 Preston, *Spanish Civil War*, 256.
66 Ibing, "Reminiscences," LAC MG 30 E173 Vol. 4, 80.
67 Ibing, interview with Petrou.
68 Ibing, "Reminiscences," LAC MG 30 E173 Vol. 4, 86.
69 On Republican strategy, see Preston, *Spanish Civil War*, ch. 6 and 9.
70 Ibing, interview with Grenke, LAC R11667-0-6-E.
71 Beevor, *Battle for Spain*, 312–14.
72 Rhodes, *Hell and Good Company*, 212.
73 Ibing, interview with Grenke, LAC R11667-0-6-E.
74 Rhodes, *Hell and Good Company*, 216–17.
75 Ibing, "Reminiscences," LAC MG 30 E173 Vol. 4, 78.
76 Ibing, interview with Grenke, LAC R11667-0-6-E.
77 Ibing, "Reminiscences," LAC MG 30 E173 Vol. 4, 78.
78 Ibing, interview with Grenke, LAC R11667-0-6-E.
79 Ibing, interview with Petrou; see also Carroll, *Odyssey of the Abraham-Lincoln Brigade*, ch. 12, "The Great Retreats."
80 Beevor, *Battle for Spain*, 361–64. See also Howard, *Mackenzie-Papineau Battalion*, ch. 16, "The Retreats."
81 Beevor, *Battle for Spain*, 405.
82 Ibing, interview with Grenke, LAC R11667-0-6-E.
83 Ibing, "Reminiscences," LAC MG 30 E173 Vol. 4, 79.
84 Ibing, "Reminiscences," LAC MG 30 E173 Vol. 4, 77.
85 Ibing, "Reminiscences," LAC MG 30 E173 Vol. 4, 77.
86 Ibing, "Reminiscences," LAC MG 30 E173 Vol. 4, 78.
87 Ibing, "Reminiscences," LAC MG 30 E173 Vol. 4, 78.
88 Ibing, "Reminiscences," LAC MG 30 E173 Vol. 4, 78.
89 Eby, *Comrades and Commissars*, 351; see also Rhodes, *Hell and Good Company*, 185.
90 Hochschild, *Spain in Our Hearts*, 113.
91 Orwell, *Homage to Catalonia*, 162.
92 Roderick Stewart and Sharon Stewart, *Phoenix: The Life of Norman Bethune* (Montreal: McGill-Queen's University Press, 2011), ch. 9, "Blood"; Adrienne Clarkson, *Norman Bethune* (Toronto: Penguin, 2009).
93 Ibing, "Reminiscences," LAC MG 30 E173 Vol. 4, 82.

94 Orwell, *Homage to Catalonia*, 147.
95 Carroll, *Odyssey of the Abraham-Lincoln Brigade*, 104.
96 Rhodes, *Hell and Good Company*, 184.
97 See, for example, Ibing, interview with Grenke, LAC R11667-0-6-E.
98 Hochschild, *Spain in Our Hearts*, 118.
99 Ibing, interview with Grenke, LAC R11667-0-6-E.
100 Ibing, interview with Grenke, LAC R11667-0-6-E.
101 Eby, *Comrades and Commissars*, 351.
102 Hochschild, *Spain in Our Hearts*, 123.
103 Ibing, interview with Grenke, LAC R11667-0-6-E.
104 Ibing, interview with Grenke, LAC R11667-0-6-E.
105 Ibing, interview with Grenke, LAC R11667-0-6-E.
106 Ibing, "Reminiscences," LAC MG 30 E173 Vol. 4, 81.
107 Ibing, "Reminiscences," LAC MG 30 E173 Vol. 4, 78.
108 Beevor, *Battle for Spain*, 317. See also Hochschild, *Spain in Our Hearts*, 107.
109 Orwell, *Homage to Catalonia*, 36.
110 Ibing, interview with Grenke, LAC R11667-0-6-E; Ibing, "Reminiscences," LAC MG 30 E173 Vol. 4, 78.
111 Ibing, interview with Grenke, LAC R11667-0-6-E.
112 Ibing, interview with Grenke, LAC R11667-0-6-E; Ibing, "Reminiscences," LAC MG 30 E173 Vol. 4, 79.
113 Ibing, interview with Grenke, LAC R11667-0-6-E.
114 Beevor, *Battle for Spain*, 361–64; Petrou, *Renegades*, 90–91.
115 As they would be later on the Eastern Front in World War II.
116 Beevor, *Battle for Spain*, 317.
117 Ibing, "Reminiscences," LAC MG 30 E173 Vol. 4, 82.
118 Ibing, interview with Grenke, LAC R11667-0-6-E.
119 Ibing, interview with Petrou.
120 Ibing, "Reminiscences," LAC MG 30 E173 Vol. 4, 82.
121 John C. Firmin's account of the war, LAC MG 30 E173 Vol 1, File 18.
122 Ibing, "Reminiscences," LAC MG 30 E173 Vol. 4, 82.
123 Ibing, interview with Grenke, LAC R11667-0-6-E.
124 Ibing, "Reminiscences," LAC MG 30 E173 Vol. 4, 82.
125 Ibing, "Reminiscences," LAC MG 30 E173 Vol. 4, 82.
126 Ibing, interview with Grenke, LAC R11667-0-6-E.
127 Ibing, "Reminiscences," LAC MG 30 E173 Vol. 4, 80.
128 Rhodes, *Hell and Good Company*, 187.
129 A long excerpt from the pamphlet can be found in Roderick Stewart and Jesus Majada, *Bethune in Spain* (Montreal: McGill-Queen's University Press, 2014), 79–85.
130 Paul Preston, *The Spanish Holocaust: Inquisition and Extermination in Twentieth Century Spain* (London: Norton, 2012), ch. 9 and 12.
131 David Wingeate Pike, *France Divided: The French and the Civil War in Spain* (Eastbourne: Sussex Academic Press, 2011), 207.
132 Rhodes, *Hell and Good Company*, 236.
133 Preston, *Spanish Civil War*, 294; Preston, *Spanish Holocaust*, 323.
134 Preston, *Spanish Civil War*, 307–9; Preston, *Spanish Holocaust*, 323.

135 Wingeate Pike, *France Divided*, 197, 205.
136 Carroll, *Odyssey of the Abraham-Lincoln Brigade*, 175–76; Petrou, *Renegades*, 88–89, Eby, *Comrades and Commissars*, 367.
137 Eby, *Comrades and Commissars*, 372. See also Howard, *Mackenzie-Papineau Battalion*, 196–204.
138 Petrou, *Renegades*, 48.
139 Ibing, "Reminiscences," LAC MG 30 E173 Vol. 4, 81.
140 Beevor, *Battle for Spain*, 311.
141 Ibing, interview with Grenke, LAC R11667-0-6-E.
142 By the summer of 1937, the Communists had a number of disciplinary camps, the largest of which, Camp Lukacs (named for the general of the XII International Brigade), had 4,000 volunteers sentenced to it between August and October alone. (Petrou, *Renegades*, 125–30; Beevor, *Battle for Spain*, 321.)
143 Ibing, interview with Petrou.
144 "Documents on Volunteers of the International Brigades," LAC MG 10 K2, Mackenzie-Papineau Fonds 545, File List 6, Microfilm Reel K 263.
145 See, for instance, Preston, *Spanish Holocaust*, 406–7. According to some scholars, discipline was fairly light in the American Abraham Lincoln Battalion. Carroll (*Odyssey of the Abraham-Lincoln Brigade*) claims that there was little coercion in that battalion, mostly due to the deeply felt ideological commitment to Communism of most of its volunteers (see, especially, 108). Eby, however, offers a much different assessment; his book is full of stories of heavy-handedness on the part of the commissars. (See, in particular, *Comrades and Commissars*, ch. 16, "In the Penal Colonies.") Petrou argues that discipline was a common problem for the Mackenzie-Papineau Battalion, in part because of an anti-authoritarian culture that took hold in its rank and file, and in part because of tensions with the officers, most of whom were from other countries, especially the U.S. and to a lesser extent Britain. Still, Petrou writes that only a minority of Canadian volunteers (about 150) were charged and punished during the war. Most of these received only a few days' detention; some were sent to a disciplinary camp, and a few were executed. (*Renegades*, 109–12).
146 Carroll, *Odyssey of the Abraham-Lincoln Brigade*, 132.
147 Ibing, interview with Petrou.
148 Carroll, *Odyssey of the Abraham-Lincoln Brigade*, 132. It is not clear whether Clark commanded the whole Regiment or just one unit within it. According to the online database of the Abraham Lincoln Brigade Archives (ALBA) (http://edit.alba-valb.org), Clark was the commander of the 2nd Squadron of the Regiment. However, Carroll (citing information from Sennett, the political commissar) claims that he was commander of the Regiment. Clark's popularity stemmed from both his courage and his understated approach to wielding authority. Sennett remembered that Clark "imposed discipline by personal example only. . . . But nothing could have been more rigorous. [The] regiment was always haunted by the fact that [their] most valuable man was the least political." (Carroll, *Odyssey of the Abraham-Lincoln Brigade*, 132.)
149 Petrou, *Renegades*, 94; Eby, *Comrades and Commissars*, 348.
150 Ibing, "Reminiscences," LAC MG 30 E173 Vol. 4, 81; on the food supplies causing problems for members of the Brigades, see Beevor, *Battle for Spain*, 180.
151 Eby, *Comrades and Commissars*, 347–48.
152 Most histories of the Spanish Civil War and the International Brigades devote some atten-

tion to the volunteers' journey home, but only as a small part of the story. This is not surprising, since most of the major questions – whether the Republic would prevail, or whether volunteers would survive the combat – had been settled. Moreover, the stream of departing internationals in late 1938 was small compared to the flood of Spanish refugees that poured into France as the Republic started to collapse in early 1939. Nevertheless, these journeys out of Spain, through France, and back to volunteers' homes were often remarkable stories in themselves. And they feature many of the themes that were essential in the war itself: the disunity within the Republican ranks, the unreliability of Communist organizations supporting the volunteers, and the Western democracies' indifference or hostility toward the internationals.

4: The Long Trek Home

1 Petrou, *Renegades*, 93–94.
2 Eby, *Comrades and Commissars*, 382; Petrou, *Renegades*, 92.
3 John Gates of the Abe Lincolns, for example, was one of those commissars. (Carroll, *Odyssey of the Abraham-Lincoln Brigade*, 190–91; Beevor, *Battle for Spain*, 344–45.)
4 The Comintern's file on Ibing includes a notation that he "refuses repatriation." ("Documents on Volunteers of the International Brigades," LAC MG 10 K2, Mackenzie-Papineau Fonds 545, File List 6, Microfilm Reel K 263.)
5 Carroll, *Odyssey of the Abraham-Lincoln Brigade*, 191.
6 Ibing's refusal of repatriation referred to in the paragraph above was probably in response to an earlier offer, as the record's date appears (though it is smudged on the microfilm) to be Nov. 22, 1937 – months before the incident discussed here. ("Documents on Volunteers of the International Brigades," LAC MG 10 K2, Mackenzie-Papineau Fonds 545, File List 6, Microfilm Reel K 263.)
7 Tyler Wentzell, "Canada's *Foreign Enlistment Act* and the Spanish Civil War," *Labour/Le Travail* 80 (Fall 2017), 213–46.
8 Beevor, *Battle for Spain*, 344; Petrou, *Renegades*, 41.
9 Petrou, *Renegades*, 41.
10 LAC MG 30 E173 Vol. 5, File 6, Document C145311.
11 Ibing, interview with Grenke, LAC R11667-0-6-E.
12 Ibing, "Reminiscences," LAC MG 30 E173 Vol. 4, 83.
13 Ibing, "Reminiscences," LAC MG 30 E173 Vol. 4, 83. The original of the Nansen passport is in Ibing's family's possession.
14 Beevor, *Battle for Spain*, 403–6.
15 Wingeate Pike, *France Divided*, 200–201, 205–6. The Munich Accord also sounded the death knell for the Popular Front alliance in France.
16 Ibing, "Reminiscences," LAC MG 30 E173 Vol. 4, 77.
17 Ibing, "Reminiscences," LAC MG 30 E173 Vol. 4, 83.
18 Beeching, *Canadian Volunteers*, 189; Preston, *Spanish Civil War*, 293; Carroll, *Odyssey of the Abraham-Lincoln Brigade*, 204–5; Eby, *Comrades and Commissars*, 410–11.
19 Preston, *Spanish Civil War*, 288; see also Petrou, *Renegades*, 98.
20 On France's policies, see Wingeate Pike, *France Divided*, 188–91; Scott Soo, *The Routes to Exile: France and the Spanish Civil War Refugees, 1939–2009* (Manchester: Manchester University Press, 2013), 34–41. Soo's main focus is Spanish refugees at the end of the war.
21 Eby, *Comrades and Commissars*, 412–13.

22 Eby, *Comrades and Commissars*, 412.
23 Beeching, *Canadian Volunteers*, 190.
24 Petrou, *Renegades*, 102–3.
25 Ibing, interview with Grenke, LAC R11667-0-6-E. Ibing did not mention participating in events held for returning veterans in Paris, and it was unlikely that he was able to join any of them. Most were for French veterans. See Wingate Pike, *France Divided*, 373–74.
26 Ibing, "Reminiscences," LAC MG 30 E173 Vol. 4, 83. On the parade for French veterans, see Wingate Pike, *France Divided*, 374.
27 Preston, *Spanish Holocaust*, 490.
28 This sweep remains an especially mysterious part of Ibing's time in Europe, as his recollections of it were confused. He said in one interview that the raids were part of an effort to secure the city in preparation for a visit from King George VI – but the British royal visit occurred months earlier in July. He said that he was arrested by the "Police Mondaine," which he thought was the unit in charge of watching internationals – but Police Mondaine means the Vice Squad, who were unlikely to be given the task of dealing with internationals.
29 Eby, *Comrades and Commissars*, 415.
30 Petrou, *Renegades*, 104–5.
31 Ibing, interview with Grenke, LAC R11667-0-6-E.
32 John Merriman, *The Red City: Limoges and the French 19th Century* (Oxford: Oxford University Press, 1985).
33 Ibing, interview with Grenke, LAC R11667-0-6-E; Ibing, "Reminiscences," LAC MG 30 E173 Vol. 4, 83.
34 Ibing, interview with Grenke, LAC R11667-0-6-E.
35 Zuehlke, *Gallant Cause*, 276.
36 Ibing, interview with Grenke, LAC R11667-0-6-E.
37 Ibing, interview with Grenke, LAC R11667-0-6-E.
38 Ibing, interview with Grenke, LAC R11667-0-6-E.
39 Zuehlke, *Gallant Cause*, 277; Ibing, interview with Grenke, LAC R11667-0-6-E; Ibing, "Reminiscences," LAC MG 30 E173 Vol. 4, 84.
40 Ibing, interview with Grenke, LAC R11667-0-6-E.
41 Ibing, interview with Grenke, LAC R11667-0-6-E.
42 Hochschild, *Spain in Our Hearts*, xviii–xix.
43 Aside from the Soviet Union, Mexico was the biggest supporter of the Spanish Republic in international affairs. One of Mexico's most publicized gestures of support was arranging a tour of Mexico and the United States for the Barcelona football club in 1937. (See Lowe, *Fear and Loathing in La Liga*, 33–35.) Mexico took in about 25,000 Republican refugees in total; some were veterans of the International Brigades, although most were Spaniards who fled later after the war was lost. Mexico was also unconcerned about travel documents, and almost none of the refugees it accepted had government-issued papers. (Jordi Oliveres, "How the Spanish Civil War Drove My Family to Mexico," *Fusion*, April 12, 2014, http://fusion.net.)
44 Ibing, interview with Grenke, LAC R11667-0-6-E.
45 Ibing, "Reminiscences," LAC MG 30 E173 Vol. 4, 84.
46 Ibing, interview with Grenke, LAC R11667-0-6-E.
47 Ibing, interview with Grenke, LAC R11667-0-6-E.
48 Ibing, interview with Grenke, LAC R11667-0-6-E.
49 Zuehlke, *Gallant Cause*, 278.

50 Ibing, interview with Grenke, LAC R11667-0-6-E.
51 Zuehlke, *Gallant Cause*, 278.
52 Ibing, interview with Grenke, LAC R11667-0-6-E.
53 Canadian policy regarding veterans of the International Brigades – and the rather quiet way it was implemented – also shaped Ibing's long journey back from Spain. This was another aspect of the history of the Spanish Civil War that has not been fully explored by historians, and unfortunately for Ibing, at the time Communist organizations were slow in understanding and acting upon the policy.
54 Petrou, *Renegades*, 54–55, 170–72.
55 This story has been well documented in Gregory Kealey, *Spying on Canadians: The Royal Canadian Mounted Police Security Service and the Origins of the Long Cold War* (Toronto: University of Toronto Press, 2017).
56 Reg Whitaker and Gregory S. Kealey, "A War on Ethnicity? The RCMP and Internment," in *Enemies Within: Italians and Other Internees in Canada and Abroad*, ed. Franca Iacovetta, Roberto Perin, and Angelo Principe (Toronto: University of Toronto Press, 2000), 139.
57 Petrou, *Renegades*, 173–74.
58 The policy was recorded in a series of government documents kept in the Mackenzie-Papineau collection at Library and Archives Canada. It is not clear who authored most of the documents, but they do outline the position of different government departments, and crucially, they issue final directives to officials regarding policy implementation. The policy that the government did implement, as recounted by a number of historians, especially Howard, is in line with the one outlined in the memos. See LAC MG 30 E173 Vol. 5, File 6; and Howard, *Mackenzie-Papineau Battalion*, 224–47.
59 LAC MG 30 E173 Vol. 5, File 6.
60 A letter from the RCMP to O.D. Skelton, Undersecretary of State for Foreign Affairs, as quoted in "The Spanish Crucible, Episode 1," *Living Out Loud*, www.cbc.ca/radio/livingoutloud.
61 LAC MG 30 E173 Vol. 5, File 6.
62 LAC MG 30 E173 Vol. 5, File 6; Howard, *Mackenzie-Papineau Battalion*, 226.
63 LAC MG 30 E173 Vol. 5, File 6; Howard, *Mackenzie-Papineau Battalion*, 225. The Immigration Branch did not know that Ibing *did* harbour ambitions to resettle in Spain if the war was won, though this was hardly his primary reason for going to Spain.
64 Petrou, *Renegades*, 103.
65 LAC MG 30 E173 Vol. 5, File 6; Howard, *Mackenzie-Papineau Battalion*, 226–29.
66 The main officer in charge of the processing in Ripoll, Colonel Andrew O'Kelly, become the object of some veterans' scorn for the slow, painstaking approach to interviewing the veterans and assessing their answers. O'Kelly's coldness and evident lack of urgency was consistent with Ottawa's approach to the volunteers. His attitude accounted for some of the delay in getting the Canadians out of Spain – and in turn perhaps some of the delay in word spreading about Canada's policies. However, he did allegedly speed up his work after some of the volunteers gave him new incentive by stealing some food from his private stash. (Beeching, *Canadian Volunteers*, 191.)
67 Petrou, *Renegades*, 102.
68 Beeching, *Canadian Volunteers*, 191–92; Zuehlke, *Gallant Cause*, 268; Petrou, *Renegades*, 101–3; LAC MG 30 E173 Vol. 1, File 5, Doc. 1, Memo from O.D. Skelton to Mackenzie King, date not clearly marked.
69 MacLeod and Tim Buck had been the first Canadians to visit Spain just after the war start-

Notes to pages 115–118 | 181

ed, having been invited as part of the Republic's effort to gain international support. After problems with MacLeod's passport and visa requirements for travel (LAC MG 30 E173 Vol. 1, File 5, Doc. 1, Memo from O.D. Skelton to Mackenzie King), he proved an able representative, raising large sums of money for the veterans in London before focusing on arranging their voyages home.

70 Beeching, *Canadian Volunteers*, 1–3, 191–92; Petrou, *Renegades*, 102.
71 The main group of Canadians had to watch as British, American, and other veterans were able to leave Spain while they continued to sit in the gloom of Ripoll. Watching the large contingent of veterans of the Abe Lincolns depart at the start of December was especially demoralizing. (Petrou, *Renegades*, 102; Howard, *Mackenzie-Papineau Battalion*, 228–89; on Abe Lincolns returning home, see Eby, *Comrades and Commissars*, 412–17.) All the while the Republican defences continued to falter and Franco's armies were advancing. (Zuehlke, *Gallant Cause*, 268.) For Canadians in Ripoll it made for an uneasy time – and an ever colder and hungrier one as winter set in – but the tension they experienced in early December was not as severe as that which Ibing was facing around the same time.
72 RCMP Memo, Oct. 18, 1938, LAC RG 146 Vol. 1880, Mackenzie-Papineau Battalion, Part 1.
73 In all of his testimonies about his return from Spain, Ibing stated matter-of-factly that his lack of Canadian citizenship and his lack of valid travel papers made it obvious that he would not get permission from Canadian authorities to be repatriated.
74 Petrou, *Renegades*, 103.
75 RCMP Memo, Feb. 4, 1939, Nova Scotia Branch, LAC RG 146 Vol. 1880, Mackenzie-Papineau Battalion, Part 2.
76 Zuehlke, *Gallant Cause*, 269.
77 Petrou, *Renegades*, 103.
78 Petrou, *Renegades*, 103.
79 "Memo on International Brigade Work in Canada," Aug. 22, 1939, LAC R14760-0-4-E (formerly MG10-K2), Fonds 545, File List 6, File 535.
80 Beeching, *Canadian Volunteers*, 194. Petrou does not make the same claim about veterans perishing due to starvation, but does describe similarly dire conditions in the camp; see Petrou, *Renegades*, 104–5.
81 Zuehlke, *Gallant Cause*, 282; Beeching, *Canadian Volunteers*, 180–81.
82 They were left stranded in the port in late April due to a lack of funds for their trip home, and the authorities threatened to send them to a detention camp. Only after a quick response from supporters to another desperate fundraising plea from the FMPB did the group reach Canada in early May. (Memo from the Rehabilitation Fund of the Friends of the Mackenzie-Papineau Battalion, copied in RCMP Files on the Mackenzie-Papineau Battalion, April 1939: RCMP Memos April 1939, LAC RG 146 Vol. 1880, Mackenzie-Papineau Battalion, Part 3.)
83 RCMP Memos Aug. 1939, LAC RG 146 Vol. 1880, Mackenzie-Papineau Battalion, Part 4.
84 Preston, *Spanish Civil War*, 293.
85 Zuehlke, *Gallant Cause*, 283–84. The RCMP's internal report contemptuously claimed the crowd in the main waiting room in the station – which numbered about 3,000 while the rest were outside – was made up of "about 85% foreigners ... Jews as usual were well represented." (Secret RCMP Memo, Feb. 5, 1939, Toronto Branch, LAC RG 146 Vol. 1880, Mackenzie-Papineau Battalion, Part 2.)
86 These events drew 2,000 in Vancouver, 4,000 in Montreal, 4,000 in Winnipeg, and 5,000 in

Edmonton. (RCMP Memos, Feb. 1939, LAC RG 146 Vol. 1880, Mackenzie-Papineau Battalion, Part 2.) Smaller groups of returning volunteers also had welcome parties waiting for them. Paivio's group of about thirty released prisoners got a reception when they landed in Canada in early May; when about seventeen from the group arrived in Winnipeg they were met by a crowd of 600. (Zuehlke, *Gallant Cause*, 284; RCMP Memo, May 13, 1939, Winnipeg Branch, LAC RG 146 Vol. 1880, Mackenzie-Papineau Battalion, Part 2.)
87 Albert Camus, *L'Espagne Libre* (Paris: Calmann-Lévy, 1946), 9; quoted in Hochschild, *Spain in Our Hearts*, xvii (and it is part of the title of his book), and Wingeate Pike, *France Divided*, 240.

5: Settling Down

1 Ibing, "Reminiscences," LAC MG 30 E173 Vol. 4, 85.
2 "Activities of the Friends of the Mackenzie-Papineau Battalion, National Committee Report," LAC R14760-0-4-E (formerly MG10-K2), Fonds 545, File List 6, File 535, 3–4. The report also claimed that across Canada, the veterans required a total of 884 visits to the doctor.
3 Friends of the Mackenzie-Papineau Battalion, "Memo on International Brigade Work in Canada," Aug. 22, 1939, LAC R14760-0-4-E (formerly MG10-K2), Fonds 545, File List 6, File 535.
4 O.C. Doolan as quoted in Gregory Kealey and Reg Whitaker, *R.C.M.P. Security Bulletins: The Depression Years, Part V, 1938–1939* (St. John's: Canadian Committee on Labour History, 1997), 379–80.
5 Kealey and Whitaker, *R.C.M.P. Security Bulletins, 1938–1939*, 399–400.
6 The GWFA was reorganized into the German-Canadian League in 1937, while Ibing was in Spain.
7 Ibing, "Reminiscences," LAC MG 30 E173 Vol. 4, 81.
8 Kealey and Whitaker, *R.C.M.P. Security Bulletins, 1938–1939*, 379.
9 "Memo on International Brigade Work," LAC Fonds 545, File List 6, Files 535-37.
10 Ibing was missed by the FMPB's largest effort to track the veterans – which included assessments of each veteran's commitment to Communism. But he was included in several subsequent lists, including one that noted his address upon returning to Winnipeg and his place of work. (LAC R14760-0-4-E [formerly MG10-K2], Fonds 545, File List 6, Files 535 and 536.)
11 LAC MG 30 E173 Vol. 1, File 5.
12 Ibing, interview with Grenke, LAC R11667-0-6-E.
13 RCMP Memos, April 1939, LAC RG 146 Vol. 1880, Mackenzie-Papineau Battalion, Part 3.
14 Ibid; "Reminiscences," LAC MG 30 E173 Vol. 4, 85.
15 Ibing, interview with the author.
16 Although it was a successful business, Sarah longed for the cultural and political vibrancy she remembered enjoying in her youth in Eastern Europe. (Ibing, interview with the author; Ibing, personal communications with the author.)
17 Ibing, interview with the author.
18 Ibing, interview with the author.
19 Evans, *Third Reich in Power*, 580–61. Perhaps the leading study of *Kristallnacht* is Martin Gilbert, *Kristallnacht: Prelude to Destruction* (New York: HarperCollins, 2006).
20 Henry Trachtenberg, "The Jewish Community of Winnipeg and the Federal Election of

1935 in Winnipeg North," *Manitoba History* 61 (2009), www.mhs.mb.ca/docs/ mb_history; Henry Trachtenberg, "The Winnipeg Jewish Community and Politics: The Inter War Years, 1919–1939," *Manitoba Historical Society Transactions* 3, 35 (1978–1979), www.mhs.mb.ca/docs/transactions.
21 Grenke, "From Dreams of the Worker State to Fighting Hitler," 87.
22 Gregory Kealey and Reg Whitaker, *R.C.M.P. Security Bulletins: The Depression Years, Part III, 1936* (St John's: Canadian Committee on Labour History, 1997), 180–81.
23 Tony Judt, *Postwar: A History of Europe since 1945* (New York: Penguin, 1945), 58–59.
24 Grenke, "From Dreams of the Worker State to Fighting Hitler," 92.
25 Eley, *Forging Democracy*, 278–79.
26 Gerald Tulchinsky, *Joe Salsberg: A Life of Commitment* (Toronto: University of Toronto Press, 2013), 60–61; Avakumovic, *Communist Party in Canada*, 139–40.
27 Ibing, interview with Petrou.
28 Eley, *Forging Democracy*, 279–80.
29 Tulchinsky, *Joe Salsberg*, 61; Manley, "'Communists Love Canada!,'" 80.
30 Manley, "'Communists Love Canada!,'" 81.
31 Eley, *Forging Democracy*, 280.
32 Avakumovic, *Communist Party in Canada*, 140–41.
33 Avakumovic, *Communist Party in Canada*, 141.
34 Ibing, interview with Grenke, LAC R11667-0-6-E; Ibing, interview with Petrou.
35 Manley, "'Communists Love Canada!,'" 81.
36 Avakumovic, *Communist Party in Canada*, 140; John Riddell and Ian Angus, "The Left in Canada in World War II," *Socialist History Project*, www.socialisthistory.ca. The *Toronto Clarion*'s claim was not entirely fabricated out of thin air, as Communist organizations had for many years described Ottawa's use of arbitrary power as a sign that the government was developing fascist tendencies, or that fascism was subtly expanding its reach in Canada. Still, the preposterousness of calling Ottawa a greater fascist threat than Nazi Germany would have been all too evident to someone like Ibing.
37 Grenke, "From Dreams of the Worker State to Fighting Hitler," 93–94.
38 Petrou, *Renegades*, 175.
39 Petrou, *Renegades*, 174–75.
40 Ibing, interview with Petrou. A number of other Communists also tried to enlist despite the party's official line. Jack Scott, for instance, also said he went to a recruitment office but was turned away because he was too short. (Scott, *A Communist Life*, 56.)
41 Ibing, interview with Petrou. See also Ibing, "Reminiscences," LAC MG 30 E173 Vol. 4, 85; Ibing, interview with the author. In his interview with Petrou, Ibing's recollections about just when he tried to enlist are a little unclear. But in his reminiscences for the official history of the Mackenzie-Papineau Battalion and his interview with the author, he was clear that it was after the war started.
42 Ibing, interview with Grenke, LAC R11667-0-6-E.
43 Ian Radforth, "Political Prisoners: The Communist Internees," in *Enemies Within*, ed. Iacovetta, Perin, and Principe, 197–98; Whitaker and Kealey, "A War on Ethnicity?," 128–29; Kelley and Trebilcock, *Making of the Mosaic*, 274–75; Reg Whitaker, "Official Repression of Communism During World War II," *Labour/Le Travail* 17 (Spring 1986), 136–39.
44 Whitaker and Kealey, "A War on Ethnicity?," 129.
45 Ibing, interview with Grenke; Ibing, interview with the author.

46 Whitaker and Kealey, "A War on Ethnicity?," 134–37. According to some historians, particularly Robert Keyserlingk, Ibing should have counted himself somewhat lucky that he avoided internment. Keyserlingk argues that the RCMP had almost no useful intelligence on Nazi sympathizers within the German-Canadian community, and thus when it faced demands to take action in September 1939 it "threw together in great haste haphazard lists of hundreds of Canadian residents and citizens without much chance of turning up truly dangerous agents."(Robert Keyserlingk, "Breaking the Nazi Plot: Canadian Attitudes towards German Canadians, 1939–1945," in *On Guard for Thee: War, Ethnicity, and the Canadian State, 1939–1945*, ed. Norman Hillmer, Bohdan Kordan, and Lubomyr Puciuk [Ottawa: Canadian Committee for the History of the Second World War, 1988], 53–69.) Although the numbers were small and most internees were from rural areas and tended to lean to the right politically, Keyserlingk contends that many "simple workers or farmers" were interned, often solely on the basis of their "neighbours' denunciations." (55) However, Whitaker and Kealey argue persuasively that the RCMP was generally "cool-headed" in the face of political pressure to take action against perceived fascist sympathizers, and actually had a clear idea of who were the prominent Nazi-sympathizers in the German community. In fact, some of the RCMP's intelligence on Nazi supporters came from the surveillance work and testimony of leaders of the German-Canadian League. (Grenke, "From Dreams of the Worker State to Fighting Hitler," 93).

47 RCMP Intelligence Bulletin, Oct. 23, 1939, as quoted in Whitaker, "Official Repression of Communism," 139.

48 Whitaker, "Official Repression of Communism," 136–39, 141–52.

49 Radforth, "Political Prisoners," 198; Grenke, "From Dreams of the Worker State to Fighting Hitler," 94.

50 Grenke, "From Dreams of the Worker State to Fighting Hitler," 94.

51 Ibing, interview with the author.

52 Ibing, interview with Grenke.

53 Whitaker, "Official Repression of Communism," 145.

54 Whitaker, "Official Repression of Communism," 141.

55 Whitaker, "Official Repression of Communism," 144; Keyserlingk, "Breaking the Nazi Plot," 60.

56 Throughout the war, 847 were interned for suspected Nazi sympathies, and about 140 for suspected Communist connections. (Whitaker and Kealey, "War on Ethnicity?," 137–38.)

57 Keyserlingk, "Breaking the Nazi Plot," 60.

58 Whitaker, "Official Repression of Communism," 147; Keyserlingk, "Breaking the Nazi Plot," 60.

59 "List of Spanish War Veterans," RCMP Files, Feb. 25, 1941, LAC RG 146 Vol. 1880, Mackenzie-Papineau Battalion, Part 4.

60 Ibing, interview with Grenke, LAC R11667-0-6-E.

61 Ibing, interview with Grenke, LAC R11667-0-6-E; Ibing, interview with the author.

62 Ibing, interview with the author.

63 Grenke, "From Dreams of the Worker State to Fighting Hitler," 94. The RCMP also contended that the league was concocting the most absurd scenarios to defend Soviet policies, proposing, for instance, that Stalin was waiting for Germany to tire itself in Western Europe so that he could eventually launch his own attack and sweep through Europe himself. See Kealey and Whitaker, *R.C.M.P. Security Bulletins, 1938–1939*, 281.

64 Ibing, interview with the author; Ibing, interview with Grenke, LAC R11667-0-6-E.
65 Ibing, personal communication with the author. On Saltzman's life, see "Percy Saltzman, Canada's First TV Weatherman, Dies," *CBC.ca*, Jan. 16, 2007; "Biography," Percy Saltzman website, www.percysaltzman.com.
66 Ibing, interview with Grenke, LAC R11667-0-6-E.
67 Avakumovic, *Communist Party in Canada*, 148–50. See also Ian Angus, *Canadian Bolsheviks: The Early Years of the Communist Party of Canada* (Montreal: Vanguard Publications, 1981), 319–20.
68 But in a testament to the scale of the casualties suffered by volunteers in the Spanish Civil War, the total number of Canadians killed while serving in the International Brigade – at least 600 – dwarfed the numbers of CPC members killed in World War II – about 50. (Avakumovic, *Communist Party in Canada*, 150.)
69 Tulchinsky, *Joe Salsberg*, 65–66.
70 Ibing, interview with Petrou. Ibing also complained about these policy reversals in his interview with Grenke and his interview with the author, and in Ibing, "Reminiscences," LAC MG 30 E173 Vol. 4, 85.
71 Ibing, interview with the author.
72 Ibing, personal communication with the author.
73 Petrou, *Renegades*, 159; "Activities of the Friends of the Mackenzie-Papineau Battalion," LAC R14760-0-4-E (formerly MG10-K2), Fonds 545, File List 6, File 535, Reel K 261.
74 Grenke, "From Dreams of the Worker State to Fighting Hitler," 95.
75 Ibing, interview with Grenke; Ibing, "Reminiscences," LAC MG 30 E173 Vol. 4, 85.
76 Grenke, "From Dreams of the Worker State to Fighting Hitler," 96.
77 German Workers and Farmers Association Fonds, LAC R11667-0-0-E. Only a few issues of the journal are available at Library and Archives Canada. In another sign that the federation had at least some support from the Canadian government, its masthead noted that its publication was "Permitted by Wartime Press and Trades Board under Order No. 223."
78 Grenke, "From Dreams of the Worker State to Fighting Hitler," 96–97; German Workers and Farmers Association Fonds, LAC R11667-0-0-E.
79 Ibing, interview with Grenke; German Workers and Farmers Association Fonds, LAC R11667-0-6-E; Grenke, "From Dreams of the Worker State to Fighting Hitler," 95–97.
80 Interview with Petrou. Jack Scott also complained about the tight control of Communist organizations in Toronto compared to the way they could function elsewhere in Canada; see, for example, Scott, *Communist Life*, 49.
81 This opinion was shared by other federation members, and by later historians as well.
82 Ibing, interview with Grenke, LAC R11667-0-6-E.
83 Grenke, "From Dreams of the Worker State to Fighting Hitler," 97, 104; Ibing, interview with the author.
84 Ibing, interview with Grenke, LAC R11667-0-6-E. Although membership figures of the federation are not available, it was smaller than the German-Canadian League, which probably peaked at 1,800 members in 1939, let alone the German Workers and Farmers Association, which counted well over 2,000 members earlier in the 1930s. The federation's scope was limited almost entirely to central Canada – it had only a small unit in Winnipeg and no units further west. The federation also did not attract the level of support from middle-class professionals that had saved the German-Canadian League. (Grenke, "From Dreams of the Worker State to Fighting Hitler," 102, 95, 97.)

85 Ibing, interview with Grenke, LAC R11667-0-6-E; Ibing, interview with the author.
86 Ibing, interview with Grenke, LAC R11667-0-6-E; Grenke, "From Dreams of the Worker State to Fighting Hitler," 95–97.
87 "From a human point of view," is the title of ch. 4 of Tulchinsky, *Joe Salsberg*, 67–94.
88 Ibing, interview with Grenke, LAC R11667-0-6-E; Ibing, interview with the author.
89 Tulchinsky, *Joe Salsberg*, 65.
90 Whitaker, "Official Repression of Communism," 149–52, 156–59.
91 Avakumovic, *Communist Party in Canada*, 152–56.
92 Tulchinsky, *Joe Salsberg*, 67–70.
93 Dennis Molinaro, "How the Cold War Began . . . with British Help: The Gouzenko Affair Revisited," *Labour/Le Travail* 79 (Spring 2017), 143–55; Reg Whitaker and Gary Marcuse, *Cold War Canada: The Making of a National Insecurity State, 1945–1957* (Toronto: University of Toronto, 1995).
94 Tulchinsky, *Joe Salsberg*, 111–15.
95 Grenke, "From Dreams of the Worker State to Fighting Hitler," 98–99.
96 Ibing, interview with Grenke, LAC R11667-0-6-E.
97 Ibing, interview with Grenke, LAC R11667-0-6-E.
98 Ibing, interview with Grenke, LAC R11667-0-6-E; Ibing, interview with the author.
99 Grenke, "From Dreams of the Worker State to Fighting Hitler," 98–99.
100 Ibing, interview with the author.
101 Grenke, "From Dreams of the Worker State to Fighting Hitler," 100. As historian Michael Maune shows, Döhler would remain a passionate supporter of the DDR through to the 1980s, although he did offer some criticisms of DDR policy, especially in the later years of his activism in the 1960s and 1970s. (Michael Maune, "Les 'amis de la RDA' au Canada: Horst Döhler et le Komitee Kanada-DDR face à la Liga für Völkerfreundschaft," *Zeitschrift für Kanada-Studien* 1 [2007], 120–36.)
102 Ibing, interview with Grenke, LAC R11667-0-6-E.
103 Ibing, interview with Grenke, LAC R11667-0-6-E. In some interviews and written statements, he put the year at 1952, but in most he said it was 1953.
104 Ibing, personal notes.
105 Ibing, interview with Grenke, LAC R11667-0-6-E.
106 Eric Hobsbawm, *Interesting Times: A Twentieth Century Life* (London: Abacus, 2002), 149.
107 Ibing, interview with Grenke, LAC R11667-0-6-E.
108 Ibing, interview with Grenke, LAC R11667-0-6-E; Ibing, interview with the author.
109 Ibing, personal note to his family; Ibing, interview with the author.
110 Evans, *Third Reich in Power*, 13–15.
111 Judt, *Postwar*, 59, 131–33.
112 Ian Buruma, *Year Zero: A History of 1945* (New York: Penguin, 2013), 180–81.
113 Ibing, personal note left to his family.
114 Ibing, personal note left to his family; Ibing, personal communication with the author.
115 Ulrich Hahnemann, "Prof. Ing. Sigmund Israel Huppert – ein jüdischer Hochschuldozent zwischen Lehre und Antisemitismus in den Jahren 1902–1931," thesis for the degree of archivist, University of Applied Sciences, Potsdam, 2007, 55. Thanks to Christian Rousseau for help with translation.
116 Bundesarchiv, NSDAP-Mitgliederkartei, BArch R 9361-VIII Kartei/13070310. Hahnemann contends that Gustav Ibing joined the Nazi party in July 1932, even before they took pow-

er. (Hahnemann, "Prof. Ing. Sigmund Israel Huppert," 55.) But the date of Gustav Ibing's becoming a party member is clearly shown on his membership record at the Bundesarchiv.
117 Evans, *Third Reich in Power*, 14–15.
118 Hahnemann, "Prof. Ing. Sigmund Israel Huppert," 55.
119 Evans, *Third Reich in Power*, 33–40.
120 *The Trial of German Major War Criminals: Proceedings of the International Military Tribunal Sitting at Nuremberg, Germany, Part 22* (Aug. 22, 1946, to Oct. 1, 1946), 481–82.
121 Hahnemann, "Prof. Ing. Sigmund Israel Huppert." Hahnemann also suggests that Gustav Ibing published a number of anti-Semitic articles in the local Nazi-controlled press. However, Hahnemann admits this is a supposition based on Gustav Ibing's previous experience in journalism; he does not have clear evidence that Ibing was the author. He concludes that the identity of the author of the articles remains uncertain.
122 Hahnemann's thesis covers the period up to 1931 and only mentioned Gustav Ibing's record up to 1946 in a footnote.
123 Ibing, personal note to his family.
124 Ibing, interview with Grenke, LAC R11667-0-6-E.
125 Judt, *Postwar*, 176–77.
126 Ibing, personal communications with the author.
127 Ibing, interview with Grenke, LAC R11667-0-6-E.
128 Richard Harris, *Creeping Conformity: How Canada Became Suburban, 1900–1960* (Toronto: University of Toronto Press, 2004), ch. 6, 129–54.

6: Rarely Looking Back

1 Ibing, interview with the author; Ibing, personal communications with the author.
2 True to form, the RCMP monitored the trip and kept press clippings of the tour. See LAC RG 146 Vol. 1880, Mackenzie-Papineau Battalion, Part 6.
3 The RCMP also reprinted many of these newsletters. See LAC RG 146 Vol. 1880, Mackenzie-Papineau Battalion, Part 6.
4 LAC MG 30 E173 Vol. 2, File 9.
5 Ibing, "Reminiscences," LAC MG 30 E173 Vol. 4, 86.
6 Ibing, interview with Petrou.
7 Carroll, *Odyssey of the Abraham-Lincoln Brigade*, 201.
8 Ibing, interview with Grenke, LAC R11667-0-6-E.
9 He expressed similar regrets in his interview with the author.
10 Ibing, "Reminiscences," LAC MG 30 E173 Vol. 4, 86.
11 Irma and Clifford Orchard returned to Toronto in 1981 – after living in Waterloo (for Cliff's university education) and Montreal (for his work) – and bought a house in Don Mills. The Ibings delighted in seeing their grandchildren Lisa (born 1971) and Mark (born 1975) grow up.
12 Ibing, interview with Grenke, LAC R11667-0-6-E.
13 Ibing, interview with Grenke, LAC R11667-0-6-E.
14 Parks Canada, "Mackenzie-Papineau Battalion Recognized as Being of National and Historical Significance," press release, June 4, 1995, www.pc.gc.ca.
15 The group had by then been renamed the Association of Veterans and Friends of the Mackenzie-Papineau Battalion. Ibing also became an honorary citizen of Spain in 1996.
16 "Canadian Vets of Spanish Civil War Get Ottawa Monument," CBC Digital Archives, Oct. 20, 2001, www.cbc.ca/archives.

17 "Mac Paps Honoured in Ottawa," workingtv.com.
18 He was elated when his first great-granddaughter, Madeleine, was born in 2007, but unfortunately he died before the birth of his great-grandson, Max, in 2011, and his grandson Mark's wedding to Jordan-na Belle-Isle in 2012.
19 Ibing, interview with the author.
20 Karl Marx, "Eighteenth Brumaire of Louis Napoleon," 1852.

Index

Page references in italics refer to photographs.

Abyssinia, invasion of, 54
activism, 48, 135, 138, 155; Communist, 44, 51, 139; Jewish, 128; labour, 42; left, 42
agricultural labour, 25, 28–29
Albacete (Spain), 65, 70, 73, 102, 114
Alberta: net farm income in, 167n84
Allen, Jay, 58
anti-Communist sentiment, 140
anti-fascism, 41–42, 49–55, 59, 61, 63, 118, 119, 124–27, 132, 135, 139, 145, 153, 159
anti-Nazism, 124, 128, 133, 141
anti-Semitism, 123–24, 136, 140
anti-Stalinism, 71
Argentina: German emigration to, 165n41
Asia: immigrants from, 166n47
Association of Veterans and Friends of the Mackenzie-Papineau Battalion, 187n15. *See also* Veterans of the Mackenzie-Papineau Battalion
Australia: hostility toward Germans in, 166n51

Bad Frankenhausen (Germany), 14–16, *17*, *18*, 143, 146
Banting, Sir Frederick, 45–46
Barcelona, 70–73, 78–79, 82, 84, 91, 103, 105, 152; political disengagement in, 71
Barrie (Ontario), 129–31; Ibing's expulsion from, 130–31
Barsky, Edward, 80–81, 87
Beeching, William, 4–5, 57, 63, 105–6, 117, 151–52, 172n98
Beer Hall Putsch, 13
Beevor, Antony, 80, 82, 90, 92
Belchite, battle of, 79
Belgium: desire for compensation after World War I, 164n12; Nazi invasion of, 129
Belle-Isle, Jordan-na, 188n18
Belorussia, 122
Bennett, R.B., 27, 34, 44, 50, 56
Berlin (Ontario): renaming of, 23
Berlin Uprising, 148
Bethune, Norman, 86, 94

Bland, Salem, 134
Blum, Léon, 50, 55, 170n49
Bolsheviks: seizure of power by, 23, 40
Brazil: German emigration to, 165n41
Brecht, Bertolt, 148
Brennan, Bill, 68
Brest-Litovsk Treaty, 11, 164n12
Britain: attitude toward veterans, 121; confrontation with Nazi Germany, 125; democratic and union traditions in, 169n11; Free Germany Movement unit in, 136; Great Strike in (1926), 50; hostility toward Germans in, 166n51; labour and left traditions in, 46; and Spanish Civil War, 55–57, 67, 103–4, 114, 153
Brunete, battle of, 79–80
Buck, Tim, 43–44, 51–52, 115, 125–26, 129, 180n69
Burke, Lee, 172n98

Calgary: anti-Semitism protest rallies in, 123
Camp Lukacs (disciplinary camp), 177n142
Camus, Albert, 118
Canada: admission of Jewish refugees into, 123; "Anglo-preference" in immigration to, 23; anti-German discrimination in, 131; attitude toward veterans, 121; Communist organizations in, 120–21, 131–34, 139, 149: *see also* Communist Party of Canada; criticism of inequities in, 150; deportation of immigrants from, 34–35, 168n92; Foreign Enlistment Act (1937), 102, 112–13; "foreign subversives" in, 23; hostility toward Germans in, 23, 166n51; Immigration Act (1919), 23, 113; immigration policy, 20, 22–25, 27, 112–17; immigration to, 20–27, 165n41; independence of from Britain, 126; internment of "enemy aliens" in, 23, 127, 130; involvement of in World War II, 125, 127, 131, 133; Ministry of External Affairs, 113–14; nation-building, immigration as part of, 24; Nazi sympathizers in, 123, 127, 137, 141, 184n46, 184n56; population growth in, 166n48; pro-Soviet rallies in, 139; racism in, 22–23; and repatriation of volunteers, 112–17; settlement of west in, 22–25; and Spanish Civ-

189

il War, 55–56, 102; spy ring in, 140; subversive activity in, 127, 129; unemployment in, 30, 34, 49; views of German immigration in, 22–24; vigilante groups in, 130; wartime security measures in, 126–28, 130, 139; as "wide-open" place, 21; xenophobia in, 22–23, 29
Canadian Jewish Congress, 123
Canadian Labour Defence League (CLDL), 39, 44, 47, 51
Canadian League Against War and Fascism, 51–52
Canadian Lutheran Immigration Society, 24, 167n58. *See also* Lutheran Immigration Board
Canadian National Railway (CNR): and immigration, 22, 24–26, 30–31, 33
Canadian Pacific Railway (CPR), 1–2, 36, 110; and immigration, 22, 24–26, 30–31, 33
Canadian Workers' Circle, 122
capitalism, 156; "crisis of progress" in, 45; Golden Age of, 155
Carlists, 95
Carroll, Peter, 177n145
Catalonia, 70–71, 78; May Days uprising in, 129
CBC Radio Archives, 4
Cecil-Smith, Edward, 67, 125–26
chain migration, 27
Ciudad de Barcelona (ship), 67
Clark, Durward, 98, 177n148
Clarkson, Adrienne, 157
class conflict, 42
CNT (Confederación Nacional del Trabajo; National Confederation of Labour), 71–73, 78; as "splinter group," 73
Cold War, 140
Committee to Aid Spanish Democracy. *See under* Communist Party of Canada
Communism, 1–3, 40–43, 46–48, 51, 58–59, 63, 71–73, 97–98, 107, 112–13; absence of ideology and party doctrine, 47; alienation of Jewish Communists, 140; conversion to, 4; dehumanizing nature of, 149; disillusionment with, 53, 142, 148–49; and Nazis, 106; obsession with threat of, 50, 56, 120–21, 127–29, 131, 139; organizations in Canada, 120–21, 131–34, 139, 149; propaganda of, 126, 132, 141, 142
Communist International (Comintern), 117; file on Ibing, 171n57, 178n4; Popular Front, 42, 48–49, 51–53, 55, 105, 124–26, 145, 153, 170n40; Third Period, 41–43, 48–49, 52
Communist Party of Canada (CPC), 39, 43–44, 47–49, 51–53, 63, 65, 113, 115, 117, 119–20, 129, 141, 148–49, 169n14, 171n57, 172n101; authoritarianism of, 52–53; banning of, 130, 134, 139; Committee to Aid Spanish Democracy, 59–60, 134; fealty of to Soviet Union, 137–38; and Non-aggression Pact/World War II, 124–26, 131, 133; policy reversal of, 133
concentration camps: French, 107; 117; Nazi, 20, 123, 144
Co-operative Commonwealth Federation, 42–43, 46
Crefeld (ship), 25–27
Czechoslovakia, 104

Dachau concentration camp, 20
Defence of Canada Regulations (DOCR), 127
Denmark: Nazi invasion of, 129
Dick, Ernest J., 163n7
Döhler, Horst, 136–37, 142, 186n101
Don Mills (Ontario), 149

Eastern Europe: fascist-allied dictatorships in, 102; German-speaking enclaves in, 21; immigrants from, 24, 166n47; Soviet territories in, 145–46; treatment of Jews in, 140
East Germany, 142; Ibing's visit to, 143–49, 154; Ministry of State Security (Stasi), 143; Socialist Unity Party, 146; and Soviet Union, 144–48
Ebert, Friedrich, 10
Ebro offensive, 103, 105
Eby, Cecil, 105
enemy aliens, 127, 129, 131
Ethiopia. *See* Abyssinia
Evans, Richard, 10, 17–18
Eveready Printers, 132–35, 142; and Communism, 132

Falange/Falangists, 54, 95
far-right groups, 41
fascism, 39, 41, 50–51; social, 41, 43, 49; Soviet Union's position on, 124; support for, 129
Fifth Columnists, 129–30, 137
financial crisis (1929), 18–19
Finland: immigrants from, 170n32
Finnish Organization of Canada, 128
France: Communist party in, 66, 116; concentration camps in, 107, 117; confrontation with Nazi Germany, 125; desire for compensation after World War I, 164n12; expansion of security measures by, 107; fall of to Nazis, 117–18, 129; German embassy in, 108–9, 154; occupation of Germany after World War I, 11–13, 54; Police Mondaine, 179n28; Popular Front in, 105; and Spanish Civil War, 55–57, 67, 82, 103–4, 153; Spanish refugees in, 177n152
Franco, Francisco, 55, 62, 65, 67, 71, 77–79, 81–82, 89–91, 96, 100, 101, 106, 117–18, 152–54; and battles of attrition, 80; emergence

Index | 191

of, 54; violence of, 57–58; and "war of annihilation," 94–95
Free Germany Movement, 136
Freikorps (Free Corps), 18, 40
Friends of the DDR, 142
Friends of the Mackenzie-Papineau Battalion (FMPB), 115–16, 120, 172n98, 181n82; keeping track of veterans, 120–21; Manitoba branch of, 120; National Committee of, 119

Garner, Hugh, 96
Gates, John, 178n3
Geiser, Carl, 95
gender identity, 17
German-Canadian Federation, 135–40, 185n84; inability of to gain traction in German-Canadian community, 137; loyalty of to Communism, 136–37, 142; problems for, 140–42
German-Canadian League, 120, 123, 126, 128–29, 132, 135, 185n84; Jewish members of, 128; Toronto chapter of, 131. *See also* German Workers and Farmers Association
German Revolution (1918–19), 8, 40
German Workers and Farmers Association (GWFA), 36, 39, 47, 60, 120, 123, 171n57, 172n101, 185n84; Winnipeg unit of, 47, 52. *See also* German-Canadian League
Germany: aggression of in international affairs, 53; black Africans in, 12; break-up of, 141; collapse of imperial state system in, 10; Communism in, 13, 18, 41, 61, 106; counterpropaganda, emigration-related, 22; depletion and demoralization of army, 11–12; and disarmament clauses, 53–54; economy of, 13–14, 16, 41; emigration from, 20–27, 46, 165n39, 165n41; "enemy aliens" from, 23; faltering war effort in, 8; French occupation of, 11–13, 54; housing shortage in, 21; national humiliation in, 11; nationalist "fighting leagues" in, 18; Non-aggression Pact with Soviet Union, 124–25; "November criminals," 164n15; paramilitaries in, 18, 40, 41, 159; postwar reparations by, 11, 13; refusal to accept defeat in World War I, 10–12; remilitarization of, 54; resistance in, 14; and Spanish Civil War, 54, 56, 82, 102; street violence in, 17–18, 41, 159; structure of postwar, 141; ultra-nationalist extremism, 11–12; unemployment in, 19; and World War II, 104, 127. *See also* East Germany; West Germany
The Globe and Mail, 142
Goutor, Madeleine, 188n18
Goutor, Max, 188n18
Gouzenko, Igor, 140

Great Depression, 3, 19, 25, 27–37, 39, 44, 46, 50, 57, 62–63, 115, 159
Grenke, Arthur, 4, 31, 47, 80, 163n8
Guadalajara (Spain), 78; battle of, 87

Hadesbeck, Frank, 116
Hahnemann, Ulrich, 146, 187n121
Halifax: Immigration Office, 26
Heaps, A.A., 42–43, 169n16
Himmler, Heinrich, 106
Hindenburg, Field Marshal Paul von, 12
Hitler, Adolf, 19, 51, 61, 64, 67, 104, 126, 131, 136, 138; appointment of as chancellor, 146; attack on Soviet Union, 132–33; destruction of left by, 50; "Hitler salute," 108–9; ideology of, 123; invasion of Poland by, 125; and persecution of Jews, 124; and *pronunciamiento*, 54; rebuilding of armed forces by, 53; rise of, 49; and Soviet Union, 125; and Spanish Civil War, 55; support for, 36, 56, 137
Hitler Youth, 20
Hoar, Victor. *See* Howard, Victor
Hobsbawm, Eric, 45, 49, 59, 143
Howard (Hoar), Victor, 163n7
Hungary, revolution in, 50

Ibàrruri, Dolores: "La Pasionaria," 105
Ibing, August, 143, 155
Ibing, Berta, 7–8, 13
Ibing, Else, 17
Ibing, Gustav, 40, 143–44, 145, 146–47, 187n121; death of, 148; and Nazi party, 144–47, 186n116; as opponent of French occupation, 13; political career of, 8, 10, 14, 16; as printer, 7, 132; "pull" in Communist government, 147
Ibing, Hans, 15, 17, 19, 26, 29, 33, 88, 99, 145, 156, 158; attachment of to Canada, 150; as Canadian citizen, 150; and CPC, 49, 51–53, 129, 137, 141, 148–49, 159; death of, 157; disenchantment of with Communism, 142, 148–49; early life of, 7–20; emigration of to Canada, 20–27; as "enemy alien," 127; expulsion of from France, 107–12; and German-Canadian Federation, 135–40, 141–42; and German-Canadian League, 120, 126, 129, 132; and Great Depression, 27–37; gymnasium (high school) years of, 17, 20; health of, 99–100, 119; as honorary citizen of Spain, 187n15; in International Brigades, 65–100; lack of Canadian citizenship, 60, 103, 116, 181n73; misplaced faith in Soviet system, 149; in Paris, 104, 106–10, 154; passport problems of, 103–4, 108–12, 116, 181n73; politicization

of, 39–64; refusal of repatriation, 102, 178n3, 178n6; rejection of from Canadian military service, 126–27; reporting to RCMP, 127–29; retirement of, 155, 156; return from Spain, 101–18, 119; riding the rails, 36, 62; sense of justice, 154; silence about involvement in Spain, 151; and Spanish Civil War, 53–64, 65–100; suspicion surrounding, 127, 130; and sympathy for underdog, 57, 153–54; as truck driver for Regiment de Tren, 1, 74–75, 80–81, 82, 84–94, 97–98, 102–4, 153, 163n10; visit to East Germany, 142–49, 154; work in Canada, 28–37, 121, 129–31, 132–35, 142, 149, 155, 159
Ibing (Orchard), Irma, 134, 149, 155, 187n11
Ibing, Sarah. *See* Kasow, Sarah
Ile-de-France (ship), 66
Independent Labour Party (ILP), 42, 169n11, 169n14, 169n18
Indigenous peoples, 22
International Brigades, 1–3, 59–60, 62, 65–100, 101–3, 106–7, 111, 113, 117, 120, 129, 134, 151–52, 154; Abraham Lincoln Battalion, 73, 98, 101, 174n45, 177n145, 177n148, 181n71; *La Despedida* for, 105; Dimitrov Battalion, 74; Dombrowski Battalion, 74; Mackenzie-Papineau Battalion, 61, 67, 73, 77, 79, 93, 95–96, 98, 125, 130, 134, 174n45; and NKVD, 97–98; Ottawa monument to, 105, 157; as "scum of the earth," 95; Thaelmann Battalion, 60–61, 74, 174n48; withdrawal of, 104–5, 112, 177n152. *See also* veterans; volunteers
International Printing Pressmen and Assistants' Union, 132
Italy: aggression of in international affairs, 53; Communist party in, 66; and Spanish Civil War, 54, 56, 82, 102, 171n76; and World War II, 104, 127

Jewish people: in Canada, 123–24; German, plight of, 123; German-Canadian, 124; in German-Canadian League, 128; Nazi killing of, 123–24; in Toronto, 135
Judt, Tony, 44–45, 53, 146

Kanadai Magyar Munkás (*Canadian Hungarian Worker*), 134
Kardash, Bill, 125
Kasow, Bessie, 122, 134–35
Kasow (Ibing), Sarah, 121–22, 134–35, 138, 140, 148, 149, 155, 182n16; death of, 155
Kealey, Gregory, 112, 127
Kershaw, Ian, 13
Keyserlingk, Robert, 184n46

King, W.L. Mackenzie, 56, 113, 125, 139
Kitchener (Ontario), 23; anti-Semitism protest rallies in, 123
Korean War, 142
Kristallnacht, 123, 147

labour movement, 42
Labour Progressive Party (LPP), 139–40
labour socialists, 169n11, 169n18
leftism, 12, 20, 39–64, 71–72, 78, 106–7, 112, 122, 131, 145, 154; and immigration, 46–47; and Nazis, 106; radical, 50; and RCMP, 121
Lenin, Vladimir, 11
Library and Archives Canada: Mackenzie-Papineau collection, 180n58
Liebknecht, Karl, 41
Limoges (France), 107
Liversedge, Ron, 61–62
López, Juan Negrín, 104
Ludendorff, Major General Erich, 12
Lutheran Immigration Board, 28, 167n68
Luxemburg, Rosa, 41

Mackenzie-Papineau Battalion, official history of, 4–5, 133, 152–53. *See also under* International Brigades
MacLeod, A.A., 115, 139–40, 180n69
Madrid, 77, 82
Mainz (Germany), 7–8, 9, 10, 12, 16, 54; expulsion from, 13–15
Mainzer Volkszeitung, 8, 10
Manitoba: Hunger March (1932), 44; immigration policy in, 29; net farm income in, 167n84; per capita income in, 33
Manley, John, 52, 170n40
Marshall Plan, 141
Marx, Karl, 159
Marxism, 47–48
masculinity, 17–18
Maune, Michael, 186n101
McKay, Ian, 169n14
Mexico: Communist insurrection in, 130; Free Germany Movement unit in, 136; openness to refugees, 110; and Spanish Civil War, 179n43
middle class: German-Canadian Jewish, 124, 128; suburban development, 149
Mola, Emilio, 172n82
Mulock, Sir William, 129
Munich Accord, 104, 178n15
Mussolini, Benito, 49–50, 54, 56, 78, 104

National Capital Commission, 157
Naylor, James, 168n8, 169n11, 169n18
Nazi extremism, 17

Nazis/Nazism, 41, 49, 61, 136–37, 144–47, 159; Canadian sympathizers with, 123, 127, 137, 141, 184n46, 184n56; concentration/death camps, 20, 118, 123, 144; as enemies of the Reich, 61; hunting of German Communists and leftists by, 106; and Jews, 123; occupation of France by, 117–18; resistance to, 129; rise of, 3, 13, 20, 34, 57; Spring Offensives, 129; Sturmabteilung (SA; Storm Division), 18, 144, 147; support for, 56
The Nazi Scourge, 136
Netherlands: Nazi invasion of, 129
New Democratic Party (NDP), 154, 157
Night of the Long Knives, 147
Non-intervention Agreement, 56, 59, 67
Non-intervention Committee, 68
Norddeutscher Lloyd company, 25
North Bay (Ontario), 31
Norway: Nazi invasion of, 129
Nuremberg International Military Tribunal, 147

O'Kelly, Andrew, 116, 180n66
On-to-Ottawa Trek, 44, 49, 62
oral history, 163n7
Orchard, Clifford, 155, 187n11
Orchard, Irma. *See* Ibing, Irma
Orchard, Lisa, 155, 187n11
Orchard, Mark, 155, 187n11, 188n18
Orwell, George, 71, 79, 86, 90; *Homage to Catalonia*, 86

Paivio, Jules, 62, 69–70, 117, 151, 157, 181n86
Paris, 104, 115–17; Ibing's escape from, 1–2, 4, 107–12
passports/travel documents, 103–4, 108–12, 114, 116
Perpignan (France), 104
Petrou, Michael, 133; *Renegades*, 4, 62–63, 96, 98, 113, 126, 163n9, 172n98, 173n105, 177n145, 181n80
Picasso, Pablo: *Guernica*, 77
Poland, Nazi invasion of, 125
Popular Front. *See* Communist International
POUM (Partido Obrero de Unificación Marxista; Workers' Party of Marxist Reunification), 71–73, 78–79, 174n38; as "splinter group," 73
Preston, Paul, 55, 57, 105; *The Spanish Holocaust*, 94–95
Pyrenees, crossing of, 66–70

Queen, John, 42

racism: in Canada, 22–23; in Germany, 12; in Nazi ideology, 124

Rae, Bob, 157
Railway Agreement, 22, 24–25, 30, 166n55
"Red Express" train, 66
Red Front Fighting League, 18
Red Scare, 140
Red Terror, 40
Regiment (Regimiento) de Tren, 1, 74–75, 80–81, 82, 84–94, 97–98, 102–4, 153
Regina Riot, 61–62
Reich Banner Black-Red-Gold, 18
religion, 8, 24
Reynolds, Mac, 4, 163n7
Ripoll (Spain), 105, 115–17, 180n66, 181n71
Robertson, Norman, 128
Rose, Fred, 125
Royal Canadian Air Force, 126
Royal Canadian Mounted Police (RCMP), 44, 112–14, 116, 124, 137, 187nn2–3; Communist suspicions of, 120, 127–31, 139; and enemy aliens, 127; obsession with leftists, 121, 129–30
Rudolstadt (Germany), 143–44, 147
Russian Revolution, 23

SA (Sturmabteilung; Storm Division). *See under* Nazis/Nazism
Salsberg, Joe, 125, 138–40
Saltzman, Percy, 132
Saskatchewan: net farm income in, 167n84
Saul, John Ralston, 157
Scott, Jack, 48, 183n40, 185n80
Seattle General Strike, 50
Sennett, Bill, 98
Skelton, O.D., 121
Slovakia, revolution in, 50
social democracy, 41–46, 49
Social Democratic Party (Sozialdemokratische Partei Deutschlands; SPD), 8, 10–16, 18, 40–43, 144, 146, 164n2, 169n11; *Vorwärts* (*Forward*), 10
socialism, 39, 43, 48, 52, 71, 148, 156; "hall," 47, 120, 170n32
Socialist Party of Canada, 46
social justice, 47
South Africa: hostility toward Germans in, 166n51
Soviet Union, 39–40, 44–46, 48, 50, 53, 63, 97, 110, 122, 153–54, 164n11(ch.1); CPC fealty to, 137–38; and East Germany, 144–47; Free Germany Movement unit in, 136; Gulag labour camps in, 110; Hitler's attack on, 132–33; Jewish Anti-fascist Committee, 139; Non-aggression pact with Nazi Germany, 124–25; position of on fascism, 124; and post-

war Germany, 141; and Spanish Civil War, 71, 87, 104; spies for, 102–3, 114, 140; treatment of Jews in, 140; and World War II, 127
Spain: Communist party in, 58, 71–73, 78–79, 97, 101–2; left tensions in, 70, 72–73; map of, 76, 83; *pronunciamiento* in, 54
Spanish Civil War, 53–64, 65–100, 128, 136, 151; apathy about, 71; Great Retreats, 81, 90, 92, 95, 98, 101; May Days, 78–79, 129; misery of, 82–100; Non-intervention Agreement, 56, 59, 67, 125; passports surrendered during, 102–3; prisoners of war in, 95–96; repatriation of volunteers from, 101–18; right-wing militias in, 95; volunteers in, 60–64, 65–100. *See also under* International Brigades; veterans
"The Spanish Crucible" (CBC), 163n7
SPD. *See* Social Democratic Party
Stalin, Josef, 45, 59, 87, 104, 110, 137, 140, 153, 154, 184n63; Great Terror, 97; Non-aggression Pact, 125
Stalingrad, Battle of, 138
Stalinism, 52, 171n58
Steel Helmets combat league, 18
Stornoway (Saskatchewan), 28–29, 122

Teruel, battle of, 79–81
Third Period. *See* Communist International
Toronto, 2, 4, 129, 131–35, 155–56; character of, 156; Jewish Communist circles of, 138; Jewish community in, 135; May Day march (1939), 120; socialist circles of, 148
Toronto Clarion, 125–26
Toronto Star, 142, 149, 155, *156*
Trotsky, Leon, 103
Trotskyism, 78

Ukraine: collectivization of agriculture in, 45; Stalin's treatment of, 140
Ukrainian Labour-Farmer Temple Association, 128, 139, 172n101
unemployed associations, 44
unemployment: in Canada, 30, 34, 49; in Germany, 19
unions, 46, 71
United Jewish People's Order (UJPO), 122, 138, 140, 148
United States, 50–51; aggression by, 142; attitude toward veterans, 121; Free Germany Movement unit in, 136; German emigration to, 165n41; hostility toward Germans in, 166n51; immigration policy in, 166n55; joining World War I, 11–12; and postwar Germany, 141; Socialist party, 98; and Spanish Civil War, 55, 114

Valencia, 82, 100
Vancouver: May Day march (1939), 120
Versailles, Treaty of, 11–12, 54
veterans, of International Brigades/Spanish Civil War, 130; and anti-war rhetoric, 126; and Communist organizations, 120–21, 126; events for, 179n25, 151; ongoing contact with, 120–21; recognition from government for, 151–52, 157; repatriation of, 101–18; trip to Spain (1979), 152; triumphalist tone of, 152–53
Veterans of the Mackenzie-Papineau Battalion (VMPB), 151–52, 157, 187n15
vigilantism, 130
Vochenblatt (*Canadian Jewish Weekly*), 134, 136
Volksstimme (*People's Voice*), 135–38
volunteers, in Spanish Civil War, 60–64, 65–100; immigrants as, 62; organizing of, 73; repatriation of, 101–18; secrecy of mission, 65–66; solidarity among, 67

Wagner, Jonathan, 25
war crimes, 147
Weimar Republic, 10–11, 13–14, 16, 21, 40–41, 145, 165n43; Reichstelle für das Auswanderungswesen (RA; Reich Office for Emigration Affairs), 21–22
Weinberg, Bernd, 136
welfare state, 155
West Germany, 143
Westphalia region (Germany), 7
Whitaker, Reg, 112, 127
Wilkes, Harry, 87
Wilson, Woodrow, 11
Winnipeg, 1, 2, 4, 27, 30–37, 39–40, 111–12, 119, 121, 167n76, 168n94; GWFA in, 47, 52; leftist political culture in, 42–43; working class in, 42
Winnipeg General Strike, 23, 42–43, 50
Woodsworth, J.S., 42, 46, 169n14
Workers Party of Canada, 169n14
Workers' Unity League (WUL), 44, 48
working class, 42, 46, 71; and move to middle class, 149
World War I, 8, 10–11, 21–23, 40, 55
World War II, 118, 125–40; Eastern Front, 138; Western Front, 139

xenophobia, 22–23, 29

Zuehlke, Mark: *The Gallant Cause*, 5, 69, 108, 112, 116